OASIS JOURNAL

2012

Stories

Poems

Essays

by Writers Over Fifty

Edited by Leila Joiner

IMAGO PRESS
TUCSON ARIZONA

Published in the United States of America by:

Imago Press
3710 East Edison
Tucson AZ 85716

www.imagobooks.com

Names, characters, places, and incidents, unless otherwise specifically noted, are either the product of the author's imagination or are used fictitiously.

Cover Design and Book Design by Leila Joiner
Cover Photograph: Santorini © DeVIce

ISBN 978-1-935437-67-3
ISBN 1-935437-467-4

Printed in the United States of America on Acid-Free Paper

ACKNOWLEDGMENTS

I want to thank the OASIS Institute, all the judges who have generously volunteered their time to select our contest winners and comment on the work of our authors, and all the writers over fifty who continue to contribute their work to *OASIS Journal* every year.

May we all have many successful years ahead of us.

LIST OF ILLUSTRATIONS

CONTENTS

EDITOR'S PREFACE

This eleventh annual edition of *OASIS Journal* contains the work of 91 writers over fifty from the U.S., a few from Canada, and one from France. So what's on our minds and in our hearts this year? Some of us are concerned about the changing state of our planet, and hoping that something can be done to save Mother Earth. Others are more concerned with events closer to home: our health or that of friends and relatives. Many voices are tuned to themes of romance, love, and loss. And some focus on our animal friends. Travel stories entertain, either the hitchhiking of our youth or later adventures in distant lands. Brief but memorable brushes with celebrities compete with family reminiscences. In other words, you're bound to find something here to delight and inform you. You may even find a bit of fantasy and hints of corruption.

   I think you'll also find useful perspectives on writing from our wonderful volunteer judges. I recommend reading their books as well as this one.

L. J.

NONFICTION: Judge, Hal Zina Bennett, author and writing coach
   Website: http://halzinabennett.com/

Good work, all. I also loved the story about the landlocked boat that people painted signs on, and the visits of the black cats.

WINNER: "Sierra Memories" by Bill Alewyn
   A delicious piece. I loved that it is written in the engaging style of the great nature writers such as John Muir and Norman Clyde—and that you pay homage to the latter by including him as your inspiration and spiritual companion during your backcountry adventure. You beautifully capture not only the beauty of that solitary trek into the Sierras but touch upon the crushing impact of our changing world on the wilderness landscape. Nostalgic without being sentimental, you have painted a deeply touching picture of the Sierras and what the awesome vistas of this land mean for all of us.

FIRST RUNNER-UP: "Sheru Goes to School" by Tabinda Bashir

I was deeply touched by Lisa's engagement with Sheru and her determination to try to help him better his life. The seeming futility of it, combined with Lisa's idealism and tenacity to help him, is a reminder to every reader of how difficult it can be to change what is. You did a great job of telling the story, giving a clear, realistic picture of the oppression of poverty without getting preachy or self-congratulating.

SECOND RUNNER-UP: "A Baby Lion" by Tom Engel

Very funny piece, really, and a bit of education in there too, about people raising baby animals in the city. I love your humor, almost wry at times but also compassionate. I like subtle self-deprecating humor, and you do that great. That brand of humor can reveal our humanness and allow us to laugh at ourselves when done well and not carried too far into masochism or the author beating him/herself up. Yours is disciplined and artful writing. I enjoyed it a lot.

JUDGE'S SPECIAL MENTION: "A Boat of Many Colors" by Mary R. Durfee

What a fun piece this was to read. It captures a sense of community and "common sense" that is disappearing from the American landscape. I thoroughly enjoyed reading about "Hugo's gift to the village."

JUDGE'S SPECIAL MENTION: "The Visitation of Mr. Black" by Marie Thérèse Gass

∾

FICTION: Judge, George Wasserman, Professor Emeritus of English at Russell Sage College, New York; author of the Abel Shea mysteries (*Design of Darkness* and *The Trouble on the Terrace*).

WINNER: "Cold Case: Rona" by Neal Wilgus

I am especially taken by the wit and confident voice of this writer, who presents as his narrator a psychic sleuth who can solve crimes, but can't tell us how or why he can. Not an easy trick for a writer to pull off. "Call me Ipse Dixit. No kidding," the narrator begins—preparing us for another whopping fish-story. And there is plenty of kidding in Ipse's story: in its smart, clipped dialogue, in the amusing babble of his unconscious mind, the complex relationships of his characters, and the fragments of esoteric Spanish lore.

FIRST RUNNER-UP: "The Stars in Their Courses" by Jim Foy

There is a diminishing interest in references to real-world individuals who turn up in fiction. Often, they are simply means of making fiction seem more real, and we hardly notice them. But in this story—which, in its historical opening and throughout, is firmly rooted in the real world—two individuals from this world strike one with renewed interest because they are larger than life: Stars, we call them, until, as in this story, they are set beneath the stars in their courses.

SECOND RUNNER-UP: "Growing up" by Judith O'Neill

Stories about growing up are generally dealt with at novel-length. The hero of this short story, a carefree and careless nineteen-year-old father, grows up in an hour or two. The author's compression and fast-moving narration have turned a conventional, if not hackneyed, literary theme into a truly meaningful and exciting experience.

❧

POETRY: Judge, William Mawhinney, who organizes and hosts Northwind Reading Series in Port Townsend, Washington, and performs poetry in local retirement homes through an Arts to Elders program. His books include *Songs in My Begging Bowl* and *Cairns Along the Road*.

WINNER: "Pedestrian" by Bobbie Jean Bishop

I chose this as the winner because it really nails that heart-in-the-throat fear as a parent rushes through a "ghostly bar-closing morning" to the bedside of an injured daughter where she lies "in state like a queen in the lap of Injury". Once at the hospital the speaker is subjected to hospital protocols: a body scanner, a wristband ID ("a bracelet of passage") and left to "pace for weeks in hallways too white to endure." The immediacy of the language, the accumulation of telling details, the sense of foreboding and helplessness ("everything out of my hands now") all add up to an arresting poem. I wonder how the daughter fared after the speaker's "tightrope of vigil" was over.

FIRST RUNNER-UP: "The Day She Left" by John J. Han

I like the deceptive simplicity of this poem with its enormous realms of pain shifting just below the surface. Parenting—difficult in the best of times—feels like you must pass a tough final exam without ever having taken the course. The speaker's daughter declares "she's big enough to leave her parents' shadow" and is moving "out"—ending the opening line with an abrupt short sound, like a slamming door.

For me, the poet successfully dodges a lapse into sentimentality by not mentioning tears, but by noticing that the magnolia branches outside the window "look blurry." Baby pictures still in the family room are nicely balanced by the "self portrait she drew at age ten"—obviously left behind in her haste to leave behind childish things. The last line ends with "out"—her tongue stuck out in defiance all those years ago.

SECOND RUNNER-UP: "People a la Carte" by Maurice Hirsch

I was drawn to this sharply observed encounter between two self-absorbed "well coiffed" basketball fans and an immigrant waiter from Kosovo. Much is implied in this sly poem, lots of emotional, social, religious layers are piled on top of each other. The fun is to let it resonate among all your cultural assumptions.

I sat with your entries for a long time. With such a wonderfully strong field of contenders, it took awhile to cull out what I judge to be the "Top Ten" poems. The other seven (in descending order) are:

> "Some Lies About Loss" by Kathleen A. O'Brien
> "Sex" by David Ray
> "Baby at the Table" by Carol Christian
> "Piano Mornings" by Mimi Moriarty
> "Sunday Dinner" by Una Nichols Hynum
> "Children (Not) Raised" by Connie McIntyre
> "Requiem for My Dog" Maurice Hirsch

This selection tells you the kind of poetry I admire. I have only one life to live; I come to poetry for authentic glimpses into the lives around me, into the heat of living because, too often these days, I feel surrounded by too much cool, empty language, too much political abstraction.

OASIS JOURNAL

2012

Stories

Poems

Essays

Sierra Memories in the Shadow of Norman Clyde

Bill Alewyn

> *"I sort of went off on a tangent from civilization and never got back."*
> —Norman Clyde in an *LA Times* interview

It is the middle of August, and I am on my way to yet another trailhead for a two-week walkabout into the Sierra backcountry, although where exactly I cannot say. I told the quota conscious rangers back at the visitor's center in Bishop that I would be hiking down the middle fork of the King's River, but that was a fabrication designed to assuage the Bureaucratic Beast. Truth be known, I don't know where I'll be spreading my sleeping bag over the next two weeks, nor do I see how that could possibly matter to anyone but me. Frankly, if my alleged whereabouts remains a matter of great concern to all the NPS apparatchiks in a fortnight, I will gladly fill out a more detailed and up-to-the-minute itinerary immediately upon my return.

I am not being intentionally subversive with my plans. These days, and for many years now, my annual Sierra sojourns frequently evolve into day-by-day spiritual journeys compared to more Calvinistic predestinations—and I've been a happier hiker ever since. Also, for these very same reasons, I prefer to hike alone.

It is a winding fourteen-mile ascent by two-lane highway from Big Pine to the backcountry trailhead near Glacier Lodge. Each August for several years I've made it a point to stop off at the little house on the left with the old apple tree. This all started about ten years ago when, hitchhiking out of Big Pine en route to the trailhead, I noticed a middle-aged woman raking fallen apples from the grass in her front yard.

"Headed for the backcountry, are you?" The woman seizes my attention with her smile as much as her words. After all, it isn't every day a stranger takes the time to smile at another stranger, even in Big Pine, California.

That's when I notice the apple tree, gnarled with age and burdened with the weight of its own fruit. A couple of the heavier boughs have already broken off under the strain. "That's one very old tree," I say, pilfering the nearest apple at my feet.

"The tree was here when my parents bought the house," the woman says. "Norman Clyde used to stop here and stuff his pack full of apples on his way up the mountain."

That would be the one and only *Norman Clyde*, legendary mountaineer credited with over a hundred Sierra first ascents. This pleasant woman now has my full and undivided attention. "How long ago was that?" I ask, my enthusiasm evident.

"Don't ask me to get specific. I was a young woman, then, back in the sixties, and Norman was already an old man, but he loved these mountains and he loved our apples too. Each summer he would stuff his pack with about a hundred of them."

A slight exaggeration to be sure, I thought. Then again, being the famous Norman Clyde, maybe not an exaggeration by much. Norman Clyde's gargantuan packs were almost as legendary as the mountaineer himself. Clyde was known to strap up to ninety pounds of equipment onto his battered Yukon frame pack. And unlike the ultralight aficionados of today, Clyde never left anything behind to chance, which included his axe, spare boots, up to five cameras, several hardcover books (many in Latin, German, and Greek), not to mention all those fresh apples. That's the way many a wilderness enthusiast hiked in those days.

In embarrassing contrast, I might tote along a couple of fresh oranges and maybe the slimmest of Elmore Leonard paperbacks. Suffice to say, any additional comparisons to Clyde and myself, or any other backpacker these days, will remain disproportionate at best. Clyde, after all, would spend up to six weeks alone on one of his backcountry visits into the Sierra Nevada. And Clyde—the definitive mountaineering hyphenate: climber-guide-fisherman-search-and-rescue-volunteer-amateur-geologist-consummate-peak-bagger—came prepared for any and all contingencies in those pre-cellular, pre-planned wilderness itinerary days.

I stand beside that old tree with its weighty limbs that once bore fruit for the likes of Norman Clyde and nosh on my free apple. An apple that by current bioengineering standards cannot compare to today's visually superior yet tasteless offerings.

"Take as many as you want," the woman said. She drew my attention to the cardboard box packed with apples beside the weathered tree. It felt comforting, connective maybe, to imagine old Clyde standing beside me with his hundred apples, tolerantly grinning no doubt, while I carefully weighed two against three before stuffing my final selection into the top of my pack.

Ever since that summer's day I've felt a kindred attachment for the spirit of Norman Clyde. He died in 1972, the same year I made my first pilgrimage into the Sierra Nevada when a high school buddy and I illicitly climbed Mount Whitney one June weekend. Over forty years or so I've managed to return to the eastern Sierra Nevada mountains nearly every summer, where I have encountered Norman Clyde's namesake on USGS topographical maps ever since: Clyde Peak, Clyde Glacier, Clyde Meadow, Clyde Col, Clyde Ledge, Clyde Lake, Clyde Creek, and a bit farther north toward Mammoth, Clyde Minaret.

Once, when I was in my middle-twenties, I decided to hike the length of the Pacific Crest Trail. That year I hiked as far as Echo Summit above Lake Tahoe, where I promptly assured myself I would return the following year. Instead, over the next three decades I revisited like a smitten lover the southern and central eastern Sierra backcountry. And, like that still smitten lover, I continue to discover new trails and cross country routes over this beloved mountain wilderness. These days I am in my late fifties and, even though I don't hike nearly as far or as fast as I once did, the allure of these mountains has not dulled or dimmed with the years.

In that geological nano-blink of time beginning with the year Norman Clyde passed away, I have witnessed perceptible physical changes to these mountains. Summer nights are, on the average, one or two degrees warmer than the year I first came to the eastern Sierra Nevada. And today, the once irremovable glaciers encrusted for eons below the Palisades, including Clyde's own namesake, are, by all scientific data, rapidly shrinking. Consequently, because of these global changes in climate, many long established Sierra habitats are now being threatened.

Then there are the perceptible and often peevish changes imposed upon us in the name of environmental necessity over the last thirty years, beginning with a far from equitable trail quota and a reservation system that favors wilderness visits to these mountains weeks and, in some areas, months in advance. In addition, backcountry hikers are now required to pack out their soiled toilet paper and, on some over-impacted trails like the standard hiker's route up Mount Whitney, even haul their own excrement to the nearest NFS sanctioned disposal station. When I first started visiting the Sierra backcountry, wood fires were illegal above 10,400 feet, which was later changed to 10,000 feet. Now, during the long, hazardous summer months, wood fires have been prohibited from many backcountry areas altogether. Furthermore, bear and human vehicle break-ins are on the increase at many backcountry trailhead parking lots.

At Big Pine Creek Trailhead I lock the truck, strap on my pack, and begin the hike up South Fork Creek toward unknown wilderness destinations to be announced later. On the hillside trail fifteen minutes into my hike, I see below me the fire-ravished stone and concrete foundation that was once Glacier Lodge. More physical changes wrought upon these mountains in my lifetime. I continue to hike and cannot help but wonder what Norman Clyde would have made of all these natural and man-made changes that have occurred over these recent years. In 2007, for instance, on the eastern slopes of these mountains, lightning strikes denuded a twenty-square-mile section of topsoil-retaining flora along the Oak Creek drainage. Then, in 2008, a summer deluge over the exact same area sent an overflowing wall of mud down Oak Creek, destroying homes and property, and flooding out a two-lane section of I-395 highway north of Independence.

Then there are the technological changes. Back in Clyde's day, 80-pound packs were the accepted norm, no problems. I can still remember a time not so long ago when everyone hiked with a 40- to 50-pound backpack, no problems. Nowadays, a vast majority of the New Age Wilderness Chic aficionados prefer a fully loaded 25-pound pack pared down to the latest in high-tech essentials.

This first day back in the Sierra high country is warm and cloudless. I am woefully out of condition, and progress along the South Creek Trail is steady and slow. In the evening I pitch my sleeping bag as soon as I find a suitable spot amidst the stony outcrops above Finger Lake. This ancient glacial moraine below South Fork Pass, a geological leftover from ice ages long past, is not conducive to finding the best and most comfortable of campsites. However, panoramic views to the west include both Middle Palisades and

Clyde Glaciers, both of which, the experts have alarmingly concluded, are now the waning victims of global warming.

The next morning I make a boulder-hopping ascent up to South Fork Pass. I love the metallic ping my ice axe makes as I tap it against the rocks and how that sound resonates like a tuning fork up the wooden shaft into my hand. It's been exactly ten years since I last scrambled over South Fork Pass. Receiving my first up close and personal look in a decade at the permanent ice sheet directly below the pass, I am confronted with an inescapable sight: there is far less permanent ice below the pass than there used to be. More gloom and doom evidence of global warming? I'll leave that one to the experts to decide. For me, the more tangible effects are a newly exposed layer of black ice impervious to my ice axe, plus a glacial bog of knee-deep snowmelt and scree that, when I step into it, resembles a kind of mud-colored Slurpee.

I abandon my discouraging ascent up the ice chute and choose instead a Class 3 scramble over the rocks above and to the right of the decaying ice. In a couple of hours I gain the pass and reach the talus chute on the exposed south side, where I follow the alpine drainage down the other side. Somewhere below me is the legendary John Muir Trail. High above, flanking my right, are the southern slopes of Disappointment, Middle Palisades, and Clyde Peaks. In the fading evening light I am hiking in Clyde's monolithic shadow, and more than once I look up and smile. Some twenty years ago, while hiking north along the JMT, I stepped off the well-established trail and over the next five or six hours scrambled my way haphazardly up Clyde. The view from the top, I recall now, was spectacular, although I did encounter some unforeseen technical difficulties on the route down. Reputedly, this was one of Clyde's favorite peaks. His ashes, I read somewhere, were later scattered from the summit by his son.

These days, whenever possible, I still step off established trails where I can, but I rarely climb the higher peaks today, and never alone and never beyond a technical Class 3 scramble. Conversely, the peaks and passes I scale today tend to be familiar friends, and the time I spend on their heights has grown increasingly more reflective. Also, after four decades in these mountains, I tend to shy away from the more impacted thoroughfares like the JMT, although this isn't always possible. Not that there's anything wrong with the 200-mile John Muir Trail. Ask anyone who has hiked it: mile for mile, the JMT is an empirical backpacking trail, and over any given summer you will most likely meet hikers not only from the United States but from all over the world: Japan, Australia, Great Britain, France, Russia, Germany. Chances are you will find everything you are looking for in a world class wilderness trail on the JMT. Everything, perhaps, except world class solitude.

And it is that solitude I now seek. After three days of tangential hiking, I've settled upon a destination: Darwin Bench, about twenty-five miles to the north and high above the John Muir Trail. I've camped at Darwin Bench several times. Darwin Bench: Solitude with a Vista. Call me a creature of habit: after forty years of visits into the Sierra wilderness, I find myself returning year after year to my favorite haunts. Darwin Bench is one of them.

The next morning I follow a watery path of least resistance until I reach the JMT just above Palisades Lakes. A couple hours later I descend the notorious switchbacks of the Golden Staircase, dropping down into Deer Meadow, a once shady lodgepole-lined route along Palisade Creek still recovering from the devastating aftermath of a decade-old burn. When I reach the junction to Simpson Meadow along the Middle Fork of the Kings River, I find a tree and shuck my pack. Once, there was a footbridge at this junction, but it was washed away during a high runoff spring back in the 1980s. In their wisdom the powers-that-be at Sequoia-Kings Canyon National Park opted not to replace the bridge. I am in LeConte Canyon now, imperceptibly inching my way up to Muir Pass (11,955 feet), one of the more memorable passes along the JMT, yet they are all memorable.

Also, after forty or so summers in these mountains, these hikes have become as much about the visitation of old memories as they are about creating new ones. I was hiking northbound toward the pass one September several years ago when I eyed a peripatetic coyote about a quarter-mile below the pass. Mister Coyote and I were more or less traveling in the same direction, keeping a respectful distance of about twenty yards between us. We reached Muir Hut nearly at a dead heat before mutually deciding to go our separate ways; Mister Coyote kept to the Goddard ridgeline while I hiked down to the basin around Helen and Wanda lakes.

There are no coyotes to keep me company when I reach Muir Hut the next day and make my camp in Evolution Basin, one of my favorite sections along the JMT. After spending some twenty-odd summers over the last thirty-five years up and down the eastern Sierra Nevada, nearly every pass, every ridgeline, every basin holds one kind of wildlife memory or another. I was hiking north through Evolution Basin one breezy afternoon twenty years ago when I met a southbound hiker, a pretty young woman on her way to Mount Whitney, wearing boots and carrying a full pack. That fetching young lass also wore the sheerest black dress I ever saw outside a dance floor. To this day, whenever I hike through Evolution Basin I think about that memorable young woman and her memorable black dress snapping like an ebony jib in the alpine wind.

At the falls below Evolution Basin I call it a day. The next morning I say good-bye to the JMT and start my climb up to Darwin Bench through scrub pine and dotted with lupine and mountain aster. A bench is exactly what the word suggests here: a geological ledge between Evolution Valley below and the higher peaks of the Darwin Range above. By noon I reach my destination several hundred feet above timberline and, for the first time on this hike, I set up my tent. Far below, I can see a green corner of Evolution Valley and what looks like a hobbled packhorse down in Colby Meadow.

For the next five days, my daily itinerary remains the model of Thoreauvian, or perhaps Clydean, simplicity: I do nothing more than read, write, and listen to the sounds of running water outside my new mountain home. In celebration of my arrival I pull from my pack my last green apple, which has traveled with me all the way from a generous woman's front yard in Big Pine. Core and all, I ravenously devour that apple. Then I hunt down the perfect rock for some long term reclining followed by more serious reflection. Behind me, stately Mount Goethe (13,264 ft.) keeps me properly awed and humbled, as all mountains tend to do.

By all accounts, these mountains have been generous to me, yet my own unique memories are no greater or less than anyone else who journeys into the Sierra backcountry. I have seen more than my share of rattlesnakes in Tehipite Valley and black bears along the Kern. One night just below Kearsarge Pass I had a cache of trail mix stolen from me by a sow bear and her three—count 'em, three!—hungry cubs, opportunity thieves in training.

Last year, while casting a trout pool along the upper Kern, I saw an American bald eagle glide majestically fifty feet above the river, trolling for his own free fish dinner. Another year, in northern Yosemite just below the outlet to Benson Lake, I glimpsed a rare Pacific fisher, a relative of the sea otter, quickly submerging for cover beneath the rocks. Once I had the rare and honored privilege of sharing a morning hike, sans fear or intimidation, with a full-grown mountain lion that walked parallel with me beside the upper trail above Agnew Meadows, the two of us remaining about a hundred feet from each other for several minutes.

One afternoon after a thunderstorm above Bighorn Plateau, I sat on a rock for well over an hour and watched an ephemeral double rainbow appear and then fade away in the eerie mountain light. I've watched a half-dozen bighorn sheep scramble for higher ground when I surprised them grazing at the top of Glen Pass. And I still get a thrill every time I pass a purple-blue bouquet of sky pilot (*Polemonium eximium*), which manages to thrive at higher elevations and is often found clinging to crevices atop peaks and upper passes. True to their lofty namesake, a sky pilot bouquet remains one particular wildflower that refuses to come down to you, not even by FTD.

No doubt Norman Clyde, my ubiquitous and invisible companion on this hike, had his share of exceptional memories too. Yet, accepting the bigger picture, perhaps in the end neither our memories nor our momentary selves, and maybe not even these ever-changing mountains, really quite matter in that infinite and incomprehensible grand scope of all things. Truly, in the end, everything physical remains impermanent; all existence is but the same fallen apple.

My five days of rest and contemplation interspersed with a few leisurely day hikes along this idyllic alpine ledge has come to an end all too quickly. Once again, I can't help but speculate as to what my shadowy companion on this hike would have gathered from all these changes that have transpired since his passing. Not just these warmer summers and drier winters, incredibly shrinking glaciers, and the endangered wildlife habitats these climatic changes have affected. Over these same four decades I have also witnessed the technological advances of mountaintop cellular communication, three-course freeze-dried dinners, plus the aforementioned current generational obsession for all things ultralight, including those quick-dry nylon hiking shorts that weigh about as much as an overseas envelope.

On the morning of my sixth day at Darwin Bench I pack up the tent and begin a gentle ascent along Darwin Canyon, skirting several lakes along my way to Lamarck Col. From the boulder-pocked notch of Lamarck the route is predominantly downhill all the way to North Lake, where I eventually hitch a series of rides back to my truck at Big Pine Creek trailhead.

So where, o where did my two precious weeks—not to mention my all-too-ephemeral forty summers in the Sierra Nevada—finally go? "Time," a haunted Tennessee Williams' character once argued, "is the longest distance between two points." Sometimes the shortest distance too. Eventually it all fades away from us like boot prints in a patch of warming glacial snow.

In my darker and more introspective moments, I am glad I won't live to see all the inevitable changes and the impending constraints that will only grow more and more restrictive as the human impact on these mountains exponentially increases: snowless peaks, stricter quotas, 24-hour video camera surveillance of all trailhead parking lots, and wilderness permits filed by computer several years in advance. It's enough to make one stay at home and watch a virtual reality tour of the JMT on his iPod, or is it IMAX, 360 Palm-Pilot instead.

Other times, sitting on a rock in the Bighorn Plateau and watching a receding double rainbow or reclining in my tent along Darwin Bench, I still feel a connective and energized hope, indelibly etched by forty years of memories and wonder, for all those who journey into these mountains and discover their transitory greatness for the first time.

Early next morning, I return to that old apple tree in Big Pine and scoop up about a dozen free apples waiting for me on the front lawn. I also return to the closed NPS ranger station in Bishop, where I carefully fill in those blank spaces to my itinerary that now read *Sierra tangents still unknown* before dropping the two-week old wilderness permit into the overnight box. An attention to detail, after all, must be paid to the Bureaucratic Beast. I know Clyde would surely approve this afterthought of attention.

I can't help but smile when I take the first bite from my breakfast apple.

THE LAST WAR

Ellaraine Lockie

The woman I meet on the street
leaving her SUV wears a sable coat in August
Tomorrow sweat will slide
down her sundress like butter in the sun
The weather as out of balance
as the California budget
She may or may not know the trees
lining the cul-de-sac are dying before their time
Already the acacia has told hummingbirds
it's too tired to serve their fourteen meals every hour

If she had been in Montana last month
she'd have known that the sky cried long and hard
in record breaking depression and the ten year
droughted ground couldn't absorb the tears
That ensuing floods washed
the Rocky Mountain Reservation down
the Bear Paw Mountains into a national disaster

The woman walks toward her Eichler
Ancestor cousin to the ancient houses in Pompeii
with no connection to the street
other than the door through which she disappears
Architecture that turns its back to the world and looks
into an atrium, entire walls of glass and private garden
The kind of isolation that money can buy in a city

So maybe the woman doesn't know Mother Nature
is revolting all over the world
We sink mine shafts into her body
in order to boast shiny baubles on our fingers
We drag out the rest of her entrails
if we haven't already dumped poison down them
Drain her lifeblood for bigger and better
Kill her offspring for sport and strip her naked
Who can blame her if she shakes with anger

Pours her wraths over us
Fights back with any weapon she possesses

Mother Earth will win this war
when she leaves cells of her spawn alive
After the descendants of the woman
whose sprinklers flood the sidewalk are all
swallowed, starved, smashed or buried
by the holocaust of consequences
Any mother would do the same

APRIL IN THE SONORAN DESERT

Claire Livesey

Clattering down the path
    I walk into a wall of silence.
Peace falls upon my shoulders.
    I relax completely into myself.

Ears ringing with quiet,
    transfixed in the growing light,
I stare at plants still closed in sleep.
Nothing moves.
I hardly breathe.

Through the thin, blue distance
    I can almost see an inland sea shimmering.

Primordial tides cover the desert…

I hear Kokopeli's conjure flute singing.
    That brings this vision to mind
        In the great puddle of hush.

In layered light
    each plant begins to pulse.
Engleman prickley pear stretches its fins
    stands to attention.
Fairy dusters nod in the small breeze.
Mexican poppies turn orange faces
    toward the sun.
Smells of earth and growth are in the air…
And now I see the soul burning in each stone.

Ocean Corral

Jeffrey Widen

Embers from the fire glowed throughout the valley. Dusk shrouded our canyon as the sun kissed the day goodbye. We had been taken hostage by a three-day inferno: the dreaded Santa Anna winds had once again taken a spark from a campfire and fanned it to a giant burn. The conflagration was so unpredictable that many residents were evacuated, then returned to their homes only to be evacuated again, while exhausted firefighters challenged the ebb and flow of attacking flames in hundred-degree weather.

Many residents of the canyon owned horses and boarded them at Topanga Stables. Three of us were chosen to rescue the trapped animals before they succumbed to the smoke and fire. Our backpacks were filled with wide bandanas to cover the frightened animals' eyes. Dampened kerchiefs covered our faces to filter the ever-present smoke. We looked like bandits.

Hiking up ash-covered trails, we reached the stables. We gently slipped bridles and saddles on our own horses, conscious of their fear. Silently, we strung the remaining animals together, blindfolding them as we went. Bales of hay smoldered around us. Sparks danced on the roofs of their shelters.

The plan was to lead fifteen horses out of the canyon to the Pacific Ocean. There they would be safe and cared for by veterinarians and volunteers. We hoped the ocean would create a natural corral. I would lead because I see well in the dark and because the golden coat of my large Palomino would reflect light from the rising half moon. The glow this night had turned to blood red because of the canyon's smoke, making our visibility to the other riders more difficult than we had planned. The other rescuers would space themselves amongst our nervous animals.

We mounted. I leaned forward and whispered into Tanya's highly sensitive ears, "Time to move out, girl." As she moved, the line rope tugged at her saddle horn, where it was tied. I reassured her with a pat on her neck and gently tapped her flanks with the heels of my boots. Off we went, the trailing blindfolded horses snorting from the fear caused by the smell of smoke. My fellow riders talked softly to the unseeing animals to calm them.

After several hours of wending our way down smoldering roads, our heads snapped up when our nostrils caught the mist from the ocean as it replaced the acrid smoke through which we had traveled. We pulled down our kerchiefs and sucked in the cooling ocean air. Our uncovered faces reflected moonlight as breezes dissipated the dense smoke. Our clothes were obscured by layers of soot.

We rounded the final switchback of the canyon and spotted the refuge that had been created for us. We dismounted and removed the bandanas from the horses' eyes. Remounting, we led the animals across the Pacific Coast Highway toward their safe haven.

Once on the sand, our steeds were released. Our mission was completed as volunteers threw piles of hay at their ash-covered hooves. The sound of horses chomping let us know our wards were all right.

After unsaddling our mounts, we let them enjoy food and water with the others. Volunteers brought us coffee and chow. Too tired to sleep, we all shed tears at what was lost and won that night. A lot of relieved laughter was heard, too.

Dawn broke several hours later. What a sight! Our magnificent animals were frolicking in the waves of the mighty Pacific.

THE LINES OF LIQUID CARE

Mark Stephen Fletcher

The gentle waves break along the shore
in a never ending rhythm that speaks of the nature of life.

The full moon hovering out to sea makes each wave shimmer as it breaks,
as if lifting their eyes to Heaven, their voices ring out,
then they finally come to rest on the shore.

Then sister and brother, each in their turn, rise up out of the sea
and sink in the sand of the shore.

Oh these waves, living under the moonlight, gently lapping at the shore.

Each following, and then leading, along a path that is right.
Doing what they were created to do.

As the moonlight shines brightly, through the froth of the surf,
it makes a smile on the face of the shore.

The sea birds that soar, so high overhead,
look down from their heavenly place.
They are so renewed by the majesty, order, and grace
that they cry for the joy in their life.

The song of the waves, and the smiles that they paint,
flow into the hearts of man.

They sing of soothing, and peace, the order in life,
for beasts,
and the land,
and for man.

Fallen

Joan T. Doran

And when the people could no longer see
the heavens, for a cloud had overtaken them,
they fought amongst themselves, even over stones
that lay about their feet, though nothing grew among the stones,
and in their emptiness, the people yearned for nourishment,
but only stones lay silent in their midst,
so from them, they sought fulfillment.

Behold, they said, *these stones are ours,*
let us gather them and build a mountain
which will guard us, and beneath its height
this will become our happy valley which
no cloud will overtake, so from the stones
they built a mountain, and into it they breathed
their wishes and their dreams
which sunk down roots, and from these roots
green shoots sprang forth and thrived,
and to the mountain's slopes
came creatures of the fields and of the air,
and over all they placed a man to oversee the mountain.

Then in his care the mountain's riches grew
and all the people reveled in their valley
and raised the overseer so high above them
that he knew not a raider in their midst
because the raider's visage was so fair
and even when spring lambs began to disappear
the overseer said *The mountain god must need these*
lambs to eat so the people will still prosper and will not
cry out against me and send me to a lower place
and thus I will not see and I shall thrive
and he stayed silent as the lambs.

But lo, one day a lamb itself cried out
and the people heard its cry and cried out themselves
and recognized the raider in their midst

and vanquished him and the overseer as well
and their cries pierced the cloud and the heavens
rained down torrents on their hill of stones
which fell back as it once had been.
And the gladness of their valley was no more
for they saw themselves now to be as other men
so they grieved and rent their garments over what was lost,
and forever on the fallen stones, their sorrow glistened.

WILDERNESS BLOOMED THERE

Susan Cummins Miller

Wilderness bloomed there
in the curve of the driveway
in the shadow of a post
hidden from dog-walkers and commuters
and the curtained windows
of cinder-block homes: a pincushion
cactus, *Mammillaria,* wearing a crown
of purple blossoms. The nondescript plant
has been hiding in plain sight, small
and all but forgotten

like a student from a foreign land
(Afghanistan, perhaps, where girls
are taught their place) who sits silently,
all semester, at the back
of the lecture hall, the force
within her building
until one day she raises her hand
speaks aloud
and the world turns to stare
in surprise
in awe.

Sheru Goes to School

Tabinda Bashir

Our daughter, Lisa, left Pakistan early in childhood and had her schooling mostly in Nigeria. For higher studies she went to the United States, completed her Information Technology major, and is now settled in Chicago. She lives the usual life there, with emphasis on hard work and good work ethics.

Lisa visits Lahore for vacations, loves Pakistan, and reads about the history and culture of that region. She enjoys family gatherings and the lavish wedding parties. But she has no experience of everyday life in Pakistan. She has little idea that people in such old civilizations, who have seen countless natural catastrophes and have been conquered by innumerable invaders, have a hard core. Grownups and children alike have an uncanny understanding of the human psyche. They can gauge a person's depth at a glance. Sometimes, they use these abilities to the detriment of others. Foreign visitors often get duped into parting with their money.

Home help is easily available in Pakistan. The family has a resident cook, Umer, a cleaning woman, Bashiran, a part time gardener, a watchman, and Sheru, the boy who comes to collect the garbage. Lisa stood chatting with Umer and Bashiran one day when she saw a dirty, barefoot boy about six years of age standing at the far end of the back yard. He looked curiously at Lisa and hesitated to come forward. When Umer brought the garbage bag out, he grabbed it and ran, looking back once.

"Who is he? Doesn't he wash? He looks like he has come out of a mud bath. And why is he alone?" Lisa inquired, amazed at his appearance.

"He is Sheru," Umer told her. "His family comes daily to collect garbage."

"Shouldn't he be in school?"

"No. They are poor wretches," Bashiran blurted out with disdain. "They only worry about getting the next meal and any money they can hoodwink from anyone. They will never learn and never progress. You have to work hard to defeat poverty." She had single-handedly educated and settled her eight daughters.

"But still, we should do something about him. Where does he live?" Lisa asked.

"We don't know. They come from some faraway place on their donkey cart, collect garbage, and go away," Umer told her.

The next day Lisa was ready for Sheru. He saw her and ran away. This continued for a couple of days, but gradually he came around when she offered him a cup of milk. That became a daily routine. He would almost snatch the cup from her and swallow it in one gulp. When other children of his clan were around, he would give a strange primordial cry that did not belong to any language Lisa knew. They would come running and share sips from the same cup.

Sheru was dirty, as if he had never had a bath in all his life. His body was covered with muck. He wore no shoes. His feet were covered with fresh and scarring scabies and small wounds. He constantly pulled out some scabs from the scars or dirt from the cracks, then tried to clean the spot with his spit. His pants and T-shirt, caked with mud, were two sizes too small for him.

Lisa asked him to call his father, who came the next day. He was a tall man, equally unclean except for his face, on which he might have splashed some water. He was wearing old, torn sneakers. His name was Haider.

Their clan was the poorest of the poor. They lived some fifteen kilometers away near Hanjarwal. Various members of Haider's family hopped on their donkey cart around 3:00 a.m. and reached their place of work about three hours later. We saw men, women, and children from age fourteen down to suckling babies on that cart. Haider evaded questions about how he disposed of the garbage. Lisa asked around and discovered that each family had their designated area of garbage collection allocated by those who bought the waste from them. Having gathered the rubbish, they sorted out different items and sold those to the corresponding dealer. The waste that could not be recycled was thrown into the river after paying a fee to another dealer. It turned out that there was probably a whole mafia that extorted money and controlled the garbage collectors' lives.

"Why don't you send Sheru to school? He is too young to be doing such work." Lisa asked the typical question of any foreigner unfamiliar with the perils of life in poor countries.

"What will he do in school? Even then, he will be collecting garbage. And besides, I will lose the salary he gets now. We are poor people." Haider looked at her in a way that indicated he knew well how the rich people come, advise them how to improve their lives, and then go away.

"He can get some job, start a business, and have a respectable life. He could help all of you to live better."

"What job can he get? If he studies, he will go abroad like you, and I will lose a son."

However she tried, she could not convince Haider of the benefits of education. He only knew that those who go to school ultimately leave the country, come back on holidays, and give people like him huge tips. So Lisa asked Umer, who had done eight years of schooling himself, to explain to Haider. Umer told him that if Sheru went to school he could keep accounts, see where they could make more profit, and know if they were being cheated. That clicked with Haider, and he looked a bit inclined to listen.

The next day Lisa asked Sheru, "What did you eat yesterday?"

"Roti." (Flat bread.)

"And what did you eat it with?"

"Nothing."

"You must have eaten it with something!"

"Water?"

Lisa was shocked. Roti is not eaten by itself. Apparently, roti with meat or vegetable curry was a luxury for him.

Days passed. After some more cups of milk for Sheru and constant talks with Haider, Lisa and Umer convinced him to find out the expenses from a school near where they lived. He tolerated their verbal barrage and agreed perforce. He still looked clueless about what a school was, and why it should be paid for. Lisa wondered if she was wasting her time. But she had made up her mind and was not ready to give up just yet. She assured Haider that she would pay for Sheru's education until the end and compensate for the pay he lost.

Haider brought a brochure from a school near his house, with English as the medium of instruction. Although run by Pakistanis, it was very expensive for the average person. The school expected its students to have Western

standards of hygiene and discipline and to converse in English. That was just
not right for Sheru or his father, who did not even know what the brochure
said. Sheru needed to go to a government school. Such schools are present in
all localities and are cheaper. They have dedicated local teachers who know
most residents and are aware of their shortcomings. The medium of instruction in such schools is Urdu, Pakistan's national language.

Haider didn't know the difference between an English medium and a
government school. After having spoken to a teacher in the clean environ-
ment of a private seminary, he looked more willing for Sheru to be educated.
However, he repeatedly asked about the amount of money he would get in
lieu of Sheru's salary.

Lisa had kept her father, Hamid, and me informed about her progress
with Sheru.

"Dad, I think I have to go where Sheru lives and try to find a school that
is suitable for children like him."

"Your intentions are noble," he said. "You have already been helping
him with food and money. It will be difficult for you to move around in the
slums where they live. You have never seen anything like it. The weather is
getting hot, and you may have to walk in the open. Besides, they could fleece
you easily."

"Please, Dad. Now that I have started it, I would like to finish this
project. Please."

"She won't give up easily," I said to Hamid. "I think it will be a good idea
if you accompany her."

"All right, I will. But be prepared for any disappointment," he cautioned
Lisa.

"Thanks, Dad." Lisa smiled and hugged him.

They hired a car for the next day with Yasser, our trusted driver. Haider
and Sheru were to bathe and come in clean clothes. Both of them looked
totally different the next morning. Haider, a tall, well-built, rather fair-
complexioned man, wore a faded T-shirt, jeans, and worn-out moccasins
without socks. Sheru, clad in black *shalwar qameez* (tunic and baggy pants),
wore no shoes because he didn't have any. One felt like cradling his pretty
face with his blondish hair all combed back. Possibly some genes from an
Afghan warrior had been passed down to him. Sheru looked and probably
felt lighter with all that muck washed away as he hopped and jumped in the
compound.

The car came at the appointed hour, and they got ready for their quest. Haider and Sheru sat in the front passenger seat. Dad, Lisa, and Umer squeezed in the back. I had advised Umer to carry some water, salt, and a packet of cookies. At the peak of the day it is possible to feel faint and get a heat stroke.

It took them about twenty-five minutes to reach the village of Hanjarwal. A left turn from the main road brought them to a thickly populated area of smaller, lower income houses. The narrow, convoluting tarred roads had hardly any space at the shoulders. Yasser's driving expertise took them through because, at times, it felt like the car would scrape against the front of a house. After what seemed like an interminable roller coaster ride, they emerged into an open area of a few acres. It was a large garbage dump with shops and houses on one side. They parked the car in a blind alley. Yasser stayed with his car; the rest got out and walked towards Sheru's house.

Under a burning sun in a cloudless sky, with flies and insects buzzing around and an incredible stench, they walked on dry dung. They saw human and animal excreta, either dry or less dry or fresh.

Haider walked a couple of steps behind. He was aware of the contrast between that area and the area Lisa came from. But Sheru was on his home turf. He led the way. He walked, sometimes hopped, his head held high, his arms swinging. He knew exactly which spot was dry enough to put his foot on.

In front they saw a settlement of a few hundred huts built on the garbage dump. It was a collection of shabby shacks standing up against each other. They were fashioned out of bamboo poles or scaffolding bent into a rough rounded shape and covered with scrap tarpaulin, reeds, plastic, or iron sheets. With no drainage, each hut had a low mud barrier around it to keep the rainwater out. During the rains, people walked through slimy dung to go to work. Who could question the state of Sheru's feet?

Electricity and running water were out of the question. A wall surrounded the settlement. The residents paid rent to someone, no one said who, to be able to live there.

They arrived at Sheru's shack. It was a hovel like the others with its space roughly divided into two enclosures for Haider's and his brother's families. The place was littered with old dented pots and pans, some rotting food, and soiled clothes. Lisa met with Sheru's mother and aunts. Surprisingly, they were a happy lot and greeted her with smiles.

As it often happens at such occasions, men, women carrying babies, and children came out gradually to look at the strangers. They whispered among themselves, "Now the Madams have started coming to our area."

Some of them asked Lisa if she was going to give them money. Probably some NGO had visited them. Mostly foreign, these non-government charity organizations visit such places. They take copious notes and pictures, survey the area, and distribute money. They promise to come back, but seldom do.

Lisa met with giggles when she tried to ask how they cleaned and washed their clothes. They didn't know how to converse with city people, nor did they understand what she said. The boys laughed out loud and threw mud at each other. Sheru just stood on the side.

The group proceeded from there and kept asking if there was a school in the vicinity. No one knew or cared about a school. Some gave sarcastic glances and walked on. Some pointed in different directions. At last, a man took them near the center of the settlement. A bigger hut, not very different from the others, was the local school. It was clean inside, even had a carpet and some rudimentary furniture. A few students sat there. But the school had no teacher. Quite obviously, no teacher would like to go to such a place.

They traced their steps back to the car in search of another school. The sun and the stench had gotten to Lisa. She felt faint and dizzy. The water and salt and the cookies came in handy. After that, Umer made it a point to make Lisa drink salt water periodically.

Hamid said, "Let's go back. We have had enough."

Umer voiced his consent.

"I am not giving up now, Dad. Please! After having been through so much, we have to be able to find some respectable school. If the government can establish a school in that hell hole, then there has got to be another one around," Lisa begged.

So they decided to push on. The car began cruising through tortuous narrow lanes, where the buildings threatened to crush it, but Yasser proved himself again. They stopped at every corner store and asked about a government school in the area, receiving no satisfactory answer. Tired of the repeated stopping and their slow progress, Umer decided to get out and walk in front of the car. He asked every passerby or shopkeeper and followed their directions. The car followed him. They could not have driven any faster than

Umer could walk, anyway. Eventually, a man led them to an open space between the houses. Their faces lit up because right in front of them was the Hanjarwal High School.

They got out of the car and heaved a sigh of relief. The unpaved ground in front of the school had been swept clean. The surrounding wall had a closed iron gate. Umer knocked. Someone opened a peephole and, after satisfying himself, let them in. It was a student dressed as a watchman in a clean grey uniform of *shalwar qameez,* a cap and a staff tucked under his arm. He was wearing polished shoes.

Yasser had to stay with his car, and Umer decided to sit with him.

Hamid, Lisa, Haider, and Sheru were shown into the principal's office.

The school presented a stark contrast to Sheru's habitat. Its walls had been freshly painted; it had a clean compound with areas for sports and tidy flower beds. Students walked around in clean uniforms with books in their hands.

The principal's office had a table, three chairs, a bookshelf, and a bench along the wall. Lisa and Hamid sat on the chairs at the table; Sheru and his father sat on the bench. They were welcomed by Abdus Sattar, the Physical Training master. He seemed to be a straightforward, simple teacher. After the usual greetings and a tour of the school, he asked about the purpose of their visit.

"We are here to admit Sheru in a school," Hamid said. "I am afraid he knows no reading or writing or anything else, for that matter. He comes to collect our garbage and lives near here in Hanjarwal."

"Don't worry, sir. We have all kinds of students here. There are no requirements of reading and writing for admission. We just ask the children to walk in." Then Abdus Sattar turned towards Sheru. "What is your name?"

Sheru, our barefoot garbage boy, stood up tall and pronounced his real name. "My name is Sher Ali. My father's name is Haider Ali." Impressed by his confidence, Abdus Sattar turned to Hamid and said, "Consider him admitted. I would like to see his parents."

Haider stood up. Abdus Sattar asked him to be seated and inquired about Sheru's age, their residence and family. Haider told him, "Sheru is seven years old. I have four more children. My brother's family and mine live in the settlement of garbage pickers nearby. Bibi Lisa has been kind enough to suggest that Sheru be admitted to a school. We have no money to educate our children and are thankful for any help."

Abdus Sattar explained what they had to do. "The first thing you require is a birth certificate. You can get that from the local Councilor (government representative). They will ask for a bribe of Rs.200/-, about $2.50. Regardless of his real age, get Sheru registered as five years old because by the age of sixteen we have to get the students out of school. By that time, he should have finished class ten. Books are free. You have to buy the uniform, tie, shoes, and socks from the local bazaar. That might come to Rs.1000/-, under $13.00. The monthly fee is Rs.20/-, a few cents. You have to deposit five months fee in advance, that is Rs.100/-, about $1.25."

They paid the fees and set off for the bazaar. Now it was easy to get directions. People knew the Councilor's office and the shops. They got the birth certificate and proceeded to buy the rest of the things.

Hamid wondered, while Haider browsed around the shops, "Who will get Sheru ready for school every morning? This will be a regular ongoing process."

"They don't know a thing about cleanliness. Is it possible his parents will get fed up with the routine and give up? They are in the garbage business, and this is the antithesis," Lisa said.

"I think Haider and the others will pocket the money," Umer declared in his street-smart voice. "He never misses a chance to mention compensation for Sheru's salary. I won't be surprised if the shopkeepers and the Councilor are in on it."

"I wonder if Sheru himself will get fed up with the discipline and run away. He is such a free spirit. I do hope he finishes school and becomes an example for the others. I shall give Haider some extra money instead of Sheru's lost salary before I go back to the States." Lisa visualized the realization of her dream.

Shopping at different stores was fun. Sheru looked nice in a uniform and tie. At the shoe shop he was placed in a chair. The attendant looked at his feet in amazement for a while. Then he asked Lisa, "Please clean his feet."

"I have nothing here to clean his feet with. Please do something."

The attendant looked confused. He had probably never seen such a sight. Those who could afford to buy shoes knew how to wash their feet. Unable to figure out what to do, he just grabbed a rag and quickly wiped Sheru's feet, but avoided touching them. A couple of shoes had to be tried on for size, which made the attendant uncomfortable. Nevertheless, the task was done. Then they got the socks.

Lisa's mission had been accomplished after a grueling exercise of about four hours, and at a fraction of the cost of the private school whose brochure Haider had brought. Sheru would be looked after better at the Hanjarwal High School.

Lisa, Hamid, and Umer got in the car to go back home. Sheru and Haider went along because their cart was parked by our house.

Soon it was time to say good-bye. Sheru climbed up and stood in the cart, and Haider sat in front, their faces calm as if nothing out of the ordinary had happened. Haider pulled at the reins, the donkey moved, and the cart slowly disappeared around the corner.

A Tale of the Oasis Tutor

John J. Candelaria

Once upon a time, the Oasis Tutor came to life
in cities where schools allowed children more
chances to read, to write, to talk; where tutor
sessions became places of refuge: a venue
where kids learned to read better. So together
with teachers, tutors mastered how to encourage
a child to read forever.

Today, tutor training enriches that zest to learn
the details and methods that make reading,
talking, and writing important for progress
in the classroom. Gathering with seasoned tutor
staff, new and skilled mentors attend ongoing
sessions to grasp neat insights that sharpen
a child's reading.

Each child takes her, his own time to gain
a love of reading and to build a tally of books
read. The tutor learns to be patient, reads every
day with zeal and a sparkle of joy to the voices
in every story. New words bring meaning
to the child's reading; a fresh vocabulary builds
a child's savvy.

Youngsters like the one-to-one talk, often missing
at home. Each session with talk helps them hear
words in full bloom. The tutor asks open-ended
questions that explore new ideas, new words
a child can absorb. When the full meaning
of nifty words from text and pictures unfolds,
a child smiles.

A good session has the child say, "Today I read
a book, wrote in my journal, listened to my tutor,
and talked with my friend." Words tutors cherish
as they master how to encourage
a child to read forever.

THANK YOU, MISS ERMA

Vivian Bullock

It is September, 1922, and even though I won't be six until December first, I will soon be on my way to school. I can see the little two-room country school from our kitchen window. It is close enough that I can even hear the children playing. Mama is telling me I will like school, that I will learn to read and have lots of children to play with. She stands outside with my little sister, Helen, and they watch me until I reach the school and wave goodbye to them.

Entering the schoolyard, I don't see a teacher, just children running and playing. I decide to sit on the school steps and watch them. Suddenly, I hear a loud angry voice ordering me to "Get off these damp steps now!" I look up to see a mean face glaring at me, and I say, "I don't have to." The face belongs to a woman who happens to be the principal of the school. She grabs my arm, takes me to a tree, breaks off a switch, and begins hitting me on the legs. We hear a school bell. She looks surprised, but stops hitting me, and we both follow the children up the steps to the schoolrooms.

I'm trying to hold back tears when a pretty woman puts her arm around me and dries my eyes with her handkerchief. The Principal scolds her, saying I deserved the switching, then heads towards her room, where she teaches the older children. The pretty women, holding my hand, takes me to her room, where she teaches the younger children. This women is Miss Erma, who later made learning a pleasure. Eighty-eight years later, I remember her kindness and smile, because I know now that she saw what was happening in the schoolyard and decided to ring the bell a little early.

Thank you, Miss Erma.

Mud Pies

Virginia G. Barrows

When I was a little girl,
How I loved making mud pies!
I would squat next to the dripping back yard faucet
With an old tablespoon,
An ice cream stick,
And a toy tin plate or two,
To place my finished "creations" on

I would entertain myself for hours,
My mother, tolerant soul that she was,
Didn't mind much if I got muddy,
My grungy sunsuit would be dumped
Into the washing machine
Just inside the back door,
And I would be "dunked"
A few steps further on into the bathtub

"It never rains in sunny California"
So my days were warm and toasty outside,
And I could choose that fun
Just about anytime I wanted to
As I grew older, school interrupted
My creative endeavors
Later, I got even!

I attended high school and college ceramic classes,
Learned to use the potters' wheel,
Spinning doughy clay into bowls,
Vases, pots, plates, what have you,
Dried, dipped into glaze, and fired in a kiln,
They were transformed from
Fragile, crumbly clay,
To strong vitreous ceramics
From dull mud color into brilliant glistening hues
Later in life I had my own
"Wheel and kiln," finding hours

Of joy creating my own ceramic designs
Perhaps more sophisticated, refined,
Nevertheless they were still my
"Mud Pies"

Muddy Seasons

Rebecca Ann Rouillard

Summer Time

Mud pies made out of water and dirt.
I wear sleeveless shirts and shorts.
My hot feet are bare in the cool grass.
There is dirt all over me.
Ah, the freedom of summer!
Lots of light these days.
Lots of time to play!

Autumn Time

Splashing in the mud puddles.
Rain. Rain. Rain. Come again some other day.
I wear my yellow raincoat and boots.
Falling leaves I throw back to the trees.
I can't seem to stay out of the mud!
But there is school to attend.
I have homework to do.
No time to play today.

Winter Time

Muddy boots leave tracks in the house.
My feet are soaking wet from the slush
Of the occasional melting snow.
I wear layers of clothes.
So bundled up I can barely move.
It takes so long to go out.
Red cheeks and dripping nose from the cold.
The ground is too hard to make some mud.
Maybe it's too cold to go outside today.

Spring Time

Cow paddies in the fields
Helping nature bring new life.
I wrinkle my nose at the smell.

Gentle breezes come with warmer days.
More time these days to play outside.
I wear short sleeved dresses with sweaters.
On my feet are pretty Mary Jane shoes.

I am older now, a young lady in fact.
I am 10, a whole decade have I lived.
I don't like the dirt anymore.
I like being outside with my dolls having a tea party.
I like reading a book under the shade of a tree.
I like having a glass of lemonade and cookies nearby.
I count the days until school is out.
I'm looking forward to the freedom
That summer often brings.

I am now in my fifth decade.
I look back to those summer days
Knowing it will never be the same.
But I'm still here.
I can be a child if only for a while.
I'll go outside with my feet bare and walk on the grass.
Maybe make a mud pie or two.
Just to see.

Younger Sister

Esther Brudo

like knowing that the sight of me
would light up grandma's eyes

i knew my brother hated me
but i didn't know why

he could whistle anything
play the piccolo, march in a band

collect baseball cards, save money
dislocate his elbow, break his nose

he was a boy, did brave things
i wanted to be brave, too

he pushed me away
i followed him so close i walked on his heels

he punched my arm
i kicked his shins

i wanted to be with him
help, applaud, do it too

he would have none of it

finally i didn't care
went to parties, wore lipstick
had boyfriends who liked me

then one day he wanted to learn
to dance and asked me to teach him

just in time we discovered each other
before he left to be a soldier

and i, the younger sister
stayed home

THE HORSEHAIR BRIDLE

Janet Thompson

Imagine…
Proudly leading all the other marchers, a little kid astride a beautiful copper-colored horse carried the huge American flag as high as he could hoist it.

My younger brother, Jere, was small for his age. An accomplished rider, he had a head of bouncy blonde curls, a fetching smile, and a bubbly personality. Everyone adored him. For several years, he was invited to ride at the head of the Memorial Day, College Day, and the Fourth of July parades in town.

In the mid-forties, our family lived in Fort Collins, the home of Colorado State University. We owned a tiny acreage and three horses: Brownie, Kelly, and Rocket. Brownie was an old mare that, if she got a chance to look over her shoulder, high-tailed it like the wind back to the corral. Bad-tempered Kelly, finding herself behind either of the other two horses, would obnoxiously bite them in the butt, or she might take the rider under a low branch… or both.

Rocket was a beautiful sorrel gelding, 5-gaited, part American Saddlebred and part quarter horse with a little Morgan thrown in for character. A classy animal, he was a glowing rust color with a white blaze on his face. Especially when he paced, he was a dream to ride, just an easy sliding forward and back, almost a slithering movement. Why only three horses? I didn't usually ride with the family. As a junior, then senior in high school, I preferred cheerleading, dancing, parties, and boys.

When my dad's stepfather died in the early 1940's, Daddy was given the horsehair bridle. It had never been used. When Jere was first asked to lead a parade, we all decided Rocket should wear it. Later, every ceremonial day when Rocket saw the fancy bridle, he would bow his neck, perk up his ears, and arch his tail even more than usual. *Rocket was going to be on parade!* How he must have basked in the cheers as he high-stepped down the main street in town, carrying the American flag with his beloved rider, Jere, on board. Rocket seemed to know that only exceptional horses wore this special gear. We never put it on either of the other two horses—only on Rocket and only for parade days.

We learned that a notorious train robber had made the bridle when he was imprisoned in the Wyoming State Penitentiary in Rawlins. Jailed there for years, he hand-dyed and braided the bridle. During the Depression, when the robber got out of the Pen, he sought a place to stay and work at one of the two family sheep ranches near Medicine Bow. It was common during those hard times for needy travelers "on-the-road" to receive food and shelter from caring folks who fared better. When sometime later he left the ranch, in thanks for having received food, lodging, and work, the ex-prisoner gave the family the beautiful bridle he had made.

A few talented convicts, serving long sentences in western prisons between the turn of the century and the 1930's, would spend 700 to 1,500 hours fashioning horsehair tack. Indians had handed down the hitching and weaving art, passing it from prisoner to prisoner. Some artists only used natural-colored softer mane hair instead of coarser tail hair. Because commercial dyes were caustic and could create problems for the prison administrators, only plant dyes from flowers or vegetables were allowed. The hitching was typically done over leather or wood.

My bridle is crafted from seven colors of horsehair. The reins are woven in a herringbone pattern of black and gold, ending with tassels of blue, green, burgundy, and gold. Four half-circle rosettes like conchos in a four-color zigzag pattern are at the sides of the brow-band and earpieces. Throughout the piece are other smaller multicolored rosettes and turnings covered in patterned woven horsehair.

Daddy gave the bridle to me in 1956, when our family fell apart after Jere went into the Navy, Mother and Daddy got a divorce and moved out of state, and we sold our horses. A couple of small chomps in the reins result from the horsehair being scratchy when Rocket wore it…but he was smart; he knew how a little pain brought big gains!

From 1956 to 1977, I kept the bridle packed away in tissue. Having newly restored an old Victorian house, I learned that they often featured Indian decor in some of the rooms. So I displayed it as the "pièce de résistance." Since then, it has always hung on my office wall as the lovely art object that it is.

Daily, as I see the bridle, the memories of those holiday parades flood back and linger. I forever imagine dear Jere, now in his heavenly home, proudly hoisting our beloved American flag high in a breeze, happily astride prancing Rocket, with our old "Spotty" dog, chasing along at Rocket's heels.

Digging

Tilya Helfield

When he was a kid, my brother Ray loved to climb. He bragged that he could travel the entire block from Augusta to Chapel without ever once setting foot on the ground. He crawled along fences, across roof tops and around telephone poles, swinging from one perch to the next, pounding his chest like Tarzan the ape man, shouting, 'Creega bundolo tarmangi ud yark!' which he said meant 'Slay and kill white man now!'

And he loved the movies. Every Saturday afternoon after lunch, my mother made my sister Joan and me take him with us to the Nelson Theater on Rideau Street. Mum gave us money and a clean handkerchief to wipe his nose, but as soon as we turned the corner out of sight, we tied the handkerchief over his eyes and made him walk blindfolded the rest of the way so he'd be used to the dark and could find us seats quickly in the dim crowded theater. We always had a terrible time getting him to leave when the feature was over. He loved to watch reruns of *The Perils of Pauline* over and over again, especially the episode where the heroine was tied to the railway tracks in front of an oncoming train.

"Next week she's really gonna get what's coming to her," he'd say with satisfaction. "Stupid dame!" He was really disappointed the following week when the hero galloped up on his white horse and saved the heroine in the nick of time. "He should've taken off on that horse and never looked back," he muttered, shaking his head in disgust all the way home.

One day a photographer came by carrying a camera and tripod, leading a Shetland pony by a frayed cord. When he saw Ray sitting on our front steps, he asked, "Take yer pitcher on the pony, Sonny?" Ray climbed right up into the saddle, but the minute the photographer clicked the shutter, Ray dug his heels into the pony's sides and trotted off down the street. The photographer yelled and took off after him but it was hours before he found him and brought him back. I still have the photo of Ray sitting astride that pony, a wicked grin of satisfaction on his face.

Ray was sent to his room without supper after that escapade. He didn't seem to mind, which was just as well because he got sent to his room a lot. He spent the time reading his extensive collection of comic books, which he kept in stacks on a shelf in his cupboard exactly one-quarter of an inch apart so he'd know if they'd been touched. The comics disappeared when we moved a few years later, and a few weeks ago—out of the blue, after sixty years!—Ray accused Joan and me of stealing them.

Ray was fascinated by the war. He drove my mother crazy leaving coded messages for his fellow secret agents in the hollow newel post in the banisters at the foot of the stairs, and every Saturday morning he tuned the Philco in to *L for Lanky,* a serial featuring RAF bombing missions over Germany. After the program was over, he'd climb up into the apple tree in our side yard and drop apple bombs onto the tea table Joan and I had set up under it, scattering the china and staining the lace tea cloth.

But his favourite activity by far that summer was digging a hole to China. Joan and I tried to convince him that he was wasting his time, but he maintained that if he dug deep enough, he'd come out on the other side of the world and walk upside down. He even went around muttering in an annoying kind of sing-song he insisted was Chinese, so he'd be fluent in the language by the time he got there.

The first time I actually noticed him digging was just after Grandpa Joe arrived for his annual summer visit. Grandpa didn't like females any more than Ray did and took little interest in Joan and me, especially now that Ray was old enough to help him sprinkle the tobacco shreds from his leather pouch onto the fragile cigarette paper, roll it up in the wooden cigarette machine, lick the gummed edge and stuff it into his long black cigarette holder.

While Grandpa smoked, Ray read him the stock market quotations from *The Citizen* because the print was too damned small even when Grandpa peered through the pince-nez he wore on a black cord around his neck. Then they listened to Lorne Greene reading the CBC News on the Philco. Ray loved to listen to Grandpa talk about the war and all the relatives he had left behind in Russia to die at the hands of the goddamn Bolsheviks. Ray was especially interested in Grandpa's descriptions of the beach in Florida, where he spent the winters. Maybe it was the idea of all that sand just waiting to be dug up. He was particularly fond of a snapshot Grandpa gave him of himself, his skinny bronzed body nude except for his white bathing trunks, sitting cross-legged on the beach like a swami.

When Grandpa announced that he was going to Miami again that winter, Ray asked him wistfully, "Will you take me with you to your ami, Grandpa?" Grandpa told him that he was too young and anyway he had promised to take his cousin Lenny with him this year.

That night, after supper, Ray went outside and began to dig. I was up in my room doing my homework when I heard the *thunk* of his shovel in the driveway and wondered what on earth he was up to now. I went to the window and watched him, his shirt off and one of my mother's linen guest towels tied around his forehead like a coolie, grimly shoveling. Grandpa never did take Ray to Miami. He married an American woman that winter who wasn't interested in sharing their Miami apartment with her step-grandchildren.

All that summer, Ray's friends, Stephen and Donnie, helped him occasionally, but Ray did most of the actual digging himself. Because Donnie was the oldest, he wanted a say in the design and planning of the hole, and they often argued about it. But Ray was adamant. Everyone was welcome to come and help him dig, but the hole was his project and he was in charge. Sometimes they pretended the hole was a German U-boat with a periscope made from a broken pipe, through which Ray yelled, "Achtung! Gewar nicht alles macht!" and other threats in simulated German at everyone passing by. But when the other boys got tired of the game and went home, Ray always went back to digging his hole to China.

Ray wouldn't let any girls in on the dig. He hated girls, especially Joan and me, because we never let him play with us. I was only two years older than Joan, but seven years older than Ray—a vast gulf at that age. Besides, he was a boy. We had nothing in common and Joan and I had as little to do with him as possible. We talked to each other in pig Latin, which made him crazy because he didn't understand what we were saying, and we were allowed to stay up to listen to *Charlie McCarthy* on the Philco after he was sent to bed. When my mother had a party she let us get dressed up and help serve the hors d'oeuvres to the guests, but she made Ray stay in his room because he once drank all the liquor out of the half-empty glasses and threw up on her Chinese rug.

Ray might have gotten his taste for liquor from his friend Stephen, whose father was a commander in the navy overseas. Stephen's mother spent every afternoon wrapped in an afghan in the living room, even in midsummer, sipping Canadian Club from a Royal Doulton teacup. One afternoon, the boys sneaked swigs from the bottle while Stephen's mother snored, oblivious, on the chesterfield. When he came home, my mother held his nose, forced down a good dose of ipecac and put him to bed, where he muttered, "Goddam stupid dame!" over and over like a mantra until he fell asleep. When my father got home, he took off his belt and gave Ray a whipping for drinking whiskey and swearing at his mother.

That night Ray snaked downstairs on his stomach, commando-style, crawled behind the chesterfield and shot rolled-up pieces of paper at Joan and me with a slingshot he'd made out of popsicle sticks and a rubber band. He made Joan cry and my mother lost her patience and sent all three of us to our rooms in disgrace.

The next day, to get even, Joan and I locked Ray out of the garage, which was our playhouse since we had no car. But Ray broke the lock and burst in, scattering our dolls and breaking all the doll furniture. Joan started to cry and knelt on the cement floor, gathering up the broken toys, but I was furious at the damage he'd caused. I ran out into the garden and grabbed my skipping rope and chased him through my mother's flower beds, hitting him with the rubber handles. He kept dodging away from me, taunting me as he avoided the flailing ropes, but I trapped him in the corner beside the summer-kitchen and Joan held him while I tied his hands with the rope. I grabbed the garden hose and turned the the spray on him until he was soaked to the skin. He struggled and cursed and finally got loose and ran off. We went back to straighten out the mess in the garage, completely forgetting to turn off the hose. We never noticed as it soaked the garden and flooded the cellar. When my father came home from a business trip and saw the damage, he assumed Ray had done it and took off his belt and gave him a good thrashing.

I was worried that Joan and I would get into trouble, but Ray never told him it was our fault. He tried to scrabble up the attic stairs, with my father after him, desperately trying to escape that slashing belt, but there was no way out. We could hear the thwack of leather on bare flesh all the way down in the living room, where we sat pretending to read, red-faced with guilt, not looking at each other. That night, I had a terrible stomach ache and couldn't eat any supper.

"If he'd only cry, or show some remorse, I'd let him go," Dad told Mum. "This hurts me more than it does him. But it's my duty to straighten him out and if I have to beat it out of him, then by George, that's what I'm going to do." But Ray just curled up in a tight little ball and took it until my mother begged Dad to stop before he had a heart attack. Dad stood there panting, mopping his red face with his handkerchief and glaring at Ray who glared right back.

Then Ray marched out the kitchen door to the hole he'd begun in the driveway and resumed digging, the red welts on his back and legs blazing in the hot sun like badges of honour.

As the summer passed, Ray's hole grew deeper. Every night my father peered over the top of *The Citizen* and shook his head. "That hole is a danger to life and limb," he said. "I want it filled in first thing tomorrow." Ray ignored him. My father absolutely forbade him to dig any further. However, Dad was often out of town on business and Mum spent every afternoon playing tennis or mahjong, so I was the only one who noticed that the hole was getting deeper. Ray shored it up around the sides with pieces of wood from the cellar, and he put on Mum's gardening gloves and Dad's old Stetson to keep the dirt out of his hair and eyes. Soon the hole was so deep he was completely hidden from view. When passersby heard the thunk of the shovel and looked down the driveway, all they could see were clumps of dirt flying in the air onto a steadily growing mound.

Several weeks after Ray began digging his hole to China, Ti-Guy started coming over nearly every day with his little pail and shovel, squatting at the edge of the hole and wiping his dirty nose on the back of his sleeve. His name was Guy, but everyone called him Ti-Guy, (pronounced 'Tzeegee' with a hard 'G') to differentiate him from his father, after whom he was named. He was only four, too small to be of much use in the digging, and he spoke no English, but Ray bullied him mercilessly, giving him constant orders in simulated French, which Ti-Guy did his best to obey.

Ti-Guy had just moved with his parents from the Beauce to his grandparents' house, two doors down, until they could find a house of their own. His mother was having a difficult second pregnancy, and Mme. Dupré, his grandmother, was busy with household chores, so Ti-Guy was often left on his own to roam the neighbourhood and get into trouble.

One day, Ray and his friends tied Ti-Guy up and were lowering him into the hole when it collapsed, burying Ti-Guy up to his neck. By the time my mother, Joan, and I heard their screams and ran out of the house,

Ti-Guy almost totally buried except for the top of his blond head. My mother grabbed him by the hair and pulled him out, wiped off his nose and mouth with her apron so he could breathe, and told Joan and me to take him home. Then she ordered Ray to go his room and stay there until Dad got home.

Mum met Dad at the door that evening and demanded that he take immediate action.

Dad objected. "I just got home. Can't this wait at least until I've had a drink and something to eat?" But after one look at my mother's face, he sighed with resignation, took off his belt and went upstairs to give Ray a good hiding.

Then he went out to the driveway and covered up the hole with some boards he dragged from behind the garage. That night after supper, while the rest of us were in the living room listening to *Fred Allen*, Ray climbed out his bedroom window onto the summer-kitchen roof, shinnied down the drainpipe to the driveway, removed the boards from the hole and started to dig.

"It's because of that business with the hospital," my mother accused Dad. "It's all your fault! You and that damn psychologist! He was a perfectly normal child before that."

"There's no scientific evidence for that at all," my father said. "He was far too young when it happened to remember any of it."

When Ray was four years old, he developed a terrible ear infection. Dr. Shapiro and my father carried Ray into the master bedroom and I had a last glimpse of the two men silhouetted in the yellow lamp light, bending over Ray's small body on the bed before the door closed, muffling their murmurs and the sickening smell of ether. Joan and I cowered on the stairs while my mother sat in the kitchen sipping endless cups of tea.

The next day, Ray developed a fever and spent several days in the Civic Hospital. There had been a train wreck on the CPR tracks near Alma the week before and the hospital was full of injured soldiers on leave from Camp Petawawa.

Every night when my mother had to leave him, Ray stood shaking the bars of his crib and his cries followed her down the long echoing halls— "Mama, don't leave me, Mama!"

When Ray came home from the hospital, he had terrible nightmares and became hysterical whenever my mother tried to go out. She consulted a child psychologist, who advised her to go out as usual. Ray would adjust with time.

My father, ever the scientist, insisted that the doctor knew best. So she went, despite her misgivings, leaving a drawing of a clock face with Ray, with the hands pointing to the time she'd be home. But Ray refused to go to sleep no matter what Joan and I did to soothe him. He just lay there watching the real clock's hands move to the time on my mother's drawing, whimpering, "Mama, come home, Mama."

The next year when he started school, Ray played hooky every day. Mr. Armstrong, the truant officer, came to look for him, marching up and down the neighbourhood, tracking his spoor—splashes from ice blocks melting from the milk wagon where Ray perched, clicking his tongue and flicking an imaginary switch against the horse's flanks while he accompanied the milkman on his rounds. That night Dad gave Ray his first beating.

Ray finally stopped playing hooky, but he started throwing stones at the girls in the schoolyard. Perhaps he hoped he'd be suspended and allowed to stay home to dig; instead, the principal called my father, who beat him again.

Years later, when Ray called to tell me his divorce was final, he began to talk about his normal, happy childhood. I couldn't believe it. No mention of the beatings Dad used to give him. He'd stopped digging his hole at the end of that long-ago summer. We'd moved that fall to my mother's dream house in Rockcliffe Park, an exclusive suburb of Ottawa. It had a driveway paved with asphalt—no digging possible there. No fences or drainpipes to shinny down, either. When I came home from college for spring vacation, my parents were occupied with baby Deena, Joan was busy with her high school friends, and Ray was a taciturn stranger.

Ray talked bitterly about his divorce, which he said was affecting his health. His doctor had advised him to take up swimming to release the tension. He'd started doing leisurely laps at the local YMCA on the weekend; then he began to get up early on weekday mornings to swim before he went to work. Soon he was stopping in at the pool in the evening to do more laps before he went home. He bought a log book and started to keep a record of the distances he covered.

"So far I've swum the equivalent of the breadth of the United States, all the way to San Francisco and half-way across the Pacific Ocean to Hawaii," he boasted.

I pictured him in my mind's eye, his white swimmer's cap pulled down low over his forehead, his goggles stretched tight across his face to keep the water out of his hair and eyes. His jaw was set in that old familiar grimace that I remembered so well, completely absorbed by his desperate need to shove the water from the lane before him with his huge cupped hands.

I hoped that one day he'd actually make it to China after all.

Body Search

John J. Candelaria

A wise man said at the airport,
"Just stand there and be proud of it."

Think of the machine's x-rays
as a caress to your lovely body.

Accept the male to male, female
to female hand as a touch of grace.

It's not an invasion of your privacy,
or a rake of your inner being.

Your self-esteem is not on the line,
so just stand there and be proud of it.

MIXED MESSAGE

Jacqueline Hill

Stepping away from the stark whiteness of the cruise ship, I cross the gangway, enter the second floor of a government office building, make my way downstairs, and out onto the pier. The sun is high and the air thick with humidity. The sea breezes cannot cool the perspiration streaming in rivulets down my back nor eliminate the assault of stale, fishy odors that permeate the docks. A statue of a woman in a flowing gown and with open arms welcomes me to Palermo. At a small kiosk a few steps away, I purchase a ticket for a three-hour tour. After visiting other cities in Italy, I anticipate more bustling markets, magnificent churches, and unique gardens. The affable ticket agent informs me that the tour will begin in forty minutes. "Look for the blue bus there," he says and points across the busy avenue to a corner store with a large flashing "Farmacia" sign. Deciding to explore a few blocks of the nearby business district, I also plan to search for a gelateria to purchase one of the creamy frozen desserts that I have enjoyed throughout my visit to Italy.

A huge banner, "MAI PIU SOLI CONTRO LA MAFIA, PER LA LIBERTA D'IMPRESA 1991– 2011," hanging from a three-story building on my right captures my attention, and I snap a photo, intrigued by the only word I recognize, "Mafia." The somber message of the banner, which announces protest marches throughout Italy to commemorate the murders of innocent people, completely escapes me. Straight ahead, a roundabout with a barrage of signposts indicates directions to local cities. Cars, bicycles, mopeds, daring pedestrians, and buses compete for space on the narrow street. Punctuated by piles of dried dog poop, the sidewalks burst, filled with vendors hawking knock-off designer purses and jewelry, African masks, souvenir key chains, and miniature Italian flags. Shoe stores, expensive boutiques, and flower shops share cramped store fronts of 19th century buildings. Restaurant patrons relax under multicolored umbrellas as the aromas of international cuisine tease their noses. Local office workers stride purposefully, bags tucked tightly under their arms, eyes alert and aware as carefree tourists casually stroll about.

Two smiling twenty-something girls leaning on the ledge of a walk-up window lift appetizing cups of gelato and beckon passersby to the framed window, where a glass case presents a mouthwatering palette of flavors. Opening my coin purse, I realize I've spent my last Euro for a Senegalese mask. My pockets yield several coins, but not enough to pay for the gelato.

The salesgirl reaches out her hand and asks, "How much do you have?"

"Not enough," I lament.

"Here, Signora, enjoy the best gelato in Palermo."

"Grazie." The cold, smooth, nutty chocolate glides across my tongue and instantly cools my parched throat. Much refreshed, I once again venture to the grimy sidewalk.

Suddenly, the wail of sirens cuts through the torrid air. Curiosity piqued, I hurry to the next block, where the hectic traffic abruptly halts, and a cacophony of blaring horns bleats frustration and annoyance. A face-off between screaming protesters and a line of helmeted police officers blocks traffic and impedes my progress. To make the tour on time, I must change direction. Jostling my way along the sidewalk, I glimpse at my left a quiet, tree-lined lane that provides a convenient shortcut back to the main avenue. Within five minutes, I see the "Farmacia" sign and the blue bus. A paunchy bearded man, a cigar bouncing in one hand, is gesturing to a tanned young woman in dark blue slacks and a white blouse, with large Dior sunglasses resting on her forehead. Rushing past their animated conversation and up the steps of the bus into a blast of air conditioning, I flop into a seat, the sole passenger. Immediately, the young woman appears, explaining that the tour is being postponed for an hour because numerous protests around the city are blocking the bus routes.

"Uh uh, no ma'am, no thanks. I do not care to wait. I would like my money back."

"Signora, this is a magnificent tour, with much to experience. Won't you please wait?" After a second glance at my face, she shrugs her shoulders and points toward the pier. "You must go there." I return to a now empty kiosk, searching in vain for the friendly guy who sold me the ticket for the tour. Dropping the unused ticket into the nearest trash container, I gaze first toward the ship, and then back at the business district I've just left.

I spot a sign atop a drab, nondescript building: "Apostolata Del Mare Palermo, Casa Stella Maria." A post office? Perhaps I can purchase and mail some postcards so the afternoon is not a total bust. The white entry door leads to a small, square white room with a short staircase on the right and a dark mahogany-looking door on the left. I open the heavy wooden door and step into cool tranquility. A marble altar surrounded by roses, lilies, tulips, ferns, and palms dominates the front of the room. A majestic table, covered with a delicate lace cloth, sits at the front of the altar. A five-foot wooden crucifix stands to the left of the table. Behind the altar hangs a tapestry of a golden-haloed woman cradling a child. I sit on one of the wooden benches facing the altar, the only sound the whirring and clicking of my camera. After several photographs, I place the camera next to me, bow my head, and begin to pray silently. Peace envelops me.

Moments pass; a soft voice from behind announces very clearly, "This man, this Jesus. I am mad for Him. He is wonderful, yes?" Dressed stylishly in a chic sheath with a silk scarf at her neck and golden bracelets circling her wrists, the petite woman's tiny hands flutter as her eyes flash passion.

I contemplate that this woman may be some kind of religious nut, but my trusted intuition registers only her sincerity. "Yes, I love Him too, and He loves me." For fifteen minutes, we speak quietly of our Jesus. She reveals information about a stressful job that she wants to leave, but cannot because of family responsibilities. I share my sister-in-law's struggle with lung cancer and my husband's open-heart surgery two years ago. She discloses that she drives here daily during her lunch hour to distribute religious tracts. I speak of the joyful cruise that I'm taking. Motioning toward the tapestry, she points to an image of a ship's anchor near the woman's feet, and says, "She is the patron saint of Palermo's sailors. I will pray for your safe travels." We open the door and walk together into the brightness and heat of the Mediterranean sun. Facing each other, we hold hands. "Please pray for me," she urges.

Nodding my head, I mouth, "Yes." I watch her glide across the docks to the parking area. As I turn to photograph Apostolata del Mare Palermo, Casa Stella Maria, a large, bright red, fluorescent cross in the second-story window flashes.

No Mary

Lynda Riese

Oh, she was spotless, that rose
we studied in catechism,
no bloody stain on her blue robe,
full of grace like I was
full of meanness.

"HailMaryfullofgracetheLordiswiththee
blessedbethefruit,"
we intoned as we sat at our desks
in straight rows,
heads bowed like the grapes
that hung from their stems in bunches
on my father's back fence.

"Of thy womb, Jesus,"
me aching from cramps,
I thought of my mother due in July,
the baby that grew sweet
as a mango inside her.

My mother, no Mary,
huge in her ratty blue robe
watching "Queen for a Day" on TV,
no Joseph to hold her,
no donkey to flee on.

ADOPTION

Denise Marcelli

once there were two women
who never knew each other

one you called mom
the other you would not know

one was your guiding star
the other became your sun

one gave you a need for love
the other gave you love

one gave you your nationality
the other gave you your name

one gave you your talent
the other gave you direction

one gave you emotions
the other calmed your fears

one saw your sweet smile
the other dried your tears

one surrendered you
the other prayed for a child

God led you to her

A Single Strand

Nancy Sandweiss

The Steers franchise along a highway outside Durban
is bright, scrubbed; welcomes weary tourists
seeking food, clean toilets, sterile familiarity.
I order coffee from a bored counter clerk, pull out rands
from my fanny pack. In the restroom

a silent worker wipes down counters, refills rolls
of wafer thin tissue. Does she feel lucky? Everywhere
the unemployed line streets, crowd shantytowns.
I drop small coins in the waiting dish,
hurry to the parking lot where

three men peddle sacks of kiwi, shirt-sleeved
against a passing shower. Dark eyes silently beseech
tourists and locals alike. I shake my head,
escape into the air-conditioned coach.
Peering out the window, I note the Black Africans
walk away, too.

Another day, another rest stop.
A boy approaches with polite smile, dark eyes
imploring me to buy his beads. Stabbed
by his gentleness, I buy a single strand,
depart with change I do not need.

PRECONCEIVED NOTIONS

Eleanor Whitney Nelson

Preconceived notions can land you in trouble. This thought flashed through my mind while the small plane I was riding in taxied down a remote airstrip in southern Chile. As an exploration geologist, I have spent many hours in airplanes, and the more out-of-the-way the destination, the older and more dilapidated the aircraft become. But the choice of plane is often a take-it-or-leave-it situation. You learn to inhale deeply and climb on board, ignoring the duct tape on the wings and gaping holes in the instrument panels.

I have commonly found myself in little-known places. In 1981 my husband, Frank, a geologist with years of international experience, set up a program for an American mining company to look for gold in Chile. Renowned for its huge copper mines, Chile had not been explored thoroughly for precious metals. With the entire country open for investigation, it was a jewel of an assignment for us.

A string bean of a nation, Chile stretches 2,700 miles from north to south, but averages only 110 miles in width. When we arrived, two-thirds of the country was tied together by the Pan American Highway, a two-lane paved road stretching from the Peruvian border in the north to the town of Puerto Montt in the mid-south. Settlements beyond there were accessible only by boat, light aircraft, or primitive roads from Argentina.

Late in 1982 the government opened three hundred miles of new one-lane road, the Carretera General Augusto Pinochet, now known as the Carretera Austral (Southern Highway), connecting Puerto Montt with Coyhaique, the capital of Aysen Province. Wanting to be among the first to see the newly exposed countryside, Frank and I set out in January 1983 in our four-wheel-drive vehicle to study the geology and mineral potential of the area.

Everywhere along the route, waterfalls spilled from the glaciers, carrying finely crushed rock that colored the water brilliant turquoise blue. Mats of vegetation, fed by constant mists, clung tenaciously to the glacially scoured cliffs and, scattered under the trees in the tangled forest, white and yellow ground orchids and fuchsia bushes, laden with showy red and purple flowers, thrived in the gloom.

Before long we found that what was supposed to be an all-weather gravel track had not been finished and in places was no more than scraped earth or a corduroy of hewn logs in the mud. After twelve days, our road-battered vehicle rattled into Coyhaique much in need of repair. This quiet town of 20,000 was a welcome place for a brief rest.

While in Coyhaique, we drove all the existing roads in the district, and where there were none, trekked into the mountains on horseback. Soon we realized the only way to complete our overview would be by plane. To the south travel was blocked by a mass of high peaks, topped by the Southern Ice Sheet; to the west the mountain chain plunged below the surface of the Pacific Ocean, and the land broke into a flotilla of sheer-walled islands separated by long fjords; to the east was flat Argentine *pampa*. But passage here was dependent not on geomorphology, but on the current state of international relations.

Many of our best exploration targets have been located from the air by spotting color anomalies and structures in the rock formations that are not readily visible from the ground. We were anxious to see not only the geology but the dramatic scenery.

After a week of low clouds and drizzle, we finally awoke to a sparkling clear day. Arriving at the airport early, we were surprised to find two outfits offering flights. Faced with the decision of choosing between companies I will call "Linea Aerea Ernesto Schmidt y Cia., Ltda." and "Don Pedro's Air Taxi," we had little information to go on. Succumbing to preconceived notions, we chose Schmidt. The company had the confidence to call itself an airline and it sported a good, solid German name, all of which projected an image of careful maintenance and skilled operators. In comparison, Don Pedro's Air Taxi seemed somewhat homegrown. Fortuitously, Schmidt had a scheduled flight that morning to the small town of Tortel, crossing over much of the countryside we wished to study.

Our money paid, we were escorted to the hangar, where we met the pilot. If the name of the airline profiled confidence, this pudgy, sweating young man with his shirttails hanging out profiled Don Pedro. We waited while two assistants fought to remove the seats from the port side of the twin-engine Cessna 421, leaving only those necessary for the pilot and three passengers. Into the emptied space they stuffed sacks of mail and cartons of dried milk supplement. What didn't fit was left strewn about on the floor.

I've flown surrounded by bundles of morning newspapers and crates of frozen fish—even a dead body wrapped in a tarpaulin—so milk and mail didn't seem unusual, except that no one appeared to be calculating how much weight the plane was carrying,

When the Cessna was packed to bursting with cargo, they hauled it out of the hangar. We all piled aboard and strapped ourselves in. Frank claimed the copilot's seat, I tucked in behind him, and a skinny gentleman in an ill-fitting suit squeezed in behind me, balancing his suitcase on his lap. Without a single preflight check, the pilot taxied onto the runway and took off.

Later, Frank said that right then he should have told the pilot to turn around, land, and let us off. Although he considered it, he said he didn't want to seem wimpy in front of his wife and the other passenger. In retrospect, we both agreed that wimpy far outweighed the possible alternatives.

I, in my naivete, tried to rationalize what was happening. Someone must have been making an eyeball estimate of the cargo weight, passenger weight, and luggage weight. And, of course, the pilot had done his preflight check before we boarded.

I think I knew none of this was true. Both Frank and I had allowed ourselves to fall prey to "the embarrassment factor." Against our better judgment, we privately assured ourselves that everything would be okay and said nothing.

We took off with no apparent problem and lumbered toward our first stop. After a while, Frank commented, "The pilot likes to fly rather close to the ground."

My thoughts exactly. "Perhaps it's because we're overloaded."

"Must be."

Not wanting to belabor the obvious, we remained silent, listening to the engines struggle. I couldn't help wondering what the unbalanced load did to the flying characteristics of the small plane. From treetop level we could see every blade of grass in the boulder-strewn pastures. Hugging the clearings, we snaked our way along a narrow valley past a Spanish moss-covered pine forest that crept up the sides of the craggy black mountains until loose rock and cliffs barred further growth.

After skimming across the white-capped surface of Lago General Carrera, we landed hard, but safely, in the town of Chile Chico. As the tricycle-geared plane reached the end of the runway, the overloaded tail slammed down onto the tarmac. The harried pilot yelled at Frank to jump out and lift it up. I tried not to think about structural damage.

As we taxied up to the lonely terminal with Frank supporting the back end of the plane, our fellow passenger grabbed his suitcase and fled, almost before the engines stopped. "Is there any other way of returning to Coyhaique?" I whispered. I don't know why I spoke softly; the pilot spoke no English.

We asked the agent in the waiting room. Apparently there wasn't, so we climbed back into our seats. Once more we found ourselves flying fifty feet above the surface, heading toward Tortel, only now thermals rose from the sun-warmed ground to meet cold air sliding down from the glaciers. The little plane bounced from one air pocket to another. I tried to ignore the precipitous cliffs that were slipping past us as we wound our way through steep gorges above rushing melt water. A few miles farther on I could make out the extensive sheet of blue ice, topped with a frosting of fresh snow.

The pilot seemed to delight in these tightly twisting canyons. Flying no more than yards from the vertical walls, he would head up one constricted valley, then, without warning, upend the plane on one wing and spin into a previously hidden, right-angle notch. As disconcerting as this was, I knew we had told him we wanted to look at the rocks. While neither Frank nor I had envisioned such a close-up inspection, we were pleased with the spectacular mineralization we were seeing. Trying to keep that in mind, I set about marking locations on my map for future investigation.

Just as we exited from one vertical cleft about 100 feet above a frigid-looking marsh, the engines became ominously silent, and I was aware that the plane had started to lurch and sway. Frank turned around and said, "This is it. I really think so. We just ran out of fuel."

I knew we were going to crash, that was evident, and I guess I was afraid; but more than being afraid, I was so terribly sad. I felt like, not here, not now, not out in this lonely, godforsaken bog.

"Put the camera in the bag."

Frank's words startled me. Always the optimist, I thought. I zipped up the camera in the case as I studied the wet expanse in front of us. If we had to crash, this was probably as good a spot as we were going to find. However, realistic expectations for a successful landing between the dead snags and reedy hummocks were marginal, as the badly balanced plane, now without power, wobbled forward.

On and on we skimmed, level with the ground. Why aren't we crashing? I wondered. With a jolt and a shudder, the props suddenly came to life, and we started to climb. Still clutching the camera bag, I tapped Frank on the shoulder. "What are we flying on?"

"Fuel."

"What fuel?"

"The main tanks."

I seemed to be missing something.

"The idiot took off on his auxiliary tanks and didn't know it. When they ran out, the engines stopped. While the props were feathering, he was able to shift over to the main tanks. Luck was with us, they started again." Luck indeed.

Twenty minutes and many palpitations later we set down in the village of Tortel with an impact that should have collapsed the landing gear. With full-on brakes, the Cessna skidded along the scant strip of dirt fill that jutted out into the narrow fjord. This spongy surface was the only level ground we saw within the steep-sided inlet. Not accessible by road and with few ships braving the unpredictable seas of the *Golfo de Penas* (Gulf of Misery) to the west, this settlement was a bona fide addition to my growing list of end-of-the-world places.

All thirty or so inhabitants were there to greet us. Hardly had the plane stopped before men, women, and children swarmed over it. Pushing and shoving, they grabbed the cartons of dried milk. Their arms laden, they hauled away their booty across a network of plank walkways toward wooden shacks perched on stilts along rock ledges just above the high tide mark.

Once the plane had been emptied, a small gaggle of men dressed in going-to-town clothes and carrying an assortment of rucksacks, rope-bound cardboard boxes, and tattered valises crowded around the pilot. Their fingers pointed toward the plane; their voices rose in anger. Eyes glared in our direction, then back toward the pilot. Finally, two of the men elbowed the others aside and scrambled aboard. One claimed the seat behind me, while the other stretched out on the floor. Regulations or no regulations, it was obvious he was not going to be denied his chance to escape this missionaries' paradise.

With a "hi-ho" and an airborne wheelie, our pilot spiraled us around the village in a series of banks and turns that had us pressed to our seats. Back we raced through the park-like scenery, which, by now, I had lost interest in viewing. All I wanted was to see it from a much greater distance.

It wasn't long before I got my wish. Where have I heard, be careful what you wish for? As the plane strained to gain altitude to clear the rocky fingers of Cerro Castillo, the engines seemed to be running rougher and rougher.

Frank, calling on his many hours of co-pilot-seat flying and a handful of lessons, looked at the gauges and said to the pilot in Spanish, "The manifold pressure on the starboard engine is redlining."

No response.

Frank repeated, "Señor, el *manómetro*."

The pilot appeared to be deaf.

Frank spoke more insistently. "You are going to blow the seals."

"Oh, si, si." He made some adjustments and the engine returned to a nearly steady hum.

Gradually the pressure rose again, and the process started all over.

"Señor. Señor!"

"Si, si."

All the while, my eyes were glued to the gauge. Realizing that I was missing some of the most impressive scenery in the world, I forced myself to look out the window. As my gaze passed over the starboard engine, I saw fuel pouring out close to the hot exhaust. "We're leaking fuel," I said.

"I've been watching it for the last twenty minutes," Frank replied.

"Oh."

"This is the same type of plane my boss in Arizona crash landed in—twice—when the engines caught fire."

Frank really didn't have to remind me. Why, I wondered, were we flying so high now that the engine was going to catch fire and we were going to burn up before we could get down?

Forty minutes later, we landed safely in Coyhaique. When the engines stopped, it was all I could do to crawl off the plane and wobble back to the hotel. Frank paused long enough to decline the afternoon flight.

Some weeks later, we heard that the same aircraft, while landing at Chile Chico, lost a wheel. The pilot scrounged up a spare off another type of aircraft. It didn't fit, but he managed to attach it and continued on his way.

In the years that followed, we spent many months working on projects in that area. Frank came to know the owners of Don Pedro's Air Taxi well and we utilized their services to move exploration crews to and from isolated camps. While they were not a triple-A company, judged by bush pilot standards, they were a top notch outfit.

It was through them that we learned of still another chapter in the Linea Aerea Ernesto Schmidt saga. While ferrying some charter fishermen, our pilot finally made his unscheduled water landing. Everyone survived, but the plane sank, ending its days in a watery grave. I dread to think where the pilot will surface again.

REFLECTIONS

Sarah Wellen

Sitting at the glass table
Near the window,
A cup of tea in my hand,
A reflection played a trick
Upon my tired, glazed eyes.

A plane, flying slowly
Against the sky,
Seemed an insect
Upon the glass.

Startled, I reached to kill it!
As it flew away
Out of my grasp,
I saw the plane
And felt a warm, foolish smile
Spread upon my face.

THOUGHTS ON FLYING THE FRIENDLY SKIES – 1945 TO 2012

Helen Muriel Ganopole

When I was fifteen, I took my first airplane flight. It was from Boston to Portland, Maine, to visit my cousins, and its importance in my young life was right off the charts. I spent weeks planning my flight wardrobe: pantyhose and heels, a proper traveling suit, a small hat, a jacket stylishly slung over my shoulders, and a purse filled with whatever a young girl of that day needed. I may have carried gloves. I recall that *everyone* else on the flight was dressed to the nines: the style for flying. Oh, how beautiful were the stewardesses! Of course, they were young and gorgeous, slim and groomed, with nurse's training and a manner with the public that made us feel like royalty. The little meals, set in their special compartments, were served with style and finesse. The stewardess even asked me my name, and chatted about where I might be going and why. She "cared" about me! You just felt it! Just a notch below the stewardess in those days was the movie star or model.

Good manners and civility applied when traveling. Travelers introduced themselves to their seat mates and engaged in enough conversation to be considerate and friendly. From time to time, conversing might resume as one casually read for a time or sipped coffee. Then, upon arrival, one might shake hands, even trade addresses (yes, I did) and part happily from a new friend. Plane travel had its etiquette and its social rewards. We talked about our trips to friends and recalled the pleasure of it all. It was refined and dignified. Flying was an occasion!

During Career Week at college, seniors were exposed to speakers who came from many professions, touting the joys of their work and encouraging graduates to take recommended training. Right along with talks on teaching, nursing, and elite secretarial work, we had a lovely stewardess from United, who described the glory of the sun bouncing off silver wings as she glided gloriously down the aisle tending to her passengers. She made it sound important and soul-satisfying, hinting that only the best among us might have a chance to be chosen. I considered it for a very brief time, but didn't care much for heights and knew I'd never qualify. Who could be so perfect?

This past December, I flew from Portland to Denver and back and sat there reminiscing about the classy travel of the long ago past. By then, my life had taken me on many airlines about the world, from the horrors of Olympic Air to the almost ridiculous opulence of the Saudi Arabian Airlines. I'd seen it all and watched with some relief the huge changes in airplane behavior over the decades. Economics, cultural adaptation, common sense, and many other forces caused the same "leveling" here as in our regular society. I sat crammed into my bulkhead seat with a new mom and her sweet tiny baby next to me, and on the aisle a quiet, huddled gentleman reading a book in Romanian. I was comfortable in socks and sneakers and whatever I found to wear that morning.

I had a great view of the endless stream of passengers pushing through the door and down the aisle. My, not a white glove or panty hose in the bunch. Women reflected today's styles in many strange and unattractive ways: flimsy tops designed to expose bosoms over heavy jeans or hip-length skirts, and boots one might safely wear to cross the Delaware. It was nothing short of a hoot to see little kids dragging their pink and blue cases on wheels, dolls or teddy bears strapped on top, backpacks of every vintage, blankets and pillows, carryalls with food sacks and Christmas gifts, mother and dad shepherding their tiny mob (many families of 4 or 6) down the aisle to I know not where, and trying to cram stuff into already overcrowded overhead compartments. Visits to Grandma and Grandpa were on! Everyone was on their own to get settled somewhere. Of course, Southwest was casual.

Perfunctory instructions for survival were given by a man, casually dressed for the street, nobody listening at all, and then the "staff" retired to their little pull-down seats and began to read mystery novels. I could see them from my seat. Once in the air and safe, they rose long enough to throw a miniscule bag of peanuts at each of us, and later slosh down the aisle with drinks. Then back to reading. My stewardess was rather heavy and surly and wore clothing that was not at all identifiable as stewardess clothing. Her hair was a mess, and she seldom smiled. She was, of course, seated next to the restroom, which invited a steady flow of restless passengers, perhaps an irritation. But she got the job done, in her way.

People wiggled and squirmed, produced pillows from backpacks, munched on food brought with them, and then, as settled as possible, they *all* brought out their iPods, "epods, apods, and upods." Looking down the aisle, every head was held at lap reading angle, and all eyes were glued on the miracle screen left us by Jobs. Silence took over, babies slept, and each person did his best to last the flight.

It took me seven hours to get home from Denver via Oakland to Portland, and my back was killing me. I fell into very brief conversations with the Romanian and the young mother, both on eventful trips. The gentleman lived in the U.S. now, but returned to visit his mother in the old country occasionally. His book was on the history of Christianity in Europe, and his personality was charming. Our young seatmate was about to meet her husband as he returned from Afghanistan to see his infant son for the first time. Mom was ecstatic.

So we had brief connections, and that was all we needed. The art and perks of flying didn't really concern us. Getting "there" mattered, however it was done. The airplane was a conveyance. We were glad we didn't have to walk or drive. We had a good pilot who landed on time on the right wheels, and it was over—no longer an "occasion" or a means for enjoying the pampering of old. Like all travelers now, we were just glad to board and exit. It was a streetcar in the sky. A big bus with a strap to hang onto. A ride through the blue in a crowded car. And the knowledge that each person had a need to "get there" (and bear it!) quickly in a busy, rather crazy world.

When the first tourist rocket takes off into space, it will be the same at first: wine and cheese, pillows and blankets, and a pretty Stewardess hanging from a harness somewhere to handle the gravity problem. And then, as the years pass, mayhem and disorder will rule. Passengers and peanuts will float together in a morass of luggage and babies. They will just want to "get there." Once on the new planet, they will proceed to overpopulate it and mess it up, using incredible new technical knowledge to make their way to the next part of the universe when necessary. And they will!

Coming Home

Jim Frisbie

Coming home,
after a year far afield,
I wondered, "Will they know me?"
"Will I know them?"

Ten dollars in my pocket,
flying stand-by,
planning my
tentative re-entry.

The last flight north had a seat.
I wondered, looking down
through the dusk at familiar fields,
"How do I do this?"

I wanted to slow things down,
walk the two miles to the house,
find the hidden key,
let myself in calling out, "I'm home!"

But as I started down the steps
of the turbo-prop,
I saw my father, standing
by the gate marked "Arrivals."

I found out later
he had met
every flight
that day.

I know now what it is
to have a father,
and to be
a beloved son.

I will never fear the dark,
or the coming unknown,
aware that no matter when I arrive,
He will be waiting with tears in His eyes.

How I Choose To Remember You

Lois Godel

I have a photograph of you
hitching down the highway
we were both eighteen
floppy hats and blue-jeans.
No one stopped, so
we snapped pictures of one another.
You, lifting your long hair
smiling, looking fetching
standing down the road
not fully aware of the statements we made
nor the dangers out there.

I loved your passion, but even then
when it marched into stridency
you left me, balking at its edges.
I loved your quick mind
your seeming openness to everything,
how we could talk about
anything. Now I doubt that openness
was ever more than patience
with what you saw
as my slowness to accept
doctrine.

Old friends come back sometimes
others fall away
I miss you, tho' the one I miss
left years ago, perhaps
was never there at all.
The photograph has faded
but I hold your image
full of joy and possibility
and just a little sass.

Hitchhiking

C.A. Peters

n the 1950s—and I suspect from the time automobiles were first seen on
America's highways and byways—hitching or thumbing for a ride was a
common and economical way to travel. To hitch you simply dressed as
presentably as possible and stood beside a road (or walked backwards beside
it) with your thumb out, indicating the direction you wanted to go. If you
had a long way to go, you might have held a hand-painted sign announcing
your destination. In my youth, especially if you were in uniform as most
young men were, you were guaranteed a ride. A friend delighted in telling
how, as a young Marine, he hitched from Portsmouth, New Hampshire to
Pittsburgh the day before Christmas in 1941, only a few weeks after Pearl
Harbor. Two rides got him to Erie, a distance of over 500 miles. When the
driver learned the young jarhead wanted to join his mother for midnight
mass in Pittsburgh, he continued south for three winter-road hours! As a
point of interest to future historians, veteran hitchhikers will tell you that
"he travels fastest who travels alone," and you would never endeavor to
thumb with more than two in the party.

Hitchhikers have gone the way of saddle shoes, rolled-up blue jeans,
and plain flannel shirts. Before the custom succumbed to the advent of the
interstate system, though, I had three remarkable adventures thumbing
and hitching back and forth from my home to Thiel College in Greenville,
Pennsylvania. The trip was 70 miles one way, mostly on Ohio's north-south
Route 7, which starts (or ends) at Lake Erie in the Buckeye state's northeast
corner and continues parallel to the Pennsylvania state line to East Liverpool,
Ohio. Once there, it mirrors the route of the Ohio River before it ends (or
starts) in Chesapeake in southern Ohio, where it joins U.S. Route 52.

My first memorable ride occurred in the autumn of 1951, my freshman
year in college. My father had dumped us out north of East Liverpool, where
Ohio's Route 7 turned north, away from westbound U.S. 30. I had brought a
buddy home for the weekend, which may explain why Dad was so charitable

in driving us to a fruitful spot. He seldom did that for me. He believed that challenge and adversity "build character" and was creative in finding ways to provide the same—like not driving me ten miles to where the two roads forked.

"Buddy" is not an accurate term for this drip of a guy. He had a good-looking blond older sister who found me attractive. Out of necessity, he and I became friends for as long as the romance lasted.

That Sunday afternoon found the luckless Bernie and me standing where the two highways parted. Eventually, a big white Cadillac came to a quick halt, and I jumped in the front while my pal climbed into the back seat. The driver was a well-dressed, prosperous-looking older gentleman who asked the obvious question, "Where you going?"

We replied almost in unison, "Up past Youngstown."

He said, "I'll get you to Youngstown."

Great luck! Youngstown in one stint.

As he drove, he took what appeared to be a silver dollar from the ashtray and asked if I had ever seen one. I acknowledged that until I was thirteen I received one on every birthday. He asked if I had ever seen one like his and held it closer—it was a fifty-dollar gold piece.

"No," I said. At that point he leaned over and pulled another gold coin from my ear!

"Too bad," he said. "I thought this might have been yours too."

And so it went for the next twenty-five or so miles with the driver doing one sleight-of-hand trick after another to the open-mouthed, wide-eyed "wows" and "did you see that?" of two college freshmen.

When we drew closer to Youngstown, he asked, "You boys drink?"

Not of legal age, we cautiously acknowledged we did.

In response he asked, "Want to stop at my place for a beer before you start thumbing again?"

Ah, here it comes, thought I! Every guy (except me) had stories of "those damn queers" picking them up and trying "funny stuff." We weren't sure what they wanted to do, but alarm bells went off; we started sputtering and inventing excuses. In those days, serial killers weren't in the news. Our imaginary threat was of "damn queers."

The magician sensed our discomfort and laughed. "Relax, guys, I'm not trying to make out with you. I own a bar on Market Street (Youngstown's main drag) and will get you some hamburgers to go with the beer."

He did own a bar, *The Magic Bar*. When we entered, the crowd chanted, "Trick…Trick…Trick." He set us up with two drafts, ordered our hamburgers, and then obliged the crowd with a half-dozen tricks. We were so entranced that we had two more beers before we realized it was growing dark.

Another hitching code violation was never to thumb after sundown. No one would ever, not ever, pick you up, and we still had miles to go. So, while Bernie took a last bathroom break, I thanked our benefactor and told him we had to get back on the road.

He motioned to one of the regulars and had a quiet conversation with him, after which the guy said, "I'll take you two to Greenville." We went out the back door and into the guy's jalopy, a comedown after the white Caddy. As we drove along I thanked the driver,

"Don't thank me," he replied. "The Magician said he would forgive half my bar tab if I drove you two up to Greenville. I owe $300."

We never saw the magician pull a rabbit out of his hat, but he did pull a 35-mile ride out of his wallet.

Late on a spring Friday afternoon in 1953, hitchhiking north to south on Route 7 on my way home from college, I met Mrs. Robinson—not her real name, but Ann Bancroft and Dustin Hoffman in "The Graduate" in 1967 conjured my Mrs. Robinson. On that day, my thumbing stand was at the bottom of the long steep bridge that rises from Youngstown's main square up and out of the Mahoning Valley to reach high ground south of town. This was a congested spot on the multi-lane highway. A tanker trucker had dumped me there earlier because this was such a good spot to grab a long ride. I had been there a short while when a black Buick halted just a little past me, the driver door opened, and I heard a shout: "Hurry, this is not a good spot to stop!"

I ran and jumped in to discover my Samaritan was an "old lady" of thirty-something. She was very pretty in a motherly kind of way and well dressed. "Thanks," I said, "it's really damn hot out." The "damn" wasn't required, but I wanted to convey the impression of how adult I was and not just some kid thumbing.

"You were lucky; I was downtown for lunch with some of my Allegheny college girlfriends. You go to Thiel—that's a nice little college, too."

The Samaritan had spied my hitchhiking prop, an old yellow suitcase with "Thiel" and our Tomcat mascot stenciled on it. I was amazed that a woman, a lady, had picked me up, something that had never happened to me and never had been reported by any of my fraternity brothers. Thumbing was strictly for guys.

Mrs. Robinson asked me what year I was in, agreed the weather had been unseasonably warm, then told me she had a son away at Valley Forge Military School and her husband was a pilot for Allegheny Air Lines. With a little shrug she added, "I used to fly, I was a stew." Then she lamented about how long the grass was getting at her place and asked if I had time to cut it, "for pay, of course," adding, "We have a riding mower."

I had not told my parents I was coming home (long distance calls were expensive), and on a $5.00 a week allowance I could always use more cash. I readily accepted the job. In Boardman, an affluent suburb south of Youngstown, we turned right toward Canfield and went eight or nine miles into the boondocks. She finally stopped the Buick at the end of a long drive-way in front of a four-car garage, possibly the biggest one I had ever seen. The garage was next to a grand sprawling ranch home; both buildings perched up on a little hill. Hills are rare in that part of Ohio, so this was choice real estate. One glance at the expanse of green yard convinced me they were wise to own a riding mower.

After I'd been riding and cutting grass for an hour, Mrs. Robinson came out and flagged me down. "Do you want a glass of ice water, a lemonade, ice tea, gin and tonic, or beer?" I took beer. Thirty minutes later she was back with another beer, and by the time I put the mower away I had had two or three more, all of which quickly turned to sweat—after all, it was "damn hot." I anticipated she would now pay me, drive me back to Route 7, and drop me to continue my trip south.

Instead she said, "You better shower or no one will pick you up. I'll wash your clothes." My clothes consisted of Bermuda shorts, skivvies, a tee, a dress shirt worn like a jacket, and a pair of socks. She handed me a big heavy bathrobe with the Allegheny Airlines logo on it. I blithely jumped into a really, really fancy shower and was enjoying myself immensely. The next thing I knew, Mrs. Robinson joined me. She said in a husky, whispery voice, "I'm afraid it will be awhile before your clothes are clean and dry. I'll wash your back." I had never been closer than three feet to another human in a shower, and then only in the boys' gym locker rooms. I nearly panicked as we sallied off to the bedroom, where youth, excitement, and inexperience abridged our encounter. She hugged me and quietly said, "That's okay. That was for you; the next one's for me."

I stayed for the rest of Friday, all Saturday, and into Sunday afternoon while waiting for my clothes to dry. Mrs. Robinson sent out for Chinese on Friday night, had me cook chicken on the outdoor grill on Saturday, and prepared a magnificent steak and eggs breakfast on Sunday. Then she drove me north of Youngstown on Route 7 to give me a start on my way back to Thiel, but not before saying, "Here's twenty for cutting the grass and twenty for being such a nice young man." Mrs. Robinson was indeed a generous woman. Every woman I ever slept with after that weekend should thank Mrs. Robinson, whoever she was, because I learned a lot in those three days. When I told the story to my fraternity brothers, not one believed me—a young man's fantasy come true, and no one to believe me. I quit telling the story.

If the term Redneck was used north of the Mason Dixon Line in the 1950s, I don't recall it. The equivalent pejorative of the day was Hillbilly. In my hometown, a village in the Ohio River Valley, Whoopee (silent "w") was often used for folks who today might be called Rednecks. According to urban (or at least village) legend, the term was applicable to those who came north from Kentucky and southern West Virginia on steamboats and trains during World War I and The Great Depression in search of work. Reportedly, they were called Whoopees because on Saturday night they always got rip-roaring drunk and whooped it up! We had clans of such folks up on the hill back of town.

By any of those three names, I had an unforgettable ride with a trio of them in 1952, when I hitched a ride on Ohio Route 7. The three picked me up as I was heading south toward Youngstown on my way home. These were not the folks of Hollywood Hillbilly fame or the Dukes of Hazzard. They certainly were not the jovial Larry the Cable Guy. This trio could have served as the illustration for Hillbilly or Redneck in the Encyclopedia Britannica and even for Whoopee—if there had been such an illustration. All three were drunk. The guy in the back seat had a broken, cast-encased leg stretched out between the two front seats. As the trip progressed, I learned the broken leg was the reason for their long road trip. The three had been working construction near Cincinnati when the guy with the broken limb fell from a scaffold. When it became apparent he was not going to be able to work, they determined they would all return to their home in Bug Tussle, Kentucky. For the geographically challenged, the Bluegrass State is just across the Ohio River from Cincinnati, and they were now far, far north of there. I had to ask why they were so far from home.

They told me that the guy with the cast was owed money by another fellow from Bug Tussle, who was working in Ashtabula, Ohio up on Lake Erie. They had driven nearly 350 miles north to collect it because the injured guy would be out of work and would need the cash. Fair enough. But something had happened to the three pilgrims in Ashtabula, and I never quite fathomed what. Either the other Kentuckian was not home, or he was home and had sent the money to the wife of the broken-leg guy sometime earlier. This, too, may have been known—or not. Perhaps he had already paid the debt to the broken-leg Hillbilly. I could not tell. The trek of the three pilgrims so far had been a real huggermugger. What was clear was that the guy riding shotgun was obviously drunk and extremely irritated with my broken-legged, back seat companion. Lots of tension.

I don't remember the make of their car, but do remember it was not a large vehicle, neither new nor well maintained, and looked as if they might have been living in it. In fact, as I learned, they all three had slept in it the night before. Large dice and other good luck talismans hung from the rear-view mirror. The charms included two ornate rosaries, which amazed me, as Whoopees and others of that ilk typically were not Catholic. The lucky adornments must have come with the car when it was purchased second-hand.

The radio worked all too well. It was tuned to a country station and turned up to window-rattling volume. When the trio knew the song, one or all three of them would sing along, trying to outdo the volume of the radio and each other. The driver, who seemed to be the leader of the three, had, as I recall, a good voice.

They had picked me up in the little crossroads town of Vernon Center, where the secondary road from Greenville crossed the state line to join Route 7. A buddy had driven me there. I was about eighteen miles north of Youngstown when I got in the car. Early in the ride I had determined to invent an excuse to jump ship in the city. Early on, I became increasingly wary of my fellow travelers. Periodically, the three would pass around a bottle of cheap rye whiskey or, from time to time, a mason jar of moonshine.

Having determined that this was not a jovial bunch to drink with, I tongued the bottle when it came my way to keep my intake to a minimum, but had never had white lightning, so took a healthy swallow. I learned later there are grades of 'shine and this was bottom shelf.

When we arrived downtown, it was pouring rain, so I decided to ride along until it let up. Thumbing in the rain was no fun, although some hard-core hitchhikers swore you could get a ride quicker because drivers felt sorry for you. That was never my experience.

Everyone settled down when we entered the city, and the bottle and jug disappeared as we drove carefully through Youngstown. They clearly didn't want to attract the attention of the law, which was good thinking because the local constabulary had a reputation for being corrupt, mean, and ill-disciplined. Once we cleared the city and were continuing south, the libations again flowed freely and the singing ratcheted up a few decibels. As the booze was ingested, the verbal acrimony between the broken-leg guy and his buddy in the front seat escalated. South of Youngstown, hot words were exchanged between the two, and suddenly my rear seat companion whipped out a wicked-looking knife that seemed to have a blade as large as Zorro's saber. I don't know where he had cunningly concealed it or how he had produced it so quickly. Practice, I imagine.

The guy in the front reacted to the challenge by starting to climb over the seat back past the cast-encased leg while I endeavored to shrivel into my corner of the too-small rear seat. The driver reacted to the eruption by throwing the car into a series of violent tire-screeching serpentines that made us all rock to and fro, and the highly agitated front seat rider fell back into his seat. In a Redneck drawl, the driver held out his right hand and demanded the knife from my companion, got it, and announced we were stopping "for a beer at the next honky tonk, so's everybody can cool down." I was all for it—I wanted out of that car.

The honky tonk wasn't. Instead, it was a quiet little country roadhouse in the village of East Fairfield. When we four entered, one of us on crutches, we were covertly eyed by a couple of locals much like zebras might watch lions prowling on the edge of their herd. The two regulars quickly drank up and left. Like zebras on the veldt, they could sense trouble. I bought my three traveling companions a draft and explained this was a good place for us to part company. From here, I explained, I could get a friend to pick me up and take me directly to my "hot" girlfriend, who lived over the Ohio River in West Virginia. This was a lie. To the extent that I had any girlfriend, she lived in East Liverpool, not in West Virginia, and was not hot. They insisted they would drop me there, and I could hitch over the river to West Virginia and did not need to "trouble no body." I really did not want to travel any farther with these three knife-wielding, hard drinking, serpentining hillbillies, so between our second and third beers (it is tough to fake beer drinking) I used a pay phone to send an SOS to a friend who sped to my rescue; we were only about 20 miles from my home. He arrived about the time the fourth or fifth beer was being slurped up. I bought them all another draft (they cost a quarter), told them how much I liked their white lightning, declined another sip, and fled out the tavern door to my rescuer's waiting car.

Once safely in the car I exhaled and exclaimed, "Peel rubber—get me the hell out of here."

As we sped along, my liberator asked, "Were you afraid of those guys?"

I responded with prevaricating bravado, "Hell, no!"

I hitchhiked from my sophomore year in high school until I graduated from college and rode hundreds of miles on my thumb, but these were the only unforgettable encounters of all of those rides. Mostly it was indeed a safe and cheap way to travel—and could be interesting. Hitchhiking is now lost and gone forever and should be lamented, for it seems we were a tad nicer and more trusting people back then.

THE ROAD LESS TRAVELED

Calvin Fulton

*J*im called his wife, saying he would stop overnight along the way since he was unable to leave in time to make the trip in one day. The weather was cool with ominous clouds. He stopped for lunch in a small town and, after eating, walked around the block before starting out again. Several hours later, he thought he was nearing his destination—an inn called "The Road Less Traveled," recommended by the concierge at his hotel in the city—when he came to an intersection. In addition to the perpendicular crossroad, two other roads left the intersection at diagonals. They weren't marked, but his Garmin GPS said, "Take the left diagonal in two hundred feet." The road narrowed somewhat as he turned, and he noted weeds and wildflowers bordering a ditch on either side. The road certainly looked less traveled. He had a brief memory of a long-forgotten poem. He would have to look it up on Google when he stopped for the night. The landscape changed to rolling hills, becoming more rugged in the distance. To the west, the clouds had cleared above the horizon. The sun had just set, creating a sharp, jagged horizon line that looked as if an artist had painted it to make a pleasing composition, resulting in the strange feeling as he drove on that he was entering a painting, especially as dusk changed the light to a pinkish glow.

Rounding a curve at the top of a hill, he could see a village a short distance ahead. Backlit by the late afternoon sun, the village looked like a Thomas Kinkaid painting. He had a strange thought—was it too perfect? He continued on about a quarter of a mile and saw a sign for the Inn: The Road Less Traveled – Accommodations.

He stopped at the lobby entrance. Leaving his bag in the car, Jim stepped into the lobby. There didn't seem to be many people about. A young woman at the registration desk greeted him, saying, "Mr. James Barry? We have your room ready."

He looked at the clerk questioningly and asked how she knew his name since…

"George, breakfast's on the table."

"Coming, hon." George quickly typed the rest of the sentence.

…he hadn't made a reservation.

He got up from his desk and came to the kitchen, where Olivia was just serving his favorite breakfast: scrambled eggs cooked on low heat to that perfect degree of moistness, with several leaves of chopped, fresh basil scattered over the top, a small portion of diced Canadian bacon, and half an English muffin with butter melting into it and slathered with orange marmalade. The odor was divine. He gave Olivia a quick kiss and sat down at the table. Fortunately for him, Olivia loved to cook. George's cooking skill was limited to boiling water, and even that was problematic. She served her own plate and sat opposite. Sunshine was flooding in the window, complementing Olivia's lemon yellow dress. How he loved mornings with sunlight flooding the breakfast nook. A great start to the day. What could go wrong?

"How's the writing going this morning?"

"Really well. I'm on to something this time. I've found my voice, and I have a good start."

"Good. I look forward to reading what you have so far."

"Not quite ready for that yet. Wait till I get into the heart of the story."

"Okay. I'm sure it'll come this time. Don't worry, dear."

Olivia smiled, and George knew she meant well. His attempts to write something that might be publishable someday had come to naught so far. Fortunately, money was not a problem for them. Olivia's inheritance from her grandfather and the support from George's grandmother enabled them to live in the 'burbs' comfortably. Their house looked out on landscaped grounds that Mr. Blandings in his dreamhouse would have envied. And since George didn't have to take a train into the city every day to some office, he was the envy of his neighbors, as well. He and Olivia were considered by some to be the perfect suburbanites.

"Oh, George. Don't forget. We're going to the Bennets this evening."

He groaned. "Do we have to?" He reconsidered what could go wrong.

"George! Marge and Ted Bennet are our oldest friends."

"I know. But Marge always wants to…stir things up."

"She just wants people to have a good time. Besides, we'll probably know most of the people there. I know you don't like big parties, but come on. Be a sport."

"Okay. But I really don't like Marge's big shindigs."

George wished he could play the "hail fellow/sports jock/country club type," but he was just never comfortable making small talk. His tongue froze when he tried. He had spent his childhood listening to his mother say, "Now, George, you've got to get your gumption up. You've got a mouth. Use it."—advice he had never assimilated. Many of George's friends from his bachelor days wondered how he ever got up the courage to propose to Olivia. He never admitted that it was she who proposed to him.

When George and Olivia arrived at the Bennets that evening, they could hear music and talking and laughter before they got to the door. Olivia had always enjoyed coming here; small talk was no problem for her, and she envied Marge Bennet's flair for entertaining. The house was practically a mini-mansion, and Marge's gardens were the envy of everyone in town. She usually won a blue ribbon in the annual garden tour.

George muttered quietly, "This is not going to be fun," as he rang the doorbell.

Olivia patted his arm. "You'll be fine. Tell people about the story you're writing."

Marge opened the door, hugged and kissed them both, and swept them into the library, where everyone was well into hors d'oeuvres and drinks. Olivia joined the group with enthusiasm, while George picked up a glass of wine and ambled over to three men who were replaying the previous weekend's football games and making predictions about the upcoming weekend. Ted Bennet acknowledged his presence with a brief nod as the men continued talking. George struggled for something to say, but truthfully he didn't care for football, didn't understand it, and had nothing to add to the conversation.

Marge soon announced dinner and asked everyone to proceed to the dining room and find a place card. They walked among the six small tables until they found their assigned spot—four at each table, two men and two women. George looked around for Olivia and saw her across the room, already in lively conversation with her table mates.

Olivia was right. He did know most of the people in the room, except those at his table. The man to his left extended his hand, saying, "We haven't met. I'm Gary Dunston. We're weekend guests of the Bennets. Ted and I are business associates." They shook hands. "And this is my wife, Bobbie." The woman to George's right nodded. Gesturing toward the woman across the table, Gary continued, "And my wife's sister, Bettie Barry," who also nodded. "Bettie's husband, Jim, was delayed driving up from the city, so he won't be here until tomorrow."

George frowned. He had a strange feeling, but he couldn't grasp immediately what it was.

Gary said, "Is something wrong?"

George shook his head. "Sorry, no, it was nothing. I'm George Fowler." His speech felt rushed and too loud. "That's my wife, Olivia, at that table where everyone is laughing."

The other three looked, but made no response. As they all sat down, George got up the gumption to say, "Fine weather, isn't it?" The attempt fell like a dead weight. Grasping the bottle of wine on the table, he said, "May I pour the wine for you, Bobbie?" In his haste, he knocked over her wine glass. She set the glass upright and held it firmly by the stem. He managed to pour for all three of them and himself without spilling. He tried again. "Do you folks live nearby?"

Bobbie said she and Gary were from Boston, and Bettie and Jim were their houseguests, visiting from Manchester. Marge had invited all four of them for the weekend, since the three women had been classmates at Radcliffe.

"Oh," replied George. "Manchester. That's down in Connecticut, isn't it?"

Bobbie replied, "No, the one in England."

George thought her reply sounded like a reprimand. He felt his face flush, and he hastily wiped his brow with a handkerchief, then finished his glass of wine in one gulp.

During dinner, Bobbie and Gary talked with Bettie about their last visit to England and their trip to the Lake Country. Throughout the meal, the three talked quietly or laughed at some memory of their time together. They didn't attempt to include George in the conversation.

Finally, Bettie turned and asked, "Have you been to northern England, George?"

George stammered, "I haven't been to England at all, except for a stopover in London when my wife and I went to Sweden a few years ago. And that was just a few hours at the airport."

Gary said, "If you have the opportunity, England is worth a visit."

George sensed a reprimand again. He replied, "I'm sure you're right," while thinking the evening couldn't end soon enough.

Finally, it was time to go home. As they were leaving, Marge hugged and kissed them again and said, "I hope you had a good time. It's fun to stir things up a bit, isn't it? You were a dear, George, to fill in at your table since Jim couldn't be here." She gave him a little wink.

Olivia and George walked home, arm in arm. Olivia chattered about the people at her table. "You didn't look very happy when we sat down to dinner. Did you enjoy Marge's houseguests?"

"They talked among themselves most of the time about the last time they were together in England, and I couldn't think of any way to contribute to that conversation." Olivia turned as if to respond, but George interrupted. "I know, I know…just listen and ask questions about people and places, and at least pretend to be really interested."

"I only had a chance to talk with them briefly. They seemed nice enough. Marge told me the two women are fraternal twins. Their mother was determined to make them independent, so she named them Roberta and Leticia. But when they got to school, they were dubbed Bobbie and Lettie, which soon morphed into Bettie, so they became Bobbie and Bettie. Few people know their real names."

George opened the door and stood aside for Olivia to enter first. He started to say, "I really didn't—"

But Olivia had already gone in. George called out, "Be in shortly." He closed the door, turned, and looked out across the lawn. It was a warm, moonlit night. He was so relieved to be home again and silently apologized to Olivia for his social ineptness. It was so easy for her. Marge should have put Olivia with the houseguests. People just gravitated to her, and in a few minutes they were like old friends.

He sat on the porch steps, enjoying the evening air and the scent of the gardenias planted by the front door. He and Olivia lived at the bottom of a hill—not much in the way of a view, but convenient to places they frequented. He wouldn't want the upkeep of the Bennet's estate. They lived at the top of the hill in their big house with a view of rolling hills at the back and Lake Scarborough from the front. Thinking back through the evening, he recalled that something unusual had been said. He tried to remember what it was that had momentarily caught his attention. Half laughing, he slapped his head with his hand. That was it. The coincidence of names—James Barry, the protagonist of his story, and Jim Barry, Bettie's husband—was a bit odd. But neither James nor Barry was an unusual name. He shrugged. Coincidence? Had to be.

The next morning, Jim woke early and had an early breakfast in the dining room. He returned to his room, opened his laptop, and googled the name of the inn, "The Road Less Traveled." He was directed to "The Road Not Taken," a poem by Robert Frost. Of course. He had first heard that poem when Robert Frost visited his school on a lecture tour and recited it during his presentation.

Before setting out again, Jim decided to take a short walk through the village. Nothing seemed unusual or noteworthy except the picturesqueness of all the shops and houses, as if every building and street had been planned—more like a movie set than an actual place. On his return to the Inn, he was taken ill and collapsed as he entered the front door.

George paused, not sure of where the story was going. He often said that his characters decided what they were going to do, but that wasn't happening yet with James Barry.

The phone rang, and he heard Olivia answer it in the kitchen. A few minutes later, she tapped softly on his study door, then entered. "That was Marge on the phone. She said Bobbie just received a call from the inn where Jim stayed last night. The place had a strange name." She stopped, shook her head. "Can't remember what it was. And this morning he had just returned from a walk when he collapsed as he came into the lobby. All three of them are leaving immediately. The place is about a three-hour drive from here."

After Olivia left, George sat staring at his keyboard. Was he channeling someone he didn't know? Was this a paranormal phenomenon? Who believed in that in this day and age? He put his hands on his keyboard, but didn't attempt to write anything. How could he? He didn't dare write anything more about his James Barry until he knew what was happening to the real James Barry. Had this happened before without his knowledge? He thought back over his previous writing and wondered if real life counterparts of his fictional characters were out there, living out their fate as he had written it. He had a growing sense of disquiet and urgency. Did he dare write anything more?

He had one more task to do. He turned on his computer and typed, *But Jim survived and lived to a ripe old age.* He then printed out what he had written, stapled the pages together, put them in a folder, and placed the folder in the bottom of a desk drawer.

The next morning, Olivia asked George, "Whatever happened to that story you were writing? Is it finished?"

"Nah. It didn't work out. It was turning into a fantasy, and that's not my genre."

"Marge called again this morning. You remember those guests from Boston? The husband who was delayed and stayed overnight at that inn with the strange name?"

"Yeah. What happened to him?"

"He died."

George very quietly and unobtrusively breathed a sigh of relief.

CHANGING TIDE

Sally Carper

I thought you had left for good
slipping away in the night
leaving just the shell of yourself
to be washed out to sea

Anxious for word from above
men in white hover like low clouds
floating over the beach
leaving shadowy drifts of hope

Slowly the tide begins to change
Closed eyes are startled open
Memory returns in part
The hollow fills halfway

Holding your once empty shell to my ear
I hear the question "Where am I?"
I answer with joy and happiness
"You are still here!"

She now resides peacefully
innocently naive and oblivious
to her life threatening
crash against the rocky shore

Remembering 2011

Margaret S. McKerrow

> *"To bear arms against a sea of troubles and by opposing end them?"*
> —William Shakespeare

How do I start? A list of pros and cons? I don't think so, for surely, at first glance, the cons would win! How does someone my age reconcile herself with the fact that her fifty-year-old son has been diagnosed with metastatic melanoma?

In May, when my son was first diagnosed, there was total darkness. "Chemo is not a viable cure for melanoma," we were told, "but may extend life by a couple of months." Without it, my son's prognosis was six to nine months. He had tumors throughout his body, as well as the huge egg shape that had appeared on his neck.

My son decided that, instead of delaying the inevitable, he would bring hospice into his life and let nature take its course. He became a pain pill popper, which he helped along by doses of beer and whiskey. Needless to say, this was devastating for me and our families to watch.

What did I have to lose by arming myself against that sea of troubles? Nothing! So I became a research junky: the Internet, conversations with my son's doctors, articles and e-mails sent to me by friends of friends far and wide in the research field, as well as personal stories. Eventually, I was led to Moore's Cancer Center, right here in San Diego.

A new drug not yet released by the FDA was still in the trial stage, but had such outstanding results in shrinking melanoma tumors that they were hoping for an early market release. My first hurdle was convincing my son to visit Moore's Cancer Center to see if he could be included in the trial. Unfortunately, because of his impaired liver he was not a good candidate. However, God bless those doctors and nurses because they, during the few appointments we had for testing, were able to convince him to start chemo on the chance that the "wonder" drug would be released by the time he finished his second round.

My son finished his chemo in July and Zelboraf, the "wonder" drug, was released by the FDA for general use on stage 4 melanoma patients in August. A week later, my son started on the medication. In January, 2012, Zelboraf proved itself to indeed be a wonder drug. Though he wasn't cured, some of my son's tumors did completely disappear, and some have shrunk to below a quarter of their original size. Unfortunately, there are new tumors appearing now, and new treatments to endure. But it is a year since my son's terrifying prognosis, and the researchers continue to develop new drugs, and new trials will be coming to hopefully prolong my son's life again, and we will continue to have hope for the future.

During this year poetry has relieved my stress and comforted me as I continue this journey through the dark times...the pros have it!

Metastatic Melanoma

Margaret S. McKerrow

What's in a name? Such a melodic choice, like an
exotic flower heavy with perfumed mystery.
Your vines grow rampant, your roots spread
their poison smothering life blood from innocent
victims. Like a parasite, you won't let go,
your seeds wildly scattered, remain untamed.
Deadly disease, I pray for your demise,
I wait for a cure…

SOME DAYS SHE DOESN'T REMEMBER WHO HE IS

Diana Griggs

But today when she visits him after his surgery
she places a kiss against his cheek,
sits beside his bed and takes his hand in hers.

She dozes, jaw slackens, head resting on her
pale pink cardigan spotted with morning coffee.

But he, holding her hand

is looking at a girl with cherry lips
sitting beside him on a plaid blanket
the moon spilling silver streamers
a diamond ring in his hand.

He always knew she was a jewel
dangled in front of his life,
that they were woven together with
golden thread still glittering possibilities.

Awaking from her nap
anxious eyes take in the hospital room
she pulls her hand from his clasp.

Lac Seul

Barbara Ponomareff

Acertain kind of unhappiness demands action. Any action.
I can see Peter lugging the cooler to the car. He stands there, surrounded by carryalls, various bags, his fishing gear, and now the cooler. He pauses, apparently undecided about where to start, and then begins loading the car for tomorrow morning's trip.

It wasn't easy to get to this point. He is more and more reluctant to commit himself to any plans. Since my retirement I have suggested several trips—outings to restaurants, theatre tickets—and none of these things, it turns out, have any appeal for him. Our being together has taken on more and more the look of a struggle: my pushing for doing things, his resisting almost on principle. But tomorrow we are heading off for a cabin by the water. "Lac Seul" is one of the innumerable lakes that dot the Canadian Shield. With my French being what it is, I always wondered whether it meant "single," "unique," or perhaps "lonely" lake?

We have been on the road for a few hours already. The highway winds pleasantly and repetitively through blasted rock face, deadwood swamps, and lake vistas that, in spite of their unique beauty, start to resemble each other. The small communities we pass through are more widely spaced apart now and have a desolate feel, as if time has passed them by. Peter likes to drive and the more winding the road, the better. I try to have him reminisce about other trips to the lake but he is not very receptive. Lately, our conversations have a way of fizzling out into a sullen silence.

I thought this trip might please him, and felt excited when my call to his old friend who owns a small holiday camp at the lake brought instant results. Derek assured me that he had the perfect cabin for us, right by the lake, where we would be able to view each day's sundown from our porch.

I had not quite counted on the way these many hours in the car would bring me face to face with my own dilemma. Lately, more often than not, I find myself imagining the next ten or so good years we might have left as a new opportunity, a way of experiencing the larger world out there through travel and new experiences; however, Peter is not receptive to any of this. I often wonder whether the few years' difference in our ages is now making itself felt. In any case, I have been entertaining fantasies of escape, wanting to act selfishly for once in my life, before it stops mattering.

The drive up to the camp takes us through sunlit pines. We have lowered the windows and a wonderful savoury breeze greets us. As we park, Derek appears as if on cue. He seems genuinely happy to have us show up. The outdoor life seems to agree with him; he exudes energy and good humour. The cabin, as promised, is the one closest to the lake, comfortable and cheerful. We set about unpacking for the week.

Before bedtime we sit in our Muskoka chairs facing the darkening water. Peter reminisces. Dinner with Derek, the drive up, the star-studded sky, the vast silence around us has loosened something in him that takes him right back to other summers. Before turning in, when we made ourselves the last cup of tea for the day, I sensed he was as content as I was.

I am torn out of my sleep by a series of grunts, curses, exclamations of pain as Peter, on getting up to go to the bathroom, apparently has run straight into the wall ahead of him. His knee is painful and starts swelling up. As I prepare a cold compress, I cannot help wondering how he could have missed the doorway lit up by the nightlight in the hall.

Peter has promised to make breakfast, and I wake up to his hobbling around the kitchen, opening and closing drawers and cabinet doors while muttering, sounding exasperated. He is clearly frustrated by not knowing where the kitchen utensils are kept, although we did check things out the day before. I offer to help.

From now on, his knee, swollen and tender, dictates how we spend the day. The boat trip has to be postponed; instead I lie on the dock, make lunch, and suggest to him we might invite Derek and Sylvia for a BBQ dinner. Something simple, I would just add a salad and offer fruit for dessert. Peter nods and limps off to the lodge to get his daily paper and to invite Derek.

I thought our dinner went well; the men were catching up on the latest news, and then veered off to their common past. I remember Derek talking about a common childhood friend and finishing his story with "Too bad what happened to him…" when Peter looked up and said, "What happened to him?" Derek, clearly taken aback, gave me a brief look and said, "He died a few months ago. You were the one who let me know."

In the silence that followed, I did not dare look at Peter. He had not just told Derek, but he had attended the funeral! I heard him mutter something like, "I got him mixed up, I guess…" and then, mercifully, the conversation picked up again.

The next morning, still limping, still disgruntled, he tells me to forget about his helping in the kitchen; the kitchen is organized "all wrong." He retires to the sofa inside the cabin, nursing his knee and holding a grudge against the world.

I go back to the dock to digest my observations and collect my thoughts. Yesterday's incident opened my eyes to what I had been noticing about Peter without wanting to name it. It still comes as a shock, even though at some level I must have known for many months. I suddenly remember the many times I caught him looking at his surroundings with a glaucous, vacant stare. There would be no "good ten years" ahead of us. Something had intruded into our lives that could not be ignored.

We left for home several days earlier than planned, citing Peter's troublesome knee. I drove. Peter seemed relieved to be going back home.

The weekend paper brought another shock. There had been a tornado at Lac Seul, sudden and devastating. It had swept several cabins into the lake during the night, including the one we had stayed in. Two men, fishermen, had lost their lives.

When I told Peter, he muttered, "Derek must have let someone else move in after we left…" and turned to something else. Yet I couldn't help thinking how we inadvertently choose one kind of death over another.

Katy, Texas

Anita Curran Guenin

We Sunday drive
out from Houston to Katy
where shotgun houses
have long since shed their
white paint.

My husband and I ride
in silence,
study sinking buildings,
patchy lawns, faded signs.

On sagging porches
people in rocking chairs
barely move, weighed down
by the oppressive afternoon.
From the shadows, black faces
peer out, glistened with sweat.

We ride out to escape
our life for a few hours,
look straight ahead, pretend
there is a future us,
not just a mirage
like water on the blacktop.

Morning Coffee

Jeanne Henderson

A gopher poked its head out of a pop-hole and wiggled its nose in the air as Orson made his way along the walk to Eli's front door. "You smell it too, huh?" Orson chuckled at the fearless rodent. The aroma of fresh-perked Hawaiian Kona wafted through Eli's window. "The finest Arabica grown on the slopes of Hualali" was Eli's mantra. He special-ordered it. Eli was a coffee fanatic.

Morning coffee together had become a tradition in the last three years, ever since Orson's wife passed away. It was the second best part of his day. The best part was cocktail hour, which he steadfastly celebrated every day at five o'clock—and not a minute sooner, even though Eli had given him "It's five o'clock somewhere" cocktail napkins for his birthday.

Orson tapped his cane three times on Eli's door, his signature knock.

"Come on in, Orson," Eli called from behind the door.

Orson opened the door and walked in to find Eli stretched out in the middle of the living room floor with a piece of chalk in his hand. He was reaching behind his head and making a mark on the carpet. Then he reached across his body and made a mark next to his left shoulder. Putting the chalk into his left hand, he made a mark next to his right shoulder. Orson was about to open his mouth to comment when Eli sat up and waved him closer.

"Here, take the chalk and make a mark behind my feet," he said. "I can't stretch that far anymore."

Orson bent and made a line on the carpet behind Eli's heels. "What in the blazes are you doing?" he said.

Eli rolled over onto his hands and knees, then stiffly pushed himself up off the floor. "Taking measurements," he said.

"For what?"

"For my coffin," said Eli, as he turned and headed toward the kitchen.

Orson hung his cane on the back of a chair and sat down at the kitchen table, which was strewn with sheets of paper covered with drawings of variously shaped coffins.

"Do you think a coffin should have that wider-at-the-elbows design or just be rectangular?" Eli said as he handed Orson a mug of steaming brew.

"You're really going to build your own coffin?" Orson shook his head in disbelief. "The fence between us is falling apart, and you want to build a coffin. What's the matter with you? You act like you're missing a few dendrites."

"I *am* missing a few dendrites. That's why I want to have my coffin ready. So which one do you like?"

"Don't like coffins of any kind," said Orson, and he took a sip. "I'm going to be cremated—much neater. Easier and cheaper, too."

"A coffin's cheap if you build it yourself," said Eli.

"An urn is cheaper than all that wood and nails," countered Orson, "and it's more environmentally friendly. Think of all the trees that fall to build coffins." He raised his mug again, smelling the rich aroma. Blowing a little across the top of the mug first, he took a larger sip, enjoying the way it warmed him all the way down and made the morning seem a little brighter. "Besides," he continued, "it's not good for your state of mind to be thinking so hard about dying. First things first. Let's repair the fence."

"But I could die fixing the fence. Then what?" said Eli. "No coffin."

"But while you're building the coffin, the fence could fall down. Then, instead of a little repair job, you've got a major job. Use your head, man. The fence should be number one on your to-do list. Or should I say bucket list? You've got the tools. We'll share the cost and the work. You're a long way off from needing a coffin…and we need the fence now."

"More coffee?" said Eli.

Orson held out his mug and watched the rich dark liquid stream from the pot into his mug. "You know," he said, "life is like this coffee. You've got to lap it up to the last drop…'til the pot is empty and your cup is drained. Would be a shame to leave good coffee sitting in your cup to cool while you went off building a coffin."

"You're a real philosopher, aren't you, Orson?" Eli scooped up his drawings into a pile. He pointed to the one on top. "See this here? This is my own design. See this little part at the end that's higher than the rest? That's for my feet. Why make the whole box as high as the length of your feet when your feet don't take up more than maybe five inches of space at the end? It's a waste of lumber. I figure I could build the whole thing a foot tall until the last five inches, or even six inches...keep it simple, everything in feet or half-feet. Then I'd build up the end of it, say, another six inches for my boots. Kind of like the Egyptians did."

"What kind of feet do you have?" said Eli. "Canal boats? You don't need that much room."

"Yes, I do, because I'm wearin' my cowboy boots with the spurs. You know, the ones I wore in The Lone Rangers."

Orson glanced over at the picture on the buffet. In it, Eli and the rest of The Lone Rangers strummed guitars and grinned back at him.

"You're nuts," Orson said, swinging his eyes back to Eli. "I've been meaning to ask you, anyway. Why did you call yourselves The Lone Rangers, when you weren't alone? There were four of you."

"You're off the subject. The point is, I'm wearin' my boots to the last roundup."

"Think of it this way..." Orson tapped his fingers on the maple table. "If you get cremated, you could think of it as falling into the last campfire. Have yourself cremated with a bag of marshmallows. Then you don't have to worry about your boots. Give your boots to your nephew. He's about your size."

Eli just stared at him and let out an exasperated sigh.

"You know I'm right," said Orson. "When I kick the bucket, I'm leaving very clear instructions to anyone who is unlucky enough to have to deal with my remains. Something like..." Eli looked skyward for a few moments, drumming his fingers again. "Something like 'I've lived long, and I've lived well. I pray that I'm not going to hell. When the time comes that I expire, just throw my bones into the fire.'"

"A philosopher *and* a poet," said Eli.

They each took a sip of the aromatic Hawaiian Kona.

"Good coffee," said Orson. Then he picked up Eli's drawing and flipped it over. Grabbing the pencil that lay near it, he began to make a list of the wood they would need to repair the fence. "Tell you what," he said. "We repair this fence, and I'll let you design my urn."

Eli refilled both their cups, and they each sipped in quiet satisfaction as The Lone Rangers smiled on from across the room.

ADMISSION

Joan T. Doran

My life is not a chick flick
where I wear cute guys like rings
around my little finger when not angling
for my boss' job.

I do admit to
early chase scenes in joy-ridden cars:
a hapless dog, our sober faces watching
helpless as the light bled out of trust,

and action scenes where we players
swayed together through the grainy reels,
where the barman answered only
to the ching of the cash register
and laced our ginger ale with rye
as if we were eighteen and legal
and didn't have to go to school tomorrow
to conjugate the verb être.
We wore our innocence like lipstick.

My old film flickers on in black and white.
There are no stars, just two whose roles
are ringed together till the screen goes dark,
still clutching tight
the faded tickets of admission.

Beauty Shop Therapy

Carole Kaliher

My first experience with a beauty shop occurred in 1957 at the age of nineteen. Joan, a co-worker at the Pacific Telephone Company, recommended a shop in Alhambra, near our building. It wasn't a pleasant experience, and that's a classic understatement.

I tried to explain to the beautician, "Please don't set my hair in pin curls. Use rollers because my hair is naturally curly, and pin curls don't work for my hair." (The pin curl method was used most often during that time.)

"Now, dear, I've been a beautician for ten years. I know what I'm doing. It'll be just fine."

What a lie! When she finished with me, I looked like Shirley Temple on the way to the "Good Ship Lollipop." I went home, cried, brushed, then brushed some more and cried some more. I finally had to wet it, put it in rollers, sit under the dryer, and restyle my hair. Thank God, I didn't let her cut it.

At age twenty, I bravely accepted a recommendation from another co-worker, Mary, who sent me to the House of Westmore beauty salon in Hollywood. The Westmore men were noted for being stylists to the rich and famous. They did hair and makeup. I felt like I was in good hands this time. I said, "Please don't set my hair in pin curls. It'll be a disaster."

My beautician, Nora, grinned and said, "Oh, I bet you got the old 'I've been in the business for X number of years and I know what I'm doing,' speech. Customers know how their hair reacts to styling products and methods, and it's our job to listen."

Praise the Lord, I thought, *she gets it!* She conditioned, cut, and styled my hair beautifully. I went every few months for haircuts—not often, because it was a forty-minute drive on the freeway to get to the salon, and it was rather expensive on my meager budget.

Two days before my wedding, I made an appointment to have my hair done. On the way to that appointment a woman in a yellow Buick panicked when her car slid a little on a rain-soaked freeway and pulled her emergency brake in the fast lane. I couldn't avoid hitting her. She had a small dent on her rear quarter panel, while my small foreign car was thoroughly crunched and had to be towed away. No beauty shop for me that day!

My maid of honor washed and styled my hair the next night, while giving me marital advice. "Carole, if Jim wants to have sex, just say *yes.* Ten minutes and it's done, and there'll be fewer arguments down the road. Trust me on this."

I wondered, *Why hasn't Mom given me the dreaded ten-minute advice? She didn't give me the lecture on the facts of life, so why would she start now?*

Three years went by before I attempted another trip to a beauty shop. This one had to be local because I was seven months pregnant with twins. I have a fear of drowning when water runs down my face, so I can't wash my hair in the shower like most people. I have to wash my hair while holding my head over the kitchen sink. I was so huge that, try as I might, facing front or sideways, no matter the method, I couldn't fit at the sink to accomplish this task. I finally gave up and made an appointment with a young man named John to style my hair.

I fell madly in love with him immediately. He said, "I think you need some pampering. Let me take your crutches. You sit here and relax." (I had fallen and broken my pelvic bone during my pregnancy and had to walk with crutches until the birth.) John proceeded to rub my shoulders, neck, and scalp. Heavenly! He cut, conditioned, and styled my hair to perfection.

"John, I really look forward to these shampoos."

"If you do, then I'm doing my job! You're a sweet lady, and you deserve to be treated well."

After my twins were born, I called for an appointment and was devastated to hear that he had left that shop. Those trips to John left me feeling rejuvenated and beautiful (a miracle for a hugely pregnant woman to experience).

Years went by and, by trial and error, I found many women to do my hair, but none like my first love, John. One beautician talked me into frosting my hair. She got out the perforated cap and put it on my head. With a crochet-like hook, she pulled pieces of hair through the holes.

"Nancy, remember my hair is thin, so don't pull too much through the cap."

"Oh, I've done this for years. *I know what I'm doing.*"

That dreaded phrase should have scared the hell out of me, but I went like a lamb to the slaughter. When she was through with me, my hair was almost all white.

My sons, upon seeing my hair, said, "Mom, what happened?" They looked sad.

Hell, I *was* sad. It looked like a trauma had occurred in my life and my hair had gone white from the fright. Jim came home, took one look and said in a most sympathetic voice, "Sweet P, you had to pay for that suffering? I'm so sorry." I had to go out and buy a rinse to cover the mess in order to go to work the next day.

These days, I have a lady named Virginia as a beautician. Her shop is in a retirement home in Sun City. My latest appointment was on a Thursday, and Thursdays and Fridays are the busiest days for them. What a revelation! It's wall-to-wall white-haired, elderly ladies. They're wheeled in or use their walkers if they're more mobile. Hold your feet close to your body or they may roll over them with a wheelchair.

Looking at all these women and some men, I realized there isn't a time in any of our lives when we don't need some personal attention. Frail seniors don't have a corner on the market. I remember the lines spoken by the character of Niles in the Frasier sitcom: "I've come to a time in my life that I have to pay people to touch me; how depressing."

Diane, another beautician in the shop, told me this story. "You get some odd or unusual people in our line of work. One customer came in asking to have her hair colored. I asked her, 'What color do you want?' She promptly raised her sleeve, baring her hairy underarm, and said, 'This color...can you match it?' My mouth dropped open."

While we were laughing hysterically, Virginia commented, "I guess you're lucky she didn't want you to match a lower spot on her body."

We continued laughing uncontrollably.

More than hair care goes on in a beauty shop. It's a form of therapy! Women are sometimes more candid with their hairdresser than they would be with a confessor or a counselor. We gossip, of course, but with the unspoken agreement that no names are ever mentioned, so privacy is faithfully guarded. We hear from each other what our children and husbands do *for* us or *to* us, as the case may be. We make friends, laugh, and listen to jokes and storytelling while receiving a lovely shampoo that you don't have to do for yourself.

Reliving that day triggered these memories, and I smiled. The title of beauty shop can mean a lot of different things. To me, it's pampering, friendships, listening to other people's troubles, and realizing my life isn't bad at all. After the hair is taken care of, add a pedicure, and you are in heaven. Everyone should have some beauty shop therapy.

Fairway Exchange

Barbara Ostrem

My husband and I liked golfing together, and one of our favorite courses was Glendoveer on northeast Glisan. The first hole on the less-demanding west side could be daunting because it was so visible to the parking lot and the many other golfers going to and fro. It could be intimidating to take a hefty swing—and miss!—or watch as the ball dribbled weakly off the tee sideways.

But on this particular day everything clicked, and I hit a masterful drive straight down the fairway toward the beckoning flag fluttering on the green. Not quite *that* far, but close enough to thrill me. It came to rest near some tall firs, a boundary between this and the adjacent fairway. As I strode confidently toward it, out of the trees came another golfer with club in hand, who positioned herself over *my ball,* ready to swing!

"Hey! That's mine!" I hollered. She must have heard, but whacked it anyway and followed it onto the next fairway without a backward glance. I unzipped the pocket of my bag to get another ball and saw, a few feet away, what surely was *hers* in full view, if she had bothered to look around.

Well, what the heck. I'll play hers, I mused—and did. The fact that it was a new Titleist eased my consternation. As we were putting out, back she came through the trees.

"I'm sorry. It seems I played your ball by mistake," she simpered, extending her hand to return it in exchange for hers.

"Keep it," I said.

"But mine's a new Titleist," she whined, eyes opened wide.

"Let's hope it gets me a good game," I said, smiling as I picked up my bag and headed for the next tee.

It wasn't my problem.

LAUNDRY EXERCISE

Terrie Jacks

laundry basket
overflows top
bend and stretch
do a little hop

fold five things
put them away
dance a little bit
add a little sway

hang that shirt
match some socks
fold the towels
laundry rocks

skip to my Lou
heel and toe
emptying basket
is the goal

WRINKLES

Lela Brown

I'd like to see a magazine published exclusively for women who are at least sixty-five and up to as old as women live to be. It would be called *Wrinkles* and maybe subtitled "The *Old* Ladies' Home Journal."

Wrinkles would be edited and staffed by women over sixty-five. It wouldn't accept material by writers under that age, and it would welcome articles by authors in their seventies, eighties, and beyond. *Wrinkles* wouldn't deny the realities of old age; it would explore them. *Wrinkles* wouldn't contain the kind of age-spurning medical advice so common elsewhere. It would recognize and help us with our declining abilities, chronic illness, pain, and necessary forays into the health care system. It would acknowledge the physical insults and surprises nature visits on us when we get old.

Wrinkles would contain fashion and grooming advice that is never seen in other women's magazines. What clothes suit us and where can we find them? What about hairstyles and cosmetics? What do others do about old-lady problems that younger people deem too gross or comical to consider?

Wrinkles would be literate, honest, and original. Its emphasis would be on the discoveries of this stage of our journey, as surprising and important as any of our earlier ones. In *Wrinkles* we would read about attitudes, prejudices, and lessons learned; about relationships with spouses (if we still have them), children, grandchildren, and friends; about what loneliness and loss really mean after a busy life; and about what we can make of the wisdom and opportunities we have now.

There would be guidance in how to manage our possessions and the family archives in preparation for our final departure, written from our own perspective. We'd find interviews with contemporaries. There would even be fiction, with women like us as the central characters rather than as the token old people in younger folks' lives.

Wrinkles is the magazine Oprah might publish in twenty years. I just wish I could read it now.

CRUISING

Kathleen A. O'Brien

> *The child is in me still*
> *and sometimes not so still.*
> —Mister Rogers

Lets me drive his Mustang on the Mass Pike,
"California Special," V8, top down,
sleek, candy apple red, low to the ground,
300 horses straining to be free.

Sun, silver hubcap, warms our necks
this Cape Cod-blue June morning.
Maples turn their heads to follow as
we carve our path through the Berkshires.

A black SUV keeps tailgating.
"Floor it," my friend says.
I stomp the pedal and we pull away
like the leader in the Indy 500.

85 mph. Now 70
slipping into the middle lane, satisfied.
The SUV will soon catch up, but knows
I'm not driving Miss Daisy.

Wind flops my wide-brimmed hat
and ruffles the gentleman's silver hair.
Senior citizens, we sail to the music
of the Mustang's hum; we're Thelma and Louise.

"Welcome to New York,"
sign the size of a movie screen,
signals our joy ride is nearing its end.

Wrinkled face in the rearview mirror reminds me
years are speeding by, but this memory remains:
youthful spirits alive and cruising on.

LAMB IN A LION'S CAGE

Jack Campbell

S am Lawson finished his cigarette, then vaulted up to the top bunk, stretching out for a midday snooze. His slim, six foot-four, one-hundred-and-ninety-pound frame made it in a single effort. He preferred the top bunk; it kept his possessions more or less private, and his cellmate didn't step on him in the middle of the night when nature called.

The warden had given him an assignment for tomorrow that had him reviewing his own circumstances, his mortality included. In his two and a half years in Oklahoma State Prison, he had, by choice, worked in the prison kitchen and also as Warden Charles King's go-fer guy. He was practically one of the staff. He could roam the prison grounds mostly unchallenged, the guards always assuming him to be on official business.

Sam was a fast talker with a pair of blue eyes that never seemed to blink. His father had been a neighborhood bookie in Oklahoma City. A widower, he kept young Sam busy delivering or collecting money for his book. When he died suddenly of a heart attack, Sam continued to service a few of his dad's clients and did quite well, taking on more bettors as his confidence and bankroll grew. The young bookie was doing quite well until he ran into one of the *big facts of life.*

A neighborhood Capo from the Scortino family had tolerated Sam's modest infringement on his territory until a couple of his high rollers started doing business with Sam. Retribution was swift and predictable. Without warning, Sam was framed when a cop on the take just happened to find drugs and a gun on Sam. In court, a few petty arrests for bookmaking along with the current evidence convinced the presiding judge to sentence Sam to three years in State Prison. In the end, Sam allowed that it was probably better than getting a baseball bat to both knees.

Sam took a seat in the warden's office as directed and waited to see what was needed.

The warden looked up from his work. "Sam, do you know Jarvis Tidwell in cell block B?"

Sam nodded. "Yeah, he did a hell of a job on the guy that raped his little girl, right?"

"Yes…well, his execution is set for midnight Friday, and I wanted to explain a few things about his last meal. Ordinarily, I'd have the kitchen put something nice together, but Tidwell's made an unusual request, and I want you to go over and get the details for me, okay?"

Sam scooted his chair back and rose to his full height, leaning toward the warden. "Is Tidwell in his cell?"

"No, you'll find him in the library. Get down there right away and find out what's on his mind."

Jarvis Tidwell's straight-laced deportment in his first few years on death row had been rewarded by Warden King with occasional duty in the prison library. It was unusual duty for a death row inmate, but the warden had reviewed Tidwell's file several times through the years and allowed that a lot of men, including himself, would probably have committed the same damn crime.

In almost eight years in State Prison, Tidwell had never opened up to anyone about his circumstances. The prison grapevine provided little about Tidwell's case. So, on a cold November morning, Sam Lawson was waved through the library doors by the patrolling guard and came face to face with Jarvis Tidwell, who was about to give Sam one hell of a lot to think about.

Jarvis Martin Tidwell's world pretty much fell apart the day he came home from work, slumped into his easy chair, reached for the remote, and looked up to see the three women in his life staring grotesquely at him. They had been crying and were soon unburdening themselves with news that made his blood run cold. Bonnie, his fourteen-year-old, had been raped by a neighbor a few weeks before and had just told her aunt the sordid details.

Although Lisa Tidwell's girls were two years apart in age, except for size, they could have passed for twins, both with short blond hair, green eyes you instantly took a second look at, and pleasingly slim like their mother.

Since getting out of the service, Jarvis had led a modest life in small town Oklahoma, building up a pawn shop business over fifteen years. His corner house in suburbia was surrounded by a neatly manicured yard that took up most of his free time. Jarvis had been lost after Lisa was killed in an auto accident a few years back, but he and his teenage daughters struggled along without her.

Lisa had made a modest and loving home for her family, falling for Jarvis the very first time she laid eyes on him. They were married three months later, and over the next four years the two girls were born. Fourteen and sixteen now, they were a real handful for Jarvis. Lisa's sister Grace, who lived a mile down the road, was a big help. She had been close to her nieces from birth and was their confidante.

Luther Bell lived a block away and was the neighborhood jerk. His foul mouth in consort with a horrific overbite did much to personify the jerk theory. He ran a small auto repair shop and really knew his trade. But if you were a female paying your bill, you probably got your ass pinched on your way out the door—with greasy fingers, no less.

The day Bonnie was raped, Luther had been driving the neighborhood kids around the block in a funny car he had built, and they were having a grand old time. The kids took turns, and Bonnie was the last to ride. Luther circled the block, then turned into his driveway and entered his garage, closing the door behind him with his remote.

After hearing the details, Jarvis calmed the women down, and Grace got the girls off to bed. He asked his sister-in-law to come to his shop the next morning at 9 a.m. She pleaded with him to call the police and not deal with Luther Bell himself. He walked her to her car, all the while pacifying her with, "We'll talk tomorrow, Grace—tomorrow, okay?"

Jarvis Tidwell had arrived at the decision to kill Luther Bell the instant his young daughter embraced him and whimpered, "I'm sorry, Daddy. I'm sorry." His mild manner combined with a spot-on moral compass belied a past fraught with violence and death. He was an ex-marine who had fought in Vietnam, where staying alive was a daily concern. On one occasion, while clearing the enemy out of a maze of tunnels, he had surprised two VC operating a radio set. Having left his AK 47 behind to better squeeze through the narrow openings, he quietly drew his 45 cal. pistol and killed them both as they reached for their rifles. He paused briefly to watch their blood flow into a mutual puddle before resuming his quest.

Jarvis arrived at his shop just before 9 a.m. the next morning and put on a pot of coffee. He dialed his clerk and gave him the day off. As he leaned back in his office chair and sipped his coffee, his glance went to a picture he had hung there the first day he opened his shop. Taken in Vietnam at Fire Base Outlaw, it showed his squad smiling and holding their weapons above their heads. They all looked so young.

Grace knocked on the locked door and joined him. She was dabbing her eyes with a damp tissue. Her stark resemblance to her sister, Lisa, always perplexed him. Jarvis calmed her down with a cup of coffee and began explaining his future plan for her and the girls. She would have the option of running the business as it was or selling the shop and adding it to his other savings and investments. It was clear that, with her administrative experience, they would be set for years. A sobbing Grace reluctantly left the shop, still pleading with Jarvis to let the police handle Luther Bell. He assured her he would legalize his plans for her and the girls in the coming weeks.

His pact was now in place, written in Luther Bell's blood. He walked to the gun case, which displayed an array of handguns. His favorite was the old army issue 45 cal., the same one he had used in Vietnam. He had shipped it home before departing from the war zone. As he gripped it tightly, violent flashbacks exploded in his mind, each one a nail in Luther Bell's coffin.

He spilled a box of shells across the countertop, took the clip out of the pistol, and loaded it one shell at a time. As he slammed the clip into firing position, it was indeed Sergeant Tidwell who slipped the loaded pistol into his waistband, a black leather jacket concealing its presence.

Luther Bell's wife was sweeping the front steps as he walked through their front gate. He remembered the raven-haired, dark-eyed woman from high school. Before he could inquire about Luther, she waved him toward the side of the house.

"He's back in the garage, working on something."

Jarvis smiled and continued back to the open garage door, stopping six feet from the man fiddling with a lawnmower. With a crooked grin that did much to emphasize his gaping overbite, Luther got most of "Hi ya, Jarvis" out of his mouth before a .45 slug tore into his right kneecap, bone splinters piercing the canvas bag attached to the lawnmower. He fell backwards, clutching a knee that was no longer there, shouting, "She's lying, Jarvis! She's lying!" Jarvis calmly pressed the button, closing the garage door, thus sealing off a deadly arena. Luther, now given over to panic, screamed,

"She wanted it, Jarvis! She begged me for it!" just as another slug shattered his other knee. Jarvis stood over this whimpering hulk, the stark fear in the man's eyes prompting overwhelming revulsion. "I'm sorry, I'm sorry," Luther pleaded as a third slug made him a eunuch. Writhing in a spreading pool of blood, Luther managed to prop himself up against the front wheel of his funny car. Jarvis's pistol and his hatred for this man had exacted all of the "eye for an eye" parable possible. Propping the man's head up with the gun barrel under his chin, his gaze was intense as he saw the whole fucked-up world reflected in Luther's eyes. The Marines had taught him to kill, life had shown him love, but that love could not get him through the moment. He pulled the trigger for the last time, killing Luther and puncturing the tire he was leaning on. Then he laid his gun on the blood-spattered fender just above Luther's lifeless body.

Luther's frantic wife was pounding on the small side door. Jarvis calmly dialed 911 on his cell phone, and then pressed the main garage door button. Sudden daylight splashed across a morbid scene.

Jarvis strolled out into the sunlight, down the driveway and sat on the curb, runoff from watered lawns trickling past his feet. The screams from Luther's wife resounded throughout the neighborhood, unheard by Jarvis Tidwell as he watched a fallen maple leaf float by in the gutter below.

It was not a long trial, as trials go. He pleaded guilty, much to the chagrin of his lawyer, leaving only the sentence to be decided upon. Strangely enough, the town's sympathy was with Jarvis. They did not see it as a grisly murder, but more like ridding the town of the world's biggest asshole. All that became a moot point when "hanging judge" Eli Blackwell saw it as the most heinous premeditated murder he'd ever come across and appeared to yawn slightly as he condemned Jarvis to death.

The following regimented years were mellowed somewhat as Jarvis watched his daughters marry and give him grandchildren who dazzled him with each visit. He continued to rebuff any attempts to get him a new trial, his self-imposed contrition seemingly resolute. Refusing to post appeals brought his final days on death row to an end much sooner than most. On a cold November morning in his eighth year, his execution date was set.

Sam stood in the library, shaking his head in disbelief after hearing Jarvis Tidwell's own account of his path to death row. Jarvis then handed him his last meal request. Sam's eyebrows arched as he read the menu: braised grouper in garlic sauce, sauteed artichoke hearts, asparagus with hollandaise, red mashed potatoes, and cherries jubilee. He was about to say, "How the hell are we going to do this?" until he saw the asterisk at the bottom of the page.

This last meal menu will be prepared at a restaurant, time and place to be decided at a later date, and for the person named herein (Ruth Bell). The items will be paid for in their entirety from the funds accumulated by prisoner 4592047 (Jarvis Tidwell).

Jarvis said, "It's a great meal. I had it at a pawn broker's convention one time, and I never forgot it."

Yes, it was true; Ruth Bell had visited Jarvis several times over the years and many fences had been mended. They had been casual friends in high school, and she understood what Luther had done to his family. Jarvis's request went on: "For myself, I wish only a hot cup of tea and a decent cigar in the hours before my death. I have wrought sorrow to many in my life, and now I only want to go peacefully into whatever awaits me. Please forgive me, if you can."

Sam's rugged exterior masked a soft heart that had just pumped a single tear down his cheek, which he quickly removed with the back of his hand. "Look man, you know if you file an appeal today, the warden would break his balls to get you a stay of execution."

"Sam, the day I loaded that gun and walked through Luther's front gate, I knew my life was over. It's called an eye for an eye."

"Well, I have to ask, Jarvis, why are you giving this fine meal to the Bell woman? Ain't she the enemy?"

"The enemy? Hardly, Sam. She's visited me many times through the years. I even talked her into going back to school. Believe it or not, she got her MBA last year, and now has her own little business. She's doing fine. She's really the only one out there besides my family I give a damn about, and I want her to have this."

"Well, I guess you've made up your mind. I'll give your request to the warden. Hey, if he approves it, I get out of here in a few weeks, and I wouldn't mind delivering it for you. Kind of a personal touch, ya know?"

"You don't have to do that, Sam. I think Ruth will appreciate just getting my letter and check in the mail."

"It's no problem. I've got no place to be and no one to see when I get out. Besides, the whole thing sounds intriguing."

"I don't know Sam, I—"

"Promise to be nothing but a gentleman."

"Well, let's see what the warden says first. If you still want to do this, I guess it would be okay."

The two men shook hands and Sam headed for the warden's office.

Not only did the warden approve Jarvis' request, he thought the idea of Sam delivering the gift was a great idea. On the following Friday morning just after midnight, Sam Lawson made his way back to the anteroom just off the execution chamber. He entered and stared down at a half empty cup of tea containing a partially smoked cigar. Not much left to explain a man's life. All who knew Jarvis agreed, he departed this life with the same dignity and faithful heart he had found early on as a young Marine and later as a husband and father. He had now joined forever those fallen comrades he had left behind so many years ago…*brotherhood into eternity.*

The warden stood up and extended his hand to Sam Lawson, whose lanky frame was decked out in the same civilian clothes he had surrendered the day he arrived. The two men shook hands and the warden commended him for his no-nonsense attitude while serving his sentence.

"Your work for me and this office has damn well been appreciated. If it's any consolation, I've always believed you were framed by that Scortino mob. See if you can keep clear of those guys from now on."

"Warden, I'm not going back there. After I deliver this $300 check to Mrs. Bell, I'll probably head for Houston. I've always liked that town. Besides, with my knack for figures, maybe I'll get a white collar job there… we'll see. Thanks again, Warden. You've been a square shooter."

"You sure you want to deliver that check to her? I can still mail it just as well."

"Yeah, I'll bring it to her. I got a mountain of curiosity going here."

The warden chuckled. "Good luck, Sam. Don't want to see you back her again, okay?"

Sam got a ride into town in a truck doing business for the prison. He was let out at the Greyhound terminal, where he was soon boarding a bus for Okeene, Oklahoma, Ruth Bell and Jarvis's hometown. Sliding into a seat behind the driver, he settled down for the two-hour trip, patting his breast pocket for reassurance that the $300 check was still there.

A while later, the squeal of air brakes woke a dozing Sam Lawson, and he fumbled under his seat for the small gym bag that contained his only possessions. After a few inquiries and a two-block walk, he slid into a booth at the "Steer & Beer Bar & Grill." The waitress arched her eyebrows slightly when Sam ordered three bottles of beer, but understood when she saw him down the first beer and a half in almost a single breath.

"Three years is a long time between beers," he explained.

After finishing the Blue Plate special (chicken and dumplings) and a few more beers, Sam found walking the block and a half to the YMCA a bit taxing. He hadn't counted on that 5% beer doing a job on him after a few years of abstinence. He was escorted to a room he paid for by the day and, when left alone, came to the conclusion that it wasn't much bigger than his cell but smelled a whole lot better. On his first night of freedom in three years, he sprawled out over the single bed, letting the feel of clean white sheets add to his beer high. He was soon fantasizing about meeting Ruth Bell in the morning. "I always liked her dark sparkling eyes," was what Jarvis had said. A soft purring snore soon signaled the end of a very long day for Sam Lawson.

Early next morning, the smell of brewed coffee soon had him looking for the source. A day room just off the main office displayed a continental breakfast. It was just past 8 a.m. when Sam started looking through his wallet for Ruth Bell's number. Wiping his fingers with a napkin, he proceeded to fumble with a scrap of paper bearing her phone number, eventually freeing up a finger for dialing.

After a few rings, Sam heard, "This is Ruth Bell."

"Mrs. Bell, this is Sam Lawson from—"

She interrupted with, "Oh yes, Mr. Lawson. Warden Miller at state prison told me to expect you. Where are you now?"

After he told her, Ruth suggested picking him up and bringing him to her house for further discussion. "Bring your bag along. I have a spare room you can use that's probably more comfortable than the YMCA."

Sam sat on the front steps of the Y until a neat-looking Ford Ranchero pulled up and a dark-haired woman with huge sunglasses leaned out the window.

"You Sam Lawson?"

He pushed himself up from the cold steps and walked over to greet her as she pushed up her sunglasses, revealing that pair of dark sparkling eyes.

"Yes, I'm Sam."

"Sam, if you don't mind, let's go to my place. We can have lunch and get acquainted."

"Sounds great, Mrs. Bell."

"Call me Ruth, okay?"

Sam tossed his bag in the back seat and eased into the passenger seat. A five-minute ride had them pulling into her driveway. The garage door took its time retracting, giving Sam a chance to view the former crime scene. The fully raised door illuminated a sparsely equipped double garage with only a few garden tools scattered about. No clues to the former murder remained.

"Bring your bag in, Sam. You might want to freshen up."

Later, at the kitchen table, Ruth handed him one of two cold beers and got the conversation going over lunch.

"So, Ruth, I'm just a little curious as to why you would even consider doing this 'last supper' thing in light of the circumstances. He killed your husband!"

"Yes, the circumstances…I know I don't come off as the wounded wife here, and I also know that Jarvis's punishment did not fit the crime. My husband, Luther, was a horrible man. Raping Jarvis Tidwell's daughter was the last violation he inflicted on the young girls and women in his life. If you need a prime example, it would be me. He molested me when I was only fifteen and got me pregnant. I was sixteen when I lost the baby at birth. Luther went to jail for the whole thing, then talked me into marrying him so he could get out of jail early. I had been with him for twenty years when Jarvis sent him to hell." She stared down at the table. "Sam, I'm sorry, this is probably a lot more than you wanted to hear."

"Hey, it's okay. Maybe it's time you got it all off your chest. I came here as a favor to Jarvis. Hell, the prison was just going to mail you a check for $300 with a few words of explanation. I was getting out this month anyway, so I volunteered to come here and maybe sit in for Jarvis…at least make it a little more personable. I am a bit curious as to why you stayed with Luther so long, especially marrying the guy."

"Luther wasn't always as bad as he was later in life. He had a way with him back then. Damned if he didn't sweet talk me into getting married. Like

I said, I had no idea at the time, but it was just a ploy for him to get out of prison early. I had no family to speak of, so I just went along with Luther. He was the only man I had ever been with."

Sam leaned forward, elbows on the table. "You never had any more kids?"

"No, I had a hysterectomy when I lost the baby. Luther hated kids, anyway."

"It's been almost nine years since Luther's death. You been able to find yourself a little happiness along the way?"

"I sold Luther's business and went back to school. I always liked school and really missed it when I got pregnant and had to drop out. I went all the way, Sam, and got a business degree. Right now, I have an office downtown and a small staff. We deal in real estate, but mostly taxes."

Sam gave her an approving nod. With an impish grin, he asked, "Got any openings? I'm pretty good with numbers. I did my dad's taxes until he died."

Ruth looked surprised and assured Sam she would indeed take him to her office and screen his talents.

"By the way, what's with you visiting Jarvis in prison? I was blown away by that."

"I never told anyone about this, Sam, but I knew Jarvis in high school. He was a few grades ahead of me. We never went out or anything like that, but he always said hello to me, and I think I had a small crush on him. Sometime after he went to prison, I wrote and asked if I could visit him. He was surprised, but agreed. I went to see him several times over the years, and he always seemed glad to see me. Because of Luther, I never had a lot of friends, so talking to Jarvis was kind of an oasis for me. I know that might sound a little weird, but Jarvis did much to guide my life after Luther. He talked me into going back to school. He really was quite a guy."

Sam smiled and agreed. "I'm beginning to understand why Jarvis willed you his last supper. It appears you needed each other back then and for entirely different reasons. Makes me kinda glad to be here."

"God, look at the clock, Sam. It's late…we've been talking for hours."

Ruth found Sam a clean towel and washcloth, then she took him to the spare bedroom, which had its own bathroom. "I'm at the other end of the house. If you need anything, just holler. I'm a light sleeper. I'll hear you."

"I'll be fine, Ruth. Thanks for the hospitality. See you in the morning."

Sam fell asleep with a whole new set of fantasies to deal with. Ruth Bell was quite a woman!

The smell of perking coffee brought a refreshed Sam to the kitchen table, which was already set with sticky buns. Ruth greeted him from another room, and soon they were chatting at the table, coffee in hand.

"You know, Sam, the Okeene Country Club is probably the only place in town that will serve the menu Jarvis compiled. What say we drive out there and find out?"

"Fine with me, Ruth, but I have to have a few more of these buns first. It's been a while, ya know?"

"Take your time, Sam, we're in no hurry. I took the day off."

The Okeene Country Club offered eighteen holes of golf, four tennis courts, and a workout and steam room for both sexes. The cuisine was famous in the area and the logical place to dine on braised grouper. The name board on the desk said *Allen Dean, Mgr.* After they explained the situation, he viewed their menu with a bit of consternation before pausing to speak into his desk phone. "Have chef Stefano come to my office, please." Looking up at the two visitors, he asked, "Can prisoners do something like this with their last supper?"

Sam was quick to reply. "Only with the warden's permission and using their own funds."

"I see, I see," the manager mused.

Upon arrival, chef Stefano scanned the menu and agreed that it was basically doable most days, but the grouper would be a special order. "It's kind of seasonal."

Sam handed the manager the $300 check. "Will this cover it?"

Dean's quizzical stare and pursed lips let Ruth know it fell short. "How much more, Mr. Dean?" she inquired.

"At this time, I'm not positive, but $400 to $500 should cover it nicely."

Ruth scribbled across her check book, ripped out the check, and handed it to the manager while snatching the $300 check, seemingly in a single motion. Dean's smile told her the $500 check would suffice.

"This will be a dinner for two, Mr. Dean. I'll expect champagne and your best table in a delightful ambiance. Agreed?"

"Most certainly, Mrs. Bell. It only remains for us to expedite these pro-
ceedings and give you the earliest possible date. Leave your number and my
secretary will call you post-haste."

"My number is on my check."

With that, Ruth Bell grabbed Sam's arm and made a provocative departure that even Allen Dean picked up on. She handed Sam the $300 check.
"You're going to stay for Jarvis's last supper, right?"

Sam was slightly flustered. "You should use this check to help pay for
the meal."

"Sam, unless you've got to be somewhere soon, stay at my place until
we do this thing. Hell, I'd have paid double for this meal. Yes, it's true…
Jarvis took a life, but he also put one back together." With her arm on Sam's
shoulder, she smiled. "Keep the money, Sam, and thanks for being here for
me. Wherever he is, I know, Jarvis is loving it."

Sam flashed his crooked smile as he opened her car door, not failing to
notice the symmetry of a great pair of soft white legs stretching to reach the
pedals below, the hem of her dress slightly retreating. He took his seat next
to her, and they started down the long winding driveway that led to the interstate. Leaning back, Sam pondered his immediate future. It was true that
Houston was his first choice for starting a new life, but Okeene was beginning to look pretty good to him right now.

Jarvis had been a big help getting Ruth back on track. Now, his $300
check seemed like a down payment on Sam's future. Waving it in her face,
Sam shouted, "What say we take this $300 bucks and go have a drink on
Jarvis Martin Tidwell, one hell of a guy!" Ruth, with a wide grin, adjusted her sunglasses and let her Ford Rancho burn a little rubber clearing the
driveway.

ILLUSIONS OF GRANDEUR...

Gordon Warady

Several years ago, when my wife, Phylis, received an offer from Harlequin Books for her regency romance, *Henrietta*, I asked how much money she would make with this novel and was stunned at the financial rewards. When I inquired as to her agent and was told she had none, I toyed with the idea of handling Phylis myself. Two days later, she received yet another long distance phone call with an offer from Dell.

My God! My wife was a writer in great demand. Two publishing houses were after the same book.

The wheels began to turn. I asked Phylis how many of these books she could write in a year. She told me she could write one in ninety days.

Four books per year? I could be her agent. She would write them. I would sell them.

I raced to my calculator. No matter how I did the input, it totaled six figures. Fifteen percent was the agent's share. Add that to my half of the balance and...Hmm. That's with Phylis working only one shift!

I would definitely handle her and be her agent.

Recognizing that my first hurdle must be to persuade her of the soundness of my offer to represent her, I decided we would celebrate both offers with a special gourmet dinner I would prepare that coming Saturday—complete with a bottle of Piper Heidsieck.

I would set the stage, then broach the subject of becoming her agent.

The following weekend, I spent Saturday morning shopping for the freshest produce to accompany two filet mignon steaks and the afternoon chilling the champagne, then putting the finishing touches on our special celebration dinner. As dusk deepened, I set the table. Lit the candles. Dimmed the lights. Pulled out her chair. Seated Phylis at the table. Lifted the bottle of imported bubbly out of the bucket of shaved ice. Popped its cork. Carefully filled two slender flutes.

All set to toast my talented wife's good fortune, I ventured a sip, resulting in a delicate tickling sensation in my nasal passages. I then fixed my gaze upon Phylis as she savored her own sip, her expression engagingly euphoric.

At long last, the propitious moment to seize the marital reins.

With the delicate ching of our flutes still resonating, I leaned close enough to nuzzle her delectable ear lobe and murmur, "Phylis, I would like to handle you."

Her lips quirked in a knowing smile, she responded, "Not tonight, dear."

Oh, No, My Battery's Dead!

Helen Jones-Shepherd

One summer afternoon in the late 40's, when I was about seventeen, Momma sent me to the store to pick up some onions, a key ingredient in a dish she was preparing for dinner—Beef Stroganoff, I believe.

At home also, besides my younger sister, Mary, was John, my older brother by three years. John was always bringing friends over to our house. One boy, in particular, Tommy, was quite handsome: tall and fair-haired with blue mischievous eyes. During his visits, Tommy had teased me on occasion by commenting, "John's little sister is sure growing up." And with that he would smile broadly at me. I ruled him out as a possible date because he had a fancy car, a red convertible that he sported about with much aplomb. Most of my girlfriends were "gaga" over him, and when we had group wiener bakes or other activities, Tommy always had a giggling girl on his arm. First of all, dating my brother's friends turned me off, since I overhead them gossiping about girls all too often. Secondly, his arrogance annoyed me. A sensitive beau is what I dreamed about, one who would open the car door for me, gently hold my hand, and yes, even wax poetic. At this age, I yearned for the Robert Browning who wooed his love with words. Brash or cutesy comments were not for me.

Years went by, and I started to date, seeing Tommy now and then at our dinner table joking with my brother. When he would ask me out, I would coquettishly refuse. Mother knew he lived with his mom and was very kind and considerate of her. Well, I thought, that was one plus for this conceited oaf.

Getting back to the store and the onions: I parked my car and sought out the brown onions, which I purchased. I headed for my old gray 1957 Ford, but when I turned the ignition key, I heard a terrible grinding noise and nothing happened; it was dead. Thinking it was the battery, I jumped out and lifted the hood. Now, reader, why I did that I'll never know, since my knowledge of auto mechanics was nil. However, my dad did teach me to change a tire in an emergency. Maybe I should tap the battery to wake it up, I thought, having seen my brother do it. Back into the car I went and turned the ignition key again—dead as a doornail!

No one was around to offer assistance. What to do? Momma was waiting at home for the much-required ingredients and, with time passing, she would begin to worry. Almost reduced to tears by my dilemma, I closed the hood and climbed back into the car. Suddenly, from out of nowhere came this smiling face in a red convertible who asked, "Can I help?" It was Tommy, the one person I disliked, but tolerated because he was my brother's buddy.

Looking very disconsolate and pathetic, I blurted out, "Momma is waiting for me to return, and my car won't start."

"Well, let me take a look," he offered solicitously. He parked his car and looked under the hood, perusing all the strange auto things for a few minutes. When I got out of the car, I saw him turning or tightening something around the engine. He said, "Go start it up."

Excitedly, I tried it again, but it was still dead. By now, worry had set in, as it was getting dark. Tommy then leaned toward me and stated rather officiously, "I think I know the problem. This rotor must be installed for the car to run."

Perplexed, I wondered how the part mysteriously came to be in his hand.

He grinned and, in a devilish tone, said, "If you'll go out with me Saturday night, I'll put the part back."

I was furious. This was pure blackmail! He could tell I was extremely upset with him and just stood there grinning sheepishly. As I recall, he also mumbled something about "All's fair in love and war." So, after weighing my options, since I didn't have the Auto Club at that time, I reluctantly agreed. Such a clever ploy, I thought…hmm…

And the rest of the story is history. Within a year, we had exchanged wedding vows, and later had two wonderful children, eventually celebrating thirty-four years of marriage.

Time's Promise

Vivian Bullock

His memory comes back to me like an old love song, dreamlike and sweet. We met at a bus stop, on a beautiful spring morning. I was walking around, waiting for my bus, when the man coming toward me caught my attention. I thought he moved with such grace, most likely a *good dancer*. As we were about to pass, I dropped my paper and he picked it up. When he returned it to me, our eyes met and our hands touched. The look and the touch seemed so familiar, I felt I knew him, had always known him. It seemed quite natural for us to walk to a nearby bench and sit down together.

We talked briefly…about what, I can't recall. What I do remember well was the magnetic energy between us. We learned we would not be leaving on the same bus. This didn't please him. I wanted to say, "Never mind, just come with me." But, of course, I didn't. Our time was short; my bus was in sight and his was on the way. I reluctantly broke away. He followed me and watched as I got on board. I heard him call, "Your address…I want your address." I tried to answer, but it was too late; my bus was moving away.

Time, you do so frazzle, bedazzle, and mystify me. However, my dreams have given me visions of what appear to be past lives, so when you whisper in my ear with an alluring promise, telling me I will meet this man again, in another time and place, I believe you.

The Day She Left

John J. Han

She says she's moving out.
She says she's big enough
to leave her parents' shadows.
We still have her baby pictures
in the family room.

After moving her bags to the car,
I look out the window.
Magnolia branches are now covered
with red and white buds,
but they look blurry.

Waving her hand, she drives away—
it's no big deal.
In her empty room, I find her self-portrait
she drew at age ten.
There she grins,
sticking her tongue out.

Twilight Cactus

J. R. Nakken

"**Y**ou've been trying to fix me up with Greenhouse Glenn since I was a senior," her only child spat. "If you need plant food, run next door and get it yourself."

Newly divorced, Leigh and her two little girls had moved back home to the Northwest ten long weeks ago. Her mother's house was now small and disorderly, and Edith was ashamed at her delight as they dropped clothes and toys indiscriminately into grocery boxes. Leigh's rental home was ready.

"When I was here with Grandma that summer, all he could talk about was grafting pears and peaches onto their apple tree. Not my type, Mom!" The younger woman elongated the hole in the heel of a tiny red sock and tossed it into a wastebasket.

Edith bit her tongue and did not remark on the type Leigh had chosen.

Glenn was a nurseryman, formerly the skinny kid next door. He had graduated from college the year Edith married Walt, the only father then eleven-year-old Leigh ever knew, and turned his horticulture degree and part-time business into a thriving full-time career on his folks' home place. Edith, Walt, and Leigh visited Mama often in the years that followed and in the spring always went next door for flats of annual flowers. Glenn's elderly, taciturn parents pointed and made change, but it was he who answered questions.

Glenn was shy, animated only when talking about growing things. "This guy," his baritone voice whispered as his long hands caressed a plant, "this guy wants only morning sun (or very little water, or withered leaves removed). Remember that, and he'll be happy at your house."

Edith remembered, and Glenn's plants were always content. She liked him. He was quiet and loving with his parents, fine neighbors according to Edith's mother. Before his death, Mr. Shelton appeared occasionally at eventide with a half-peck of apples or some fine pears from Glenn's grafted tree. Mama reciprocated with homemade ice cream or holiday cookies, but they were never inside one another's homes. "Best kind of neighbors," her mother twinkled.

Oh, how Edith had missed her these past six months. Mama had been her rock in the two years since Walt's death. Glenn and his fragile mother had attended the funeral, and Mrs. Shelton was gone a few days later. Edith took a meatloaf and an upside-down cake next door and spoke briefly to Glenn and a much-older sister she didn't know existed. When she slipped back through the hedge to the empty house that was now her home, she felt doubly alone.

"You could have done a lot worse," was all she said now as Leigh filled the last carton. "Glenn's a fine man." Her daughter shrugged and hoisted the box to join the others in her minivan. By mid-afternoon the little family was loaded and gone.

Edith spent the rest of the quiet July day in her neglected flowerbeds, most of them planted that spring under Glenn's tutelage. Four-inch weeds were flying from the corner of the house and freeing the soil around resplendent purple coneflowers when his face appeared over the high fence between their properties.

"Hey, Edith," he began.

"Oh, Glenn, I was just thinking about when you sold me on this flowerbed. Aren't they magnificent?"

A smile split his long face, made it nearly handsome. "They are just that! Too shaggy for most people, though. Others just want them because they're Echinacea. You know, medicinal."

Edith had never heard him talk this long without a plant in his hand. She was staring when he stammered to a stop and made his point. "Those guys over in the shady corner?" Glenn pointed to the bed of hosta under the sumac. "They've got company. Slugs. See those little holes in the lower leaves? Hosta is just about the slug's favorite food. They can eat those to the ground in a couple of weeks."

"Oh, no!" She moaned in disgust. "What shall I do?"

"C'mon over real soon. I've got some environmentally safe slug bait that really works." He slid back down the fence and was gone.

Edith stared at that spot on the aged redwood for a long time. She had used his every suggestion, and he'd been in this back yard a half dozen times since spring, designing personal flowerbeds to help make it her own. Like his parents before him, he'd never been in the house, although he did sip a soda with her and the little girls one warm spring afternoon. I wonder if he's lonely, she thought, and turned away from the fence to finish weeding the Echinacea.

Leigh was busy with her new job and didn't visit often. When she did, Edith didn't mention Glenn again, for her spirited girl was already interested in a man at work. Autumn threatened, the flowerbeds began to fade, and the leaves on her mother's ornamental fig tree curled and dropped to the tile in the entry hall. Glenn said he could come over in an hour. She brushed her frosty hair and dabbed at lip gloss.

"So glad you make house calls!" she said. He smelled of the shower instead of his usual peat moss and earth, and his damp, russet hair curled away from the comb marks on the back of his head when he bent to the pot in the hallway. "Mama loved this little tree, and I'd be devastated if it died."

"We won't let it die, Edith." His deep voice was quiet and soothing as he investigated the fig tree's molting leaves. "Look, can you see this?" He turned up a leaf. "Spider mites. I thought it might be so, and I brought this…"

He was still cataloguing all the plants endangered by the little beasties when he found himself in her kitchen nook, drinking tea while waiting to put a second coating of his homemade foam on the sick tree.

Edith made conversation about her garden. He sipped and watched her talk. Their eyes met once, and in his was a sweet kinship. She was disconcerted and bustled to the teapot, chattering.

"I thought I'd have you over for a meal, Glenn. Maybe invite Leigh. Could you use a home-cooked meal next week sometime?"

His shrug was helpless as he stood, handed over his mug, and went to his patient without answering. He finishing the second dousing and was crooning, "You get well, now, hear?" to the little tree when she joined him.

Then he was at the door, and still Edith was silent. She finally found her manners, extended a hand. "Thanks, Glenn. You're a good neighbor…and friend."

He filled the open doorway, his back to the evening, and enfolded her hand in his two. His smile was wide and guileless, and he had no struggle with the words. "Edith, do you know I am nearly thirty-five? And I have never been interested in Leigh." Then he was gone. Her hand tingled.

~

She was critical in front of the full-length mirror when she stepped from the shower that night. Maybe a little hippy, she decided, but nothing sags, and it's darn good for forty-four. What is age, anyway?

Edith put a highlight rinse on her hair the next day, and in the days that followed her back yard flowerbeds became pristine and weed-free. She gardened with one eye on the fence, but Glenn didn't appear. She was torn between manufacturing an excuse to go next door and forgetting the whole darn thing when he appeared at her door at first dark.

"Do you like cactus, Edith?" he quizzed through the screen door, remaining on the stoop when she opened it.

"Well, yes, Glenn, but…" she gestured expansively, "where would I put some?"

"Oh, yeah, right…" he mumbled and turned back to the hedge.

There's more, said a voice in her ear. *Stop him.*

She called to his retreating back. "Glenn? Glenn, did you have a cactus you wanted me to see?"

He fairly loped back. The words tumbled out. "It's a night-blooming Cereus, and it's about to open. It just blooms this one night."

She found herself following him to the greenhouse that housed his mother plants. Primal odor and the alien feel of Glenn's propagation plants assaulted her senses; lumpy, hanging monsters and living stalagmites erupted in the saucer-shaped room. Then she saw the Cereus, experienced its birth.

It was a single bloom in a thousand colors of ecru, its ten-inch trumpet radiant against ugly, twisted branches in hanging clay. Her heart leaped at its unspeakable beauty; she was mute as it unfolded its full glory to them. *He had to share this with someone he cared for*, said the voice, and her hand met his in the narrowing chasm between their bodies.

Was it minutes or hours later when he spoke? "I have tea. We can see it once more before it fades." His strong arm guided her from his first and greatest gift, around the apple-peach-pear tree and into the rest of his life.

ONE

Seretta Martin

            'Til death do us part—
The old farmer has taken this to mean his death too.
He isn't interested in meeting another woman,
doesn't want to mingle at the senior center,
gets tearful watching young couples.

A tree shines in the epicenter of his garden—
planted in his youth, it drips dozens of blossoms,
births in daylight, plumpness of avocados,
graceful in curved leaves, buttery, sassy—

slender waists, full hips. Resting beneath boughs,
he admires these shapely figures who come to him
only in summer and autumn, their smooth skin
washed by rain. He picks one.

Kachina Dance Poem

Susan Clark

Hold this day in me like a piece of fear,
a stone, the goodbye look of a lover:
they danced on the mesa together.
I did not know these dances, but wept to see them.

Children hurled coke cans
off the suicide-edge of the mesa.
Dogs foraged in the garbage
and scratched themselves.

The men danced their slow dance all day.
Kachinas, cat tails, baskets of fruit were given
to children and solemnly carried away.

These people are with themselves and each other.
I live in another country and my own heart
is divided against itself.

Presence

William Killian

"Lots of people at the mall today," my wife observes.

"I forgot to," I say.

Unaware of the length of her silence, I still feel its stare.

"Yes?" I ask.

"I said, lots—"

"Did you bring the checkbook?" I ask, turning my head away from Carol to look at the familiar woman walking by. She seems to appear in about every third female we pass. Each time, I want to go up to her, touch her face and ask her where she's been.

"The checkbook?" Carol asks.

"What—oh, uh, the checkbook. I hope you brought it. Did you?" My voice throws the words away at busy shoppers and other strangers.

"Did you know her, Paul?"

What I want to say is, "Yes, I know her better than I know you," but instead I say, "Did I know whom?"

"That thing you just gawked at."

"Oh, that was nobody. I think the checkbook is in the car," I mumble. And with that she walks by again.

I wonder why so many women look like her. I trudge on with Carol down the cold tile floor, guiding myself by the banister. I focus my eyes over the railing, down toward the floor below, x-raying bodies obscured by packages and the faces women wear to the mall. I scan gradually up and down the escalators and spot her many times. Each time I see her, something within me wants to leap and fly to her side.

Finally, I bring my eyes back to our level and notice through my peripheral vision what seems to be a shadow of her features. Light brown hair, warm face, curiously attractive and familiar. Cautiously, I allow my eyes to bring her into focus. It's Carol. I am unaware until then that we're holding hands.

"Hello," I say with a grateful smile.

"Hi," is her soft response.

"We'll just put it on Visa. You still want to eat out, don't you?"

"Sure."

During the rest of the day – lunch, movie, and shopping – I never see the woman again. I never look for her. It's been fifteen years now, and either she has moved out of town and taken all of her look-alikes with her, or she never existed at all.

But it's strange. We were at the mall the other night, and I noticed a man looking at Carol. I smiled as the man's wife jerked on his arm, and he hollered out in fake anger, "What?" It looked like us several years ago.

Carol brings me back to the present with, "I have the checkbook. I'm going in here to look at some of these dresses. Why don't you poke around for a while, and I'll meet you at Stephan's for dinner."

"Okay. Six-thirty. See you there. I want to go look at some books."

As I enter the long, narrow bookstore, the first bestseller catches my attention: *Happiness Is Wanting What You Have (Not Getting What You Want)*. "Yeah," I say. I pick up the book. It feels fresh and smells of newly printed paper. I wonder how many trees it took to publish this one.

After glancing through the jacket summary, I lose myself in the first chapter. Then from close behind me comes a sound, soft and sensual, like an old voice from the distant past.

"Paul."

I want to keep reading. I like what I'm reading. I also want to turn and embrace this voice. I like what I'm hearing, what I'm feeling. And I want to walk away; my thoughts and fears overwhelm me. I want to wake up, but I can't fool myself that this is a dream. My thoughts bump against each other. I don't know what to do, but my body does. It turns.

"You remember me from last week, Paul? You ordered the book, *When Married People Become Friends*. Do you want to take it home with you now? I'm Sally. Remember me?"

"Yes. Um, of course. Sure. I'll write a check. No, I'll just put it on Visa. I think I'll take this one, too. Yes, I'll take this one. Add this one also."

The Visa clears and there's plenty of money in the checking account if Carol decides to buy a dress. On my way to Stephan's I feel full, even before dinner.

SOME LIES ABOUT LOSS

Kathleen A. O'Brien

that time heals everything
that life will return to normal
that you can get a replacement
    a body pillow will fill the empty space in bed
    a new love can stitch up a torn heart
that eventually you'll stop thinking of him
that casseroles console

    fond memories will comfort
that sudden loss is better than slow death
that 32 years of a good marriage is enough
that "Grow old along with me,
    the best is yet to be" will come true
that grandchildren can fill the void
    keeping busy will be your salvation
that you can skirt the rim of grief and
    not have to walk through the fire
that there's such a thing as a merry widow
that money and possessions still have
    the same value

that "if only," "should have," "what if"
    will stop stalking you
that you are in control
    you could have prevented this
that by being good and following all the rules,
    you and your love
    could slip under death's radar
that the phantom pain of amputation
    will disappear

that you are a weakling
that you will never laugh again
that sanity will not return
    love was not worth the pain
that your love has ceased to exist
that love will not embrace you when you die

PIANO MORNINGS

Mimi Moriarty

When I first wake fresh from the buzz of sex,
squint at the Panasonic, roll toward you,
feel the moon trapped beneath our quilt,
prefer the warm laze of ardor and sprawl

over the difficult rise and staggered search for my pad
and pen. How much better it would be to lie next
to the honeycomb you offer even while sleeping.
It takes the discipline of an eccentric piano teacher

with only one student to pull me from your side.
She puts the metronome beside my piano, pulls
the bar to the right, then lets go. I know the
consequences of disobedience, the cozy slumber

past my early rising, the penalty for missing the
melody of my morning pages. Yes, it's all there in
black and white, each key of the sonata I'm about
to play, an exercise I am forced to follow daily,

just to say I know the scales. I'm tempted to say
enough is enough, a child's discordant rebellion on
the piano bench, her stubborn pout and rolled fists,
possibly banging the cover over the keys with a flat

"no." That's the power of your skin, softer than any
man's should be, free of the age spots that speckle
mine. I prefer the nestle of your arms to the music
from my curled fingers. But I rise, rumble naked

to the bathroom, then throw on a loose robe, find my
glasses and pad, locate a pen with just the right draw,
and begin again the monotonic early morning fugue
reluctantly composed by a neophyte poet.

Nona's Darkness

Ruth Moon Kempher

S*crew happy bird*, she thought when she first saw him, when he first came into the Knot Hole Tavern and looked down the long dark bar as if he were looking for someone special. *Don't know his ass from a hole in the wall, nor never would.*

She had one breast. Magnificent. A beautiful tubule that seemed to reach out from the rest of her, pulsating, as if it were eager for air. The other, its mate, was gone. A concave scar remained, like counterpoint. Somebody said that, once. It was a contrast, like artists strive for. A balance of hereness and goneness. And she refused to doctor herself up with rubber stuff or any of the other easily available synthetics. Tried it once, but it kept slipping. Gave her an itch. Still, in her size 42 half a bra, she was an awesome sight. "Are you freaked out enough for me?" she'd ask, sometimes, when she'd been drinking a lot. And the hurt was there, throbbing in her question.

He looked at Nona as if he'd never seen a woman before. Chose to sit at the bar beside her. It was a quiet night—a Wednesday—and would be slow until the movie across the Plaza let out. A lot of the regulars had gone over to see the reissue of *The Last Tango in Paris*. Uncut, the ads promised. Twenty minutes longer than the running time up in Jacksonville. Maybe. Nona had her doubts.

But he must have seen a woman before, she decided, watching Rick, the bartender, pour a beer for the man beside her. God help him, if he never did. "Huh?" he said to her, as if she'd spoken, which she hadn't. At least, she didn't think she had.

"I didn't say anything," she said. "You aren't from here, are you?"

He shook his head, and beer bubbled at the comer of his mouth. "Oh, no. Just a tourist. Touring…"

"I'm Nona," she announced, for no reason at all. "They all know me here. You could buy me a beer."

He did.

"Where are you from?" she asked him. She'd practically asked for the beer, after all, and was enjoying it, and you ought to be polite. At least pretend.

"Who? Me?"

"Who else?"

"I…no place special. No place you ever heard of."

"Try me."

"Omega, New Jersey."

"You know something? You're right. I never heard of it."

"Nobody else has, either, hardly. My father had a White Tower there."

"A hamburger joint?"

"I think it used to be. He rebuilt it. I was born there, upstairs."

"That makes you different," she decided, sipping her beer. "I thought you were. I just didn't know how."

"It's the white bricks." He smiled gently. "Makes all the difference."

"Do you know magic tricks, too?" she guessed.

"Sure," he nodded. "Any kind. You name it. I know it."

She snickered. "You could make me beautiful."

He shook his head. "You already are."

"Ha."

"Okay. You think you aren't beautiful, and then you're not. But you really are."

"Bird brain."

The man shrugged. He was small-built, wiry, and seemed used to being contradicted or ignored, or not believed, and generally forgotten. "You like another beer?"

"Maybe later. Tell me I'm beautiful again."

"No." He shook his head harder than before. "Not now. Because now, you're not."

"You just told me that I was."

"That was then. This is now."

Nona finished off her beer in one long swallow. "That," she said, clicking the glass down on the bar, "that is the story of my life."

He motioned to Rick, who was slicing limes up at the service end of the bar. Acrid, acid scent of the cut limes drifted to them. "Bring the lady another beer, and me, too."

"Lady." Nona giggled. "That's a hot one."

"Remains to be seen," he muttered gently to himself.

"I used to be a singer," Nona said. "Sometimes I'd sing here, when Zim played piano. I knew Zim real well, and he'd play slow for me, not his usual jazz. They said I sounded just like Sarah Vaughan. But even then…" She tried to make a joke about herself. "Even back then, when I was all here, I didn't really much like for people to be looking at me. That's why I liked singing here. At night, it's so much darker than most places."

Rick brought the two beers, smiling enigmatically at Nona, not saying anything, but evidently thinking a lot. His eyes were sparkling.

Nona looked at the new, sweating bottle. "What did I do to deserve this?"

The stranger's smile crooked out, like a lopsided *W*.

"Nothing. Yet."

"Maybe nothing, never," Nona warned.

He shrugged. "Maybe. But some things are…sort of inevitable. It doesn't matter. I enjoy talking with you."

"You don't really say much," she observed. "Except you know magic."

"Not everybody thinks to ask me about that." He studied his glass, the foam at the top, the bubbles rising in waving streamers through the clear golden liquid. "You're one of the first. Did you just guess?"

"No. It wasn't a guess." She drank, slowly. "I just knew."

"How did you know?"

"Maybe I didn't know. Maybe I guessed."

"You said you knew."

She hunched on the bar stool, which was too small for all of her weight, uncomfortable. "Okay. I thought I knew. Who in Hell cares?"

"I do." He sounded humble. "It's not important to most people, I admit. But you should look in the mirror. You'd see. With those wide eyes, you're beautiful again."

"I think you're full of bull-oney," said Nona.

"No you don't." This time he smiled a proper smile. "You could even love me, I believe."

"Oh, come on now, whoa, Nelly." She looked up at the ceiling, which was knotty pine, deeply shadowed, smoke shrouded, stained from years of drifting tars and nicotine. "What about me could possibly turn you on?"

"I guess just you, being yourself."

She chuckled. "That's crazy. And it's that crazy, I kind of like it. But I'm a fool. I guess nobody much dares tease me, in that way."

"Nobody knows you, like I do."

She shook her head. "You think I look bad now," she said. "It's shadowy in here. But you know how it is, bright, in the mornings? You know how mirrors are, in bathrooms, real well lit? Well, they ought not to allow either one. You get this film on your eyes, see, from sleeping, so you can't see really, and that's great. Then you got to wash your face, and hot damn, there you are, red lines in your eyes, sagging cheeks, the works. Forget beautiful. You think I don't know?"

He sipped his beer thoughtfully, and then he said, "You don't have to worry about all that."

"Oh?" She went back to work on her beer a while, too. "Oh? That's what you think?"

"That's what I know."

She moved on the barstool, uneasy again. "You know about dreams, too?"

"Even more about dreams than magic." He moved closer, so his knee brushed hard against hers. After the first flinching back, her knee moved close again, and their knees were pressed together.

"Tell me about my dreams," she said, and it sounded like a challenge. But there was fear in her voice, too. "I have lousy dreams. I wish I could forget them. Sometimes I dream there's something eating me, like they say, only I can see the little claws sort of, eating away somewhere inside, and then they hide and I don't know where they are and it's like they're teasing me, and that's a normal dream, they tell me, for a person who had what I did. It's a normal fear and I should forget it."

"To dream about your fears," he said. "That's supposed to keep you from going crazy."

Nona's head cocked, nervous. "I don't see how it could. Oh, I heard that, too. But I never believed it. Drive you crazy, is more like it. If you wake up and that's all you can remember. Those slithery little claws somewhere inside, still hiding. Fat lot they know, if they never dreamed it."

"That's true. That's true."

"You know what I mean?"

"Sure I do. Like I invented it, myself. That well."

"And sometimes I dream it's not inside me, at all, but it's somewhere outside, like in a bottle, but they're still eating away, scratching away at the glass, and they'll find me easy enough, when they break through. It's only a matter of time…I wake up and I can hear like an echo of that bottle's shattering, like it's somewhere in my ear."

He nodded, complacent. "Well, you know. Everything's a matter of time, in a way. We're all brought up to believe that. We spend our lives, expecting…something. We're trained to look ahead for it, something like magic. How many minutes 'til recess, how many hours 'til lunch, how many days 'til Santa Claus? How many years 'til I grow up?"

"Yeah," said Nona. "That's exactly how it is. But even so, it mixes me up, sometimes. What I think is, when it does break through that glass, whatever, maybe I'll be dead. Or maybe, when it does, it'll be that I'm just so relieved…" She brushed her hair back from her face, a harsh gesture, angry. "I don't want to talk about that, anymore. What do you dream about, anyway?"

He grinned, foolishly. "Beer," he said, and anybody who had been listening would have sensed immediately that he lied. Especially, Nona sensed that.

"Doesn't anybody ever ask you about that, either?"

"Why did you move your knee away just now?"

Nona blushed. "You're too…close."

"I should take offense. I thought you liked me."

"Forget it."

"No."

"Look, you think you bought me a beer, you bought my soul? Everything else? Forget it. Nobody asked you to, anyhow."

He nearly purred. "Why do you want to be angry? You at least liked my knee."

"You're too different," she said, decisively. "Piss on your knee."

He giggled. "Well, I have. A time or two."

She giggled, too. "You must of been awful drunk."

"Of course. I'm not all that different. Not even from you, and you're a little different, too. And I do think you're beautiful."

"You lie." Nona's face could have been chiseled out of stone—pure agate, marble, something tough. "You lie."

"Never." His voice was steady, solemn. "I do not ever lie."

"You lie, you lie, you lie," she said and, frantic, her eyes made darting movements in her face, in time with the tattoo of her words. "You lie. I know you do."

His voice was cream. "You just don't want to believe in me, do you?"

"I don't know who you are. Not anything."

"But can't you guess? Don't I, magic, hear you guessing, back in your head? You're no fool, Nona. You can guess…" Somehow, he had inched even closer without moving the barstools, had moved closer through space, 'til there was no space between them, and his hip and thigh lay pressed hotly against hers. "You're such a lovely girl, with such a lovely name…"

She was near crying. Tears welled in her eyes. "Leave me alone."

"Oh, no," he whispered. "I couldn't. And you don't want me to. Never."

Her fingers made little squirrel movements on the bar. "I asked you please just to leave me alone."

"But you want to touch me, don't you? You want to find out if I'm flesh and blood, while another part of you almost hopes I'm something…more like a dream. But I think, maybe, you'd rather find out for sure, I'm real."

She bit at her underlip. "No. No. No, I don't want to find out anything. Just go away. Thank you for the beer. Just leave."

"Go where?" He lifted his eyebrows sardonically. "Where would you suggest I go? Back to Omega, New Jersey? Well, they say we all go back to our beginnings, sooner or later. But I'd rather not, just now. Maybe you'd rather I'd melt away, into the night? Maybe you'd be happy if I slipped away like mist, like sometimes you think you'd like to do yourself, drift off into the safe darkness, where no one can see you. But you know, the night never is far away."

"It isn't?"

He shook his head slowly. "No, it isn't. It's always waiting around the next bend. It's like you said…a matter of time."

Tears glittered in streaks down her face. "Will you be there? In the dark? Will you stay?" She leaned against him heavily. "Would you stay?"

"Oh yes," he murmured. "Oh yes. I stay."

Clumsily, she swatted the tears from her face. "I must be crazy," she said. "I guess you think I'm either crazy, or some cheap pick up. That's what you think? But I'm not either one. Not for real."

"I know that."

"It's not like a beer or two and wham bam thank you ma'am. It's really not."

"I know that, too. I think you're a beautiful creature, I really do."

"Why do you say it that way? Creature?"

He moved back, but only slightly, as if to look at her more closely by adjusting the space between them, artistically, finding the sharpest perspective, balance of hereness and thereness. "I don't know why I said it that way," he admitted. "Would you rather I'd said 'animal'?"

She almost laughed. "That doesn't sound too great, either."

"Right at the moment," he said, taking hold of her hand, "I could almost say I'd never leave you. Never again."

"Damn fool," said Nona, huskily. "Damn fool, me. You'd say that, and you'd be lying, and you say you never lie. Well, everybody needs to be lied to a little, I guess."

"That's exactly right," he said, solemnly. "That's the honest truth." He still had a firm grip on her hand, although she didn't seem to want to move away, now.

"Your hands are awful cold," she said. "Must be from hanging on to that beer."

"Could be," he said. With a jerk of his head, he signaled Rick to bring the bill.

"I know I'm a fool," Nona said. "But I like to be lied to, a little, like anybody else. I do. Just like I wanted to believe in Santa Claus. Everybody wants that, Santa Claus, even if underneath, all the time they know…"

"…what they think they know." He supplied the end of her sentence demurely. He was suddenly demure, and coy. And he shrugged again, picking up the bill, whispering to himself. "Screw happy bird," he murmured, looking to see what he would have to pay.

New Year's Eve

Dolores Greene Binder

Well, we got through X-mas O.K.
Resisting the ancient lines
Of Druids and other Priests
Getting sick
To sleep out the longer nights
And days grey with blank dreams
Color-blind to glitter and tinsel
Color-blind to sound of red & green music

Remembering other years
Of baby-smells
And husbands sprawled on backs
Heads thrust from thickening necks
Watching gladiators battle
Across the line
Arrogant and distant
While we're in the next room which is
Always the kitchen
Counting the hours
And spending them on
Waiting.
Reckless.

Then
Dreaming with open eyes
Of the sea
And the horizon
Curving
Where heavy water meets air
And neither moves
And it is summer again
And there are no priests.

Here
Within us
Is the young girl

Damp with desire
Ready to give herself to
What she wills to be
The god of the moment.

And what then do women want at X-mas
Grown women like us I mean.
Sky-dreams.
Sky-scapes.
And finally
A gift of suspended disbelief
Another hour of getting high
On succulent sex
And finding a drier voice
To sing it.

Sex

David Ray

When I was that age,
whatever it was,
sex was very simple.

Simple it was, with-
out the fancy stuff,
the complicated stuff,

the techniques, the
textbook stuff, the
superfluous stuff,

the foreplay and after-
glow. Simple was sex.
I dreamed of it day

and night, how we,
she and I, would go
to the basement,

take off our clothes,
stand in the shower,
which was a stall there

in the corner, and put
our arms around
each other. And kiss.

That was sex. It was
very simple and clean,
like *Lifebuoy* and *Lux*.

And very, very ecstatic.

Bar Suez

Manuel Torrez, Jr.

It was a noisy late afternoon. Chief Bos'n Brown was hollering at some young deck hands who had recently come aboard the LST Santone County from boot camp in San Diego. They were chipping paint on a bulkhead near the opening that led to the crew's living quarters. At the same time, some gulls were swooping near the fantail where the ship's cook had dumped peelings overboard. The birds seemed to be arguing loudly as to who had first rights.

Felix Dominguez was standing near the gangway, waiting for the water taxi that would take him to the dock in Yokosuka. John Meadows was sitting on a deck bitt, checking out the shine on his shoes. Both were in their dress blues. Felix had not been ashore on liberty for several days. John hadn't been off the Santone for two weeks. He'd been kept on special work detail without liberty for fourteen straight days after snipping at Chief Brown when the Bos'n gave him a direct order to pick up some cigarette butts from the deck. Everyone on the LST Santone County knew the chief was a hard-boiled lifer and that John Meadows carried a chip on his shoulder.

John got up and looked longingly toward shore.

Felix had his eyes fixed on John. "I guess you got your mind on Michiko," he said.

John turned to look at Felix. "You guessed right, buddy. Two weeks been too long."

"Yeah…she's quite a gal."

"You took good care of her, like I asked, right? Got her the tea and canned milk from the club?"

Felix nodded, then turned and stepped away from his friend, who didn't know to what extent he had taken care of Michiko. Felix hadn't meant for his good intentions to lead to an affair with his buddy's girl, but as soon as he'd got to her place with the goods John had asked him to take her, she'd acted more than just friendly.

"Thank you, Felix," she'd said and gently grabbed his arm as he unpacked the goods and set them on the table. "You know, I've had my eye on you since John brought you here the first time and introduced us." It had escalated from that innocent touch and her surprising words to playful games in bed, where she would cross her leg over his and swear he was the one she loved and not his friend, John. Six straight liberties he'd brought her stuff from a list she'd prepared for him after every meeting—a lot of canned milk from the EM club in downtown Yokosuka. Six straight liberty nights they'd played the bed game.

He recalled her parting words on their last day together, right before he boarded the water taxi to get back to the moored Santone. "Make sure when you tell him about us to be gentle, Felix." Yeah, but that wasn't going to be easy. John could easily erupt over a lot less bad news than that.

"Felix, got something on your mind? I know you're quiet, amigo, but these last couple of days you've been morgue silent."

Felix smiled at John's remark. "Just thinking about things."

"Is it about your Mexican senorita in Texas or is it something you'd like to share with me, buddy?" John said.

They approached the gangway. They could hear the water taxi as it got close, and the water splashing against the Santone's starboard side from the taxi's wake.

"Yeah…there is something I'd like to discuss with you, but over a beer at Bar Suez."

John smiled. "It has been a long time since I've had a cold one. I can almost taste it. Just one, though, got my Michiko waiting…you tell her to expect me?"

"She knows you have liberty."

The evening was young. Felix was sitting on a stool at the bar. John went to the head and on his way back ran into three former shipmates from the Bayfield, a troop transport he'd served on before being transferred to the Santone. He sat down with them to drink a beer and share scuttlebutt.

The barmaid, a widow, was also the owner. Her name was Sallie. She was a looker. The guys referred to her with affection and desire as the untouchable fox. She took the beers to the table.

"John know yet about you and Michiko?" Sallie asked Felix when she returned. She took a cigarette from a pack she had left on the bar.

He shook his head and lowered his eyes.

"Are you nervous?" She took Felix's lighter off the bar and lit her cigarette. It quavered on her lips.

"I'm okay," he said, then took a drink from his beer and looked over where John was still seated with his friends. He noticed that their conversation wasn't inciting laughter.

Sallie had begun to tap nervously on the bar top with her long red fingernails. "You know, I don't want no trouble in here," she said and shook her head. "Not good for business. That guy John can be trouble when he drink. Why don't you take him somewhere else to give him the bad news?"

"So you know about Michiko and me?"

"Everybody knows."

"You're the one that seems touchy, Sallie. He's my friend. I can calm him down no matter what happens," he said and wanted to believe it.

"Not about Michiko…you two should never have got together," she said and nodded to where John was sitting. Her eyes sharpened. "I'm expecting big explosion when you tell that boy. What did Michiko do to make you want to go after her?"

As she talked to Felix, she also had her eyes on two marines that were with two of the bar girls in a far booth. It was still early and besides John, the Bayfield shipmates, and Felix, they were the only other patrons in the bar. John rose with a start. He'd vised one sailor's shoulders with his big hands and pulled him off his chair.

"Look!" Sallie screamed. "That boy has demons in him. I told you so. Explosion come sooner than I expect."

Felix wasted no time and rushed to lasso his buddy. He wrapped his arms around John from behind and pulled him away from the white-faced seaman. Mortified, all three crewmembers from the Bayfield fled out the door.

"What happened, man?" Felix said, as they made their way back to the bar.

John didn't reply. He shook himself from Felix's grasp. He had a sullen look on him as they sat down.

There was a round window by the door that resembled a porthole in the wardroom of the Santone. Sallie went there to look outside and shook her head. "Sailors outside arguing," she said. "What you do, John?"

John kept mum. On the water that had dripped from his cold beer bottle to the bar top, he began to scribble something with his finger. It reminded Felix of his catechism class when he was a kid, and the story the nun there had told them about Jesus scribbling the sins of the stone throwers in the Mary Magdalene parable. He flinched as he imagined his affair with Michiko being written on the wet bar top. He wondered if the sailors from the Bayfield had told John something about him and Michiko. Was John brewing some retaliatory move? He took a drink from his beer and had trouble swallowing it.

"What was it you were going to tell me?" John said.

"What?" Felix said. His heart began to pound his chest.

Sallie came to the bar, grabbed his cheeks with her fingers, and pulled on them so he would look at her. She winked at him. "Let's dance," she said and grabbed his hand to lead him to a small dance floor near the jukebox.

John lit a cigarette. He took a drag and watched them, but his expression didn't change.

Sallie laid her cheek on Felix's chest and moved her body close to his. "I like this song," she said. "What is it?"

"It's from that new movie with Jennifer Jones…and that handsome guy…"

"What guy?"

Felix shook his head. "Oh, I can't…he plays a reporter who's sent to Korea to cover the war."

"Maybe we can go see the movie," she said.

"Together?" he asked.

"Why not? Michiko gonna marry you too?"

"Bah! Why did you want to dance? I've never seen you on the dance floor with any guy."

"Maybe give John time to calm down…maybe I like you."

"What?"

"Can't a girl like me like a dumb guy like you?"

Felix lowered his head and looked at Sallie. She had a beautiful smile and ruby lips that quavered. He found himself wanting to kiss her, but he held her tighter, instead. "Why are you calling me dumb?"

"You don't know?" she said, and the tune finished. When they turned to go to the bar, John was no longer there.

"What do you know?" Felix said and snapped his fingers. "Just like that, he's gone."

"Give you two guesses where he go," Sallie said and shook her head.

"I'm going after him," Felix said and hurried to the door, but Sallie got in his way and pressed her hands on his chest.

"Don't go," she said softly.

"I have to go. He's my friend."

Sallie moved away. She crossed her arms, and her eyes got small. "Yes!" she said, grinding her words through clenched teeth, "and you stole his girl…two ways to set off explosion among friends. Anyway, you not going because of John…Michiko is who you think about."

"It's because I'm a big part of this mess that I have to go. Can't you see?" As he finished speaking, the swinging door to the bar flew open and one of the sailors from the Bayfield staggered in. He had bloody hands stretched in front of him as if he were trying to grab something to break his fall. His eyes had a hunted look, and he was breathing fast.

"What, sailor?" Sallie asked the terrified seaman. She clenched her fists and put them on her waist. "Why you come in like that to my place?"

The man dropped to one knee. The two marines from the back booth with the bar girls sprang to their feet and ran to see if they could help. Felix grabbed the man's arm.

"This is the guy that was getting the once over by John," Felix said.

"Pull him outside. I don't want the shore patrol in my place," Sallie said.

"He's about to pass out," Felix said. "Help me put him into one of the booths."

The two marines grabbed the sailor.

"He's stinko drunk," Sallie said and wrinkled her nose but nodded to the marines.

"I'm okay," the sailor said and shrugged them off. His right eye was a slit, the puffiness around it blue and purple.

"You get into it again with John outside?" Felix said. He took out a cigarette, lit it, and took a drag. He looked over at Sallie. She had her arms crossed again.

"That guy is nuts," the sailor said. "He was trying to kill me. My buddies got him off me long enough so I could get away."

"What was the beef about?" Felix said.

"Michiko," the sailor said.

Felix and Sallie looked at each other. She shook her head and lowered her eyes. "John's girlfriend?" she said.

"She's my girl!" the sailor said and beat his chest.

Felix's face paled.

"Who are you?" Sallie asked.

"What?" the man said. He touched the swollen puffiness around his eye and winced.

"What's your name?"

"Al." He had some loose cigarettes in his jumper pocket and took one out. He searched for a match. When Felix saw that he couldn't find one, he lit the sailor's cigarette with his lighter. "We've been out on operations with marines for the last month. John's been trying to move in on my gal. Michiko told me so this morning when I got back."

"Is that what you guys were arguing about in here?" Felix said.

"Yeah…I confronted him about it and he went ballistic! Said he was going to kill me."

Felix stared at Al without saying anything else and began to take backward steps until he got to a stool at the bar. He sat down. Sallie had gone behind the bar. She walked up and put her arm around his neck and pinched him gently on his cheek. He took a drink from his beer. One of the bar girls had gone to the storage room and brought back a first aid kit. She was tending the wounds on Al's hands.

"Look," Al said and raised his hands. "He cut me when I tried to take the knife away from him."

"Knife? He had a knife?" Felix asked, but the sailor had already burst out through the swinging door.

"He's running away again from John," Sallie said, "but there's no place to hide. The Hill, maybe, but that where Michiko live. Who's going to hide a Navy guy that been fighting, anyway?"

"He's going back on the Bayfield. I saw it docked when we came in on the water taxi."

"And you?" she said and smiled weakly. "Are you still going to look for John and have that talk?"

Felix grabbed Sallie's hand and pulled it from his cheek. "I have to…he's my friend."

"Not after you tell him."

"I'm going to try." He got off the bar stool. "He's my friend," he repeated and started for the door, but it swung open and John Meadows rushed in the way Felix remembered the bull charging into the plaza de toros on a Sunday afternoon when he was visiting his cousin in Monterrey. Meadows' face was crimson and he was breathing hard. He raked the room with his eyes, and then ran wildly about the room, searching every booth.

"John...why you come in steaming like that, into my place?" Sallie said.

John looked ready to blow up. "Shut up, you slant-eye pig!" he bellowed.

"Hey, man, cut the crap!" Felix said, and got in front of John. "You got no reason to talk to Sallie like that."

"You dirty Spick. You got to my Michiko, too...didn't you?"

"Get out of my place, you nasty sailor! I go get shore patrol right now," Sallie said and tried to reach the door, but John intervened, pushing her hard into the wall with the porthole window. He headed to the door, but turned to look at Felix.

"I'll deal with you later. I got a score to settle with Al first!" He stormed out.

"So what you going to do now?" Sallie said. She clasped her head with her hands.

Felix could feel his heart pounding again. He began to regret that he'd ever considered John a friend. Why was he still fighting over Michiko? He must know by now she was a bloodsucker. He looked again at Sallie, who had sat down on a stool on the other side of the bar at the far end. Her eyes had a faraway look. He went to the jukebox and dropped a coin in the slot. He selected the tune Sallie liked. He beckoned to her. She smiled faintly and walked slowly to the small dance floor. He put his arm around her waist and moved her close to him.

"How can you want to dance, after everything that happen?" she said, but turned her head and pressed it against his chest.

"Maybe I'm waiting for John to cool...or maybe I like you."

She tilted her head back, looked up at his face, and smiled. "How could you have fallen for Michiko?"

"She's sexy," Felix said.

"Dummy! She no good." Sallie muttered something under her breath in Japanese.

"What?"

"She worked here, remember? I fire her. Caught her taking money out of some drunk marine's wallet."

The Hill hugged the rocky coastline. Sallie had not wanted to go up to see Michiko, but Felix said he had to. He wanted some explanation from her, no matter how full of lies it might be.

He had to make his way past many small shacks to get to Michiko's place. Some of the guys on the Santone County referred to the Hill as Shantytown. It was difficult for him to maneuver upward on the dirt and rough flagstone path. A steady drizzle didn't make it any easier. Sallie had gotten one of her girls to tend bar. She had stayed in the cab at the foot of the hill.

When Felix got to Michiko's shack, the door was open. He hesitated outside and looked around. The light was on in the shack across the path, and the familiar crying of the baby that lived there with an elderly couple vibrated in his ears. It seemed to him that no matter when he came to see Michiko, the baby was always crying. He caught a glimpse of the old woman. She was at the back of the room so he wouldn't notice her looking at him through the window, but he did.

"Michiko, I'm coming in," he said and entered the small living space. The lone room was dark except for a candle on a table against the back wall. Michiko and Al cowered in the false sanctuary of the flickering light, holding on to each other as if they would fall into an abyss if they let go.

"Michiko, I have to talk to you," Felix said, but she shook her head and tightened her grip on Al. "What are you doing here, Al? Last time I saw you, you were running away from John Meadows."

"Yeah, well I had to come get my gal. We thought you were John," Al said and moved away from Michiko. He grabbed a suitcase by his feet, threw it on the bed, and opened it up. "Okay, babe…finish packing so we can scram."

"You knew I was seeing Michiko, right?" Felix said, and felt sorry he had said so. He didn't want any part of her now, not even memories of the days with her that had seemed so great at the time.

"Last time I left, I told her whatever she needed to do to survive was okay. She'd tried going back to Bar Suez."

Felix remembered Sallie's remarks. "Where are you taking her?" he asked.

"Away! What business is it of yours, anyway, buster?" Al snapped. He went to the entrance, stuck his head out, and looked both ways. He went back to packing. "Hurry, babe, before that crazy comes back."

"I want to talk to Michiko," Felix said.

Al's eyes narrowed and his face tightened. "There's nothing you can say to her "

"Wait. I'll talk to him," Michiko said. She closed the suitcase. Al grabbed it with a swing of his bandaged hand and hurried to the entrance.

"I'm sorry, Felix," Michiko said. "You're a good guy, but I love Al. He's been the best guy for me and my baby."

"Your…baby?"

"Yes, he's with my parents in the house across from here."

"That's your kid? The one I hear crying when I come over?"

"Yes."

Felix turned as Al entered the room. "I don't understand you, man! How come you let your gal rent out? And you guys with a kid…I don't understand!"

"We can't make it with what I get…it wasn't my idea what she did," Al said.

"I did what I had to do for my baby. Please try to understand." Michiko covered her face with her hands.

Felix turned around and walked out.

When he got back to the taxi, he was surprised to see John sitting next to Sallie in the back seat.

"John, we've been friends for a long time," he said, "but if you insult Sallie in any way again…I swear, I'm going to crush your mug!" He pulled Sallie out of the cab.

"It's okay, he not hurt me," Sallie said. "John been crying. He apologized to me…he just sad at losing Michiko."

John got out of the cab, too.

"I'm sorry, John," Felix said. "I got caught up in her game. I'm sorry if I hurt you. I know I can't make it up to you, but she made saps out of both of us."

John stared at the ground and didn't say a word.

"Al is the guy she likes…they have a kid."

John kicked at some stones.

"Sorry, man," Felix said.

John turned and crossed the street in a hurry, headed in the direction of the water taxi dock.

"That mixed up guy…you think he's going to be okay?" Sallie said.

Felix put his arm around her waist. "No, not for a long time. Hope when he's back aboard that Chief Brown don't sass him any, or John's liable to get brig time for fracturing a Chief Bosn's jaw."

Sallie laughed and laid her head on his chest.

Waiting

Steve Snyder

My sweetheart dropped me
like a body-builder drops a barbell
after the last bench press, abruptly
without explanations.

My patience was a benzedrine rush
down an endless desert highway
without off-ramps, road signs or omens.

Her rejection spawned dreams of driving
to the coast and swimming for the horizon
until surrounded by a pack of killer sharks
all hope of rescue gone.

Yet my love for her said
let her go and await from afar,
let her sunshine hair cascade over her pillow,
let her dreams drift without interruption
like snowmelt flowing downstream
to the places they're meant to go.

Romantic fool that I am,
I wait for her winter to thaw.
.
Someday she will eagerly seek me,
running barefoot through paradise,
her blue eyes wild with excitement.

SPRING BREAKUP

Tiina Heathcock

brilliantly scarfed, mitted and toqued
breathless
she struggles down the snow-laden slope

in that moment before sunset
she stands
arms outstretched
on April melt ice
inhales
scans the horizon
strikes out
alone
across the lake

safe and snug
in the traditional log cabin
on the hillside above,
seated by the window
warmed by flames from the hearth
cigars, cognac at hand,
serenaded by Dow Jones
drowsing
he notes her progress

she rounds the bend
in one yawn
beyond his reach

INTO THE DARKNESS

Tiina Heathcock

wordless
erect
fur-coated, fur-hatted
he climbs into the cutter
calms
horses pawing snow,
breaths pluming

shuddering
shawl-encircled
haloed in lamplight
she stands in the doorway
mute

a lurch
swirl of hooves
no wave
no backward glance

through cedar shadows
his image
engulfed in silent darkness,
recedes into beyond,

afterimage etched
no photograph necessary

In Between

Albert Russo

against the highrise facade
opposite my place
two men are busy
erecting a scaffold
nerves on edge
screech of metal
like the rubbing of dry bones
whilst I wait feverishly
for a friend to drop by
haven't slept a wink
my young neighbors
threw a party last night
and the music boomed
in the courtyard
till the wee hours
I can still hear it
reverberating inside my head
even the knees hurt
as if my skull were too small
to contain its echoes
the friend has just called
advising that he will be late
I'd like to cancel the visit
and slip into my bedsheets
now that the workers have gone away
but I didn't have the strength
or the will to tell him
so all that is left to me now
is to stare at the black sky
and listen to
the pummeling beat
of the rain

The Book Ended

David Braun

I came home from my never-ending hell-hole of a job at the investment company. I am one of the accountants. My job as Assistant to the Associate Director is to fill in the mystery blanks of our books, making sure they appear to tabulate our trades and other shenanigans so as to minimize our taxes and other liabilities. That would be difficult enough, but I—we—understand there is a script of half truths and obfuscations we are required to follow. If it weren't for the fact I have to pay two sets of matrimony and child support, I'd quit this job in a nanosecond. Wait, it gets worse. This job does pay for those, but it still doesn't make me enough to pay for my rags or my room and board, such as it is, not to mention that I still can't afford to treat myself in any way or save anything for a rainy day.

Other than that, I'm great, if you might perhaps think someone who is on the wrong side of fifty, overweight, suffering from allergies, type two diabetes, emphysema, heart murmurs, and probably some other things I've forgotten to mention can be great. I take seven prescription medications. On the good side, I don't party, just try to relax by myself in this run-down pretense of a house. I don't have the energy to do anything but work, eat, and sleep; well, I did forget to say I have lots of trouble getting enough quality sleep. I also forgot to mention that I do an early night shift at a hotel thirty hours a week to pay my living expenses.

So anyway, my one vice is reading; it gets me away from my grind and helps me relax enough to get to sleep. This evening I was finishing a sort of mystery. I don't really remember what it was; I just remember it was pretty creepy. The book ended and I sat quietly, contemplating the effect of its ending on me. I had chosen to read to escape from the trials and tribulations of a perfectly horrible day. I had not achieved the desired effect. I gradually shifted my focus and became aware of noises coming from the direction of the back yard. They sounded like footsteps, and then somebody kicking or stumbling over something metallic. I listened. I was getting uptight. I wondered if my imagination had been jumpstarted by the mystery. Or was there really someone out there? I couldn't stand the suspense, so I pulled myself up from the couch, went to the hall closet. and took out my Remington 30-30 lever-action rifle. The last time I used it was almost thirty years ago. It was still loaded, but the ammunition was old. I was hoping I wouldn't have to fire it.

I decided caution was in order, so before charging into my back yard I pulled my cell phone out of my pocket and called 911. The lady who answered asked who I was and where I lived in a flat, matter-of-fact voice. I told her I thought an intruder was on my property and gave her my name, Donald West. She asked if anything was happening now. Nothing was moving at the moment that I could tell, so I described what I had heard and the current scene. "I'm sure there's someone out there," I said, and explained that there had been several break-ins in the area recently. Some of my neighbors said they saw strange people acting suspiciously. The 911 lady said she'd dispatched the police and asked me to remain on the phone. She asked for a few more details about my identity, and then said a squad car was on its way.

I moved over to the sliding door and flicked on the outside light switch. Something moved over by the fence, and I heard things being hit or tripped over. I slid the door open as quietly as I could, concealing myself by pressing my body against the adjoining wall. I had no intention of playing the hero. When I peeked around the door, I saw a rake that had fallen over onto the garbage can. The outdoor light only illuminated the immediate area. The rest of my rather large back yard was still fairly dark, and this was not helped by the forest of trees and the absence of moonlight. I continued moving toward a shadowed area behind some ornamental bushes. Suddenly I heard another sharp, cracking sound, almost like a gunshot. I yelled out, "I have a gun and I will blow you away if you get closer. I've called the police and they are on the way. They'll be here in a minute."

I stopped to listen, but heard only the night sounds of locusts, crickets, and some kind of frogs. I continued scanning the yard and listening intently. Soon a siren announced the imminent arrival of the police. As I turned back toward the house, I saw a sudden movement as something burst from the corner where the fence lines intersected. Something was slinking out from the shadows, and I saw a very rotund raccoon. As soon as he spotted me, he high-tailed it to a hole in the back fence. He looked too fat to squeeze through, but somehow he managed. I breathed a sigh of relief, pulled the sliding door closed, and went back to the den to calm myself.

I was about to sit down on the couch when there was a loud knock at the front door. I moved quickly, calling out that I was on the way. Through the peephole I saw two uniformed police officers, a man and a woman, standing back from the door. I opened the door slowly and told them I was surprised they had gotten here so fast. The woman was tall, trim, and attractive. I figured her to be in her late thirties. She introduced herself as Jennifer Shepard and announced that her partner, a short, muscular and somewhat overweight guy, was Larry Almoreno. She explained they had been in the neighborhood when they got the call. They were all business.

Just then a man walked out of the shadows by the privacy fence. The gate slammed shut behind him. Officer Almoreno turned, startled, and instinctively reached for his holstered gun. He stopped when he recognized the person. He shouted out, "Jake, what the hell are you doing here?" Jake was also wearing his police uniform, though his jacket was unbuttoned and his tie was loose. He stared at me, then cleared his throat and said he had heard there was an intruder in the neighborhood, so he came over to see if he could help. He had heard a voice call out from the back yard saying, "I have a gun," and then he thought he saw a raccoon exit through the back fence. He apologized if he had disturbed anyone.

Officers Josephson and Almoreno drew their guns and split up. Jennifer asked if I didn't mind if they had a look around, but without waiting for my reply, she paraded into the house while Larry went to check the front gate of the privacy fence. I wandered after Jennifer. It's a shotgun house with no secret rooms, no place to hide anything, and after a while she concluded there was no one in the house other than ourselves. She slid the back door open, and we saw Larry standing by the fence. He didn't look like he wanted to go too far into the back yard. Finally, he came over to us, and we all went back into the house.

We encountered Jake in the front room, studying something on an end table near where I had been reading. I had a lot of junk over there, so I couldn't tell what he was looking at in particular, but he was studying something intently because he gave a little jump when he heard us. He wheeled toward the front door and we followed him out of the house. Officer Josephson gave

Jake the once over. Jake seemed nervous and quickly walked off toward the corner of the yard.

Officers Josephson and Almoreno gave each other a look. She asked me if I knew Jake. I told her I'd never met him before. She shrugged, handed me her card, and said, "If there's any more trouble, don't hesitate to call." I said thanks, and they left. By this time, though, I was a nervous wreck. I did my usual bed-time ritual, but added an extra-generous juice glass of whisky, followed by another and another, and finally dragged myself to bed. In spite of the whisky, I couldn't get the evenings events off my mind—especially Jake. What was he up to? I was tense and hot, and I tossed and turned, trying to re!ax and get comfortable. When I wasn't mulling over what had happened, I was hearing noises—noises in the back, noises in the front, noises on the sides, and noises on the roof. I even thought I heard noises inside the house. One was a loud snap. As drunk as I had managed to get, I jumped at that. I got up a couple of times, convinced that somebody—maybe Jake—was inside the house, getting ready to do me in. Finally, I put on the classical radio station at a low volume, hoping it would soothe me to sleep. That almost worked. All night long I kept drifting off, then waking up.

Next morning, I felt like death warmed over, but I managed to drag myself out of bed, dress, slam down a quart of coffee, and survive the suicidal drive to my blessed, wage-slave job. I could have called in but I didn't want to waste a day's pay on feeling bad. I figured I could do something very routine, something that involved little imagination or mental effort. Or maybe I could just hang out in my cubicle. I got to the office alive and immediately ran into Marilyn, our gorgeous, cheery-chipmunk receptionist. I managed to grunt a few syllables in her direction, and this seemed to satisfy her; she commenced talking to someone else before I finished. I got another cup of coffee and settled in. My hangover was still whacking away at my temples, but I was used to that. I went through my email, deleting as much as I could get away with and postponing responding to most everything else.

I closed my eyes for just a minute, and the next thing I knew I was hearing my cell phone playing "Ode to Joy." I wrestled my head off the desk and answered. It was Officer Josephson. She said they would like me to come down to their offices; a hearing was underway and they thought I might be interested. After due consideration, I said okay, and told them I'd be there as soon as I could. After telling my boss a very condensed version of the previous night's events and about Officer Josephson's call, he sighed and said for me to go. I descended to the parking garage and navigated my way through the downtown demolition derby.

I found the police station and located an over-priced parking garage, then groped my way to the right office. When I spotted Officer Almoreno heading down a distant hall, I dashed through the busy room after him. He heard me coming and stopped to tell me he hoped this wasn't a waste of time. He took me to a room that had a window looking into another room. I figured it must be one of those one-way mirrors. He said I.A.—I figured he meant internal affairs—had read his report about the previous night where he mentioned Officer Jackson's presence and behavior. This wasn't the first time Jake had done something out of the ordinary. They also wanted my side of the story to check the facts. I watched them through the window, and Jake looked like he was sitting in a cooking pot about to boil.

The two guys with him wore black suits, and I thought that maybe I'd fallen into one of the "Men in Black" episodes. One was sitting on the edge of the table a foot from Jake's left side, and the other was sitting catty-corner on his right side, but leaning over into his space. It was classic! They seemed to be telling him to own up to burglarizing my place and maybe all the others in the neighborhood. Jake kept saying he was just there because of the 911 call. He was rattled when they asked him how he got there so quickly, since he lives across town and it's at least a twenty-minute drive. He said he was just driving around. The suits looked like they weren't buying any of it. Then some woman pushed her way in to the room I was sitting in. She was crying a river and screeching that it was all her fault; Jake didn't do anything wrong. She was making so much noise that she halted the confrontation in the interview room.

Everybody was shocked when she ran in making all that noise. Officer Shepard put her arm around the woman and told her to calm down, which she did. Jennifer asked, "Do you know this man?" The woman caught her breath and said Jake was her friend. She said he had told her this guy might be his relative. She said she had told him to go to my house and check things out.

At that, Officer Almoreno opened the door to the interview room to tell them what was happening. The two suits and Jake crowded into our room. The woman was still crying, so it took us a minute to figure out what she was saying. Finally, she got herself together and told us that Jake had been a foster child, but he knew he had brothers and sisters. He had seen me somewhere, and somebody said we looked alike. He also said he thought he remembered that one of his brothers was named Donald. He had decided to investigate a little, and that's why he was in the neighborhood.

One of the I.A. guys asked Jake if this was true. He hesitated a minute, then lowered his head shyly. He said he didn't want to barge in if his information was wrong. He didn't want to say anything until he knew something for sure.

I said, "Well, I guess you got that out of the way."

He nodded, then he smiled. He said he was sorry if he scared me, and he shouldn't have come into my house like that. He said he was looking for a stray hair so he could run a DNA test and compare it with his.

I said I didn't think we had the same last name. He said he'd been adopted by his last foster family and took their name. He looked at me real serious and said, "It was West when I was little."

This rocked my boat. I looked at him more closely. I had to admit we looked a lot alike. I said I didn't have a brother named Jake. He looked at his lady friend, then back at me. He said his name was Francis, but he decided it was too sissy and latched on to his new last name—Jacobson—and that's how he came to be called Jake.

Well, he had me then. Francis was my youngest brother, born maybe four years after me. I couldn't remember much about him. After all, I was just nine when they split us up. I only saw him a couple of times after that, and then I don't know what happened. I was busy adjusting to my new family, trying to do well in school, and I was just a kid.

By now, Jake was looking at me intently. He said we had to be brothers—too many things added up. I said I'd be glad to give him a DNA sample, and help pay for it, too. I looked at the I.A. officers and said I didn't know what they wanted to do, but I couldn't see any point in pressing charges unless they found out something really weird. I felt like I was being sucked up in a tornado. I'm not a huggy kind of guy—just ask my exes—but part of me wanted to hug Jake. Jake, bless him, didn't have my problem. I guess he missed his family more than I missed mine, because he whipped right over to me and gave me a great big hug.

A BOAT OF MANY COLORS

Mary R. Durfee

Two years ago I visited my daughter for two weeks at her newly purchased home in South Carolina. Each day we went sightseeing, and eating out was quite a treat at the various restaurants. We always took the same route. It was then that I noticed this huge boat sitting on a grassy knoll about six feet from the main highway.

"Stop! Stop! I want to look at that boat," I said to my daughter.

"It's just an old boat," she declared. "We'll stop on the way back."

"Okay," I said. "But it looks like someone painted Happy Birthday on it."

"Oh, I know," my daughter replied. "Someone's always painting a message on it or painting a picture. They use all kinds of paint and change the colors every day."

That's odd, I thought as we continued on our way to the hairdresser's.

At the hairdresser's, I engaged in a conversation with a customer, and somehow or other I mentioned the boat.

"Oh, that boat! It's had so many colors painted over it that it's a wonder it hasn't sunk into the marsh. That awful Hugo left it here," the customer added.

"Hugo? Who's Hugo," I quickly asked.

"The hurricane. You do know we had a bad hurricane here in 1989? It was one of the worst I ever remember. They called it Hugo. What a crazy name! But oh, the damage it did. It washed up that boat on the side of the road, and nobody has ever laid claim to it. The city of Charleston was almost completely devastated, and all the beaches were washed away. It has taken us eight years or more to get our homes rebuilt and to get things back into shape the way they were. And you know that boat is still sitting there like a duck waiting for her eggs to hatch?" said the customer.

"But, here's the best part of the whole thing. The city wanted to remove the boat. It was deemed an eyesore. So they made an announcement as to its removal. Maybe float it out at high tide or just junk it in some manner. It was certainly no good. The whole bottom was encrusted with barnacles, and people had been using it as a trash bin to discard their various paint cans and brushes and garbage," the customer added.

The removal notice was published in the weekly paper, but there was such an outcry from the citizens of Folly Beach and the outlying area that the city fathers had to change their plans. Although the boat was located on a pretty busy highway (#171) connecting Folly Beach with James Island, it was back from the road far enough to cause no harm. So the town left it alone and took over the responsibility of caring for it.

It was scraped, washed down, painted white, all the debris was removed, and a weatherproof cover was put over the top. Anyone at any time has the right to use the boat to express their special message. No graffiti is ever allowed. People stop by in amazement, take pictures, and just watch. There is a new message every day, sometimes two or three. Some of the paintings are beautiful, only to be washed away or painted over by the next day.

I thanked the lady at the hairdresser's for her interesting account of the boat, and I couldn't wait to stop back for a good look. We parked our car and got out to look around. Just then, a large white professional truck pulled in and backed up to the front end of the boat. Out jumped two men, buttoning up their white coveralls, putting masks over their faces, and dragging out paint buckets and sprayers. They had been hired by someone to spray a message on the boat for someone's 50th anniversary.

My two weeks were up and it was time to go home. That boat had made quite an impression on me, and I wanted to see it once more. We made another stop. Sure enough, some people were there, painting away. I wanted to talk to them.

My daughter said, "Don't you dare!"

"It'll be okay," I said. "I'll tell them I'm a reporter and just ask a few questions."

As the two men were getting their supplies ready, I asked, "What are you painting?"

"Oh, this is going to be a surprise for my niece. She's coming to visit us, and today is her 16th birthday. I just want to surprise her."

"Where is she from?"

"Well, Syracuse. It's quite a ways from here," the painter replied.

"Oh, I used to live in Syracuse," I quickly answered.

"Well, this place is just outside of Syracuse where she lives. I doubt if you ever heard of it. It's called Verona."

"Did you say Verona?" I exclaimed in great surprise. "I only live about five miles from there. I live in Sherrill, New York. What is your name?"

"Durant."

"I knew some Durants years ago. My! What a small world! May I take some pictures? A very happy birthday to your niece, and I'm so very happy to have met you."

I knew I could use this story for journal material someday, but what should I name it? This odd boat. Then I said, "coat" to myself. A coat of many colors came to mind. Then I remembered that old story, "Joseph's Coat of Many Colors." Then I knew...so that's how it came to be named, "A Boat of Many Colors."

THE ART OF CLIMBING TREES

Seretta Martin

Given a free afternoon in early autumn,
a bicycle and a street with no traffic,
I trace tree shadows (birds, my kin).
Swerving in and out of branches,
I shift my weight, turn, glide
up one side of the shadow's treetop,
slide down the other. At the park, first falling
leaves find air currents in filtered light.

A lithe child with flaming hair catches
my eye. She toddles from her three-wheeler
to a pepper tree, tries to climb the thick trunk.
Strolling the lawn's shadowed edge,
I trace up one side to the crown, then,
down the other. Delighted, she follows,
learning the art of climbing trees.

Not Just Another Fish Story

Patricia Lent

"Let's get this show on the road!" Dad shouted down to my basement bedroom. I was twelve, and Mom, used to Dad's shouting, was not disturbed. This was my day to be alone with the handsomest man in the world

Dad's history was full of fishing. His depression diary had entries for one day after another reading: *Looked for work. None available. Went fishing.* The only exception was a day that read *Had a baby girl today. Went fishing.* I shared a place in his life.

I was Dad's fishing partner at 5:00 a.m on Saturday mornings. I would roll out, fully dressed in jeans, plaid cotton shirt, and a wool overshirt. I'd plunge into my waders, galumph up the stairs, and help Dad load the fishing gear into our blue, 1940 Ford. It was an old car, even in 1950.

We never exchanged a word on those Saturdays. We seemed to be two bodies, one mind, and I absorbed what would be the last closeness Dad and I would share. Not just because my younger brother, his first son, would grow to be companion age, but because, as I said, I was twelve. I would soon be starting womanhood, thus beginning the inevitable chasm between daughter and father that adult femaleness brings to every such relationship.

With the jump-start of adrenaline gone, I'd shuffle sleepily into the car, hunker down into the pea coat my Navy uncle, Isadore, had given me (just like the one Dad wore), and enjoy the manly company: silence, car heat, cigarette smoke, and a whistled tune now and then.

We'd stop along the way at some diner, probably named Joe's. They all smelled the same, those truck stops: more smoke, bacon grease, coffee, wet wool, and sweat. It was perfume to my young nostrils. And after ordering two "Morning Specials," Dad would chat with the drivers—fellow Union members—acting as if he finally belonged.

For 99 cents, I got a cup of real coffee (forbidden at any other time) diluted by a ton of milk and sweetened with loads of sugar, and my trucker's breakfast of two eggs, sausage, hash browns, and toast. A jukebox played away-from-home, lonesome songs. I, too, finally belonged.

After his conversation, Dad would elbow me out of my almost-mouthful and say, "Hey! Hurry! The fish bite at dawn." He'd take the $2.00 tab to the cash register, and I knew that breakfast was over, finished or not. I'd leave mine half-eaten.

Off we'd ride into the chilled darkness roofed by a crisp, star-studded sky. I would fiddle with the radio dial 'til some static-backed newscast filled the car with lulling voices. Dad would light up, and I would gaze through the foggy windows, slipping in and out of dreams in the warmth of the fan-blown heated air.

As dawn reddened the wakening sky, we would reach some unnamed river as though guided by Providence. Dad had spotted a gateway, invisible to anyone else, so we parked off the dirt road and unloaded our equipment: creels filled with gear and sandwiches, a thermos of hot cocoa, a six-pack, rods, and night crawlers gathered under sprinklers at the public park last midnight. We would trek into a secluded wooded area on the way to the water, where Dad would point out and name plants shining with dew and snail trails, "trillium, licorice fern, Oregon grape," and warn me to beware of "thistle, nettle, poison oak, poison ivy." When I got older, I came to view a lot of these as sources of medicine.

Dad knew birds, too, and would try to teach me to imitate their whistles. "Bob White. Listen to the sound. Just like the name." And he'd pucker up a perfect imitation. I'd practice every chance I got, but my Bob always blew a lot of air with my White when the sound was from the lopsided opening in my lips. I would stuff the opening with salmonberries and thimbleberries instead.

Once we had reached the sandy bank, Dad would find a shaded area, where the trees bowed over the shore to the riffled water. We would bait our hooks, threading the night crawlers, leaving enough of the worm loose on the end of the hook to wriggle, siren-like; then we'd cast out into the river.

Dad waited 'til he'd untangled my first clumsy attempts from the bushes behind us. Then he would perform his perfect cast, the nearly invisible leader flowing in a faultless half moon to the exact spot for which he'd aimed. It was always a deep hole between a fallen tree and a large rock that looked to be the home of the granddaddy of all fish.

With the hooks submerged where the bobbers could be seen, Dad and I would poke our rods into the sand. He'd pull a couple of small copper bells out of his creel and attach them to the tops of our rods with the spring-clips he'd welded to them. Dad would open a beer, lie back under the trees at the sand's edge, pull his sweat-stained grey fedora down over his face to shut out the burgeoning sun, and sip and nap, catching up on the sleep he'd left behind.

It was my job to wait for a bell to ring. While a gentle breeze caused the river to circle around the weighted bobbers, I would practice my bird whistles, or hum the latest Hit Parade songs I'd learned from the radio that week. And I would watch Dad nap, thinking, as always, *this is the handsomest man in the world*.

Green vs. Mean

Lynn Veach Sadler

Daddy pretends to be
this hot-shot environmentalist,
but he hates all green foods
(at least until drugs start coming in
"Designer Green"). Granddaddy Sam thinks
his not eating vegetables and salads
when he was a kid
is responsible for a lot of Daddy's meanness.
"Nature's vegetables and salads and fruits
fluff the meanness right out of you,"
Granddaddy Sam says.
"That's why I'm a tad leery of
all that plant engineering."

Granddaddy Sam even loves that
green Tabasco and green Heinz catsup.
(I like the purple better,
am salivating after teal.)
I explained that green Heinz
is for the kids' market,
but Granddaddy Sam went off on
the link between green nature and culture,
as in the like of
the Green Lantern and Green Hornet,
Froggie the Gremlin,
The Wicked Witch of the West, Jiminy Cricket,
Peter Pan, Robin Hood, and The Jolly Green Giant.
(I think he might have mixed his *palate/palette*,
à la Ms. Autry, my English teacher).
Nobody can best
The Jolly—Leafy—Green Giant, but I countered
(or *complemented*, Ms. Autry again)
as best I could
with Kermit, Shrek, The Teenage Mutant Ninja Turtles,
the Swamp Thing, Yoda, The Incredible Hulk…

We agree that green is not for Daddy
except as the Green-Eyed Monster
after his latest Greensleeves
and a dose of GHB,
which is Liquid G or Liquid Ecstasy.

Up in Smoke…Or Down in Flames

Mo Weathers

Summer vacation was less than a week old and already we were bored: Dillard, the oldest at fourteen and our de facto leader; me at eleven and the group geek; Dillard's brother, Allen, who at age ten pretty much went along with everyone else; and Darwin, my hard-headed eight-year-old brother who marched to the beat of his own drummer. Boredom was about to get the four of us into trouble.

We could have explored the large Douglas fir forest that covered the hill behind my granddad's house, but we weren't into exploring. We'd rather build something, or tear something down—whatever. I don't recall whose idea it was, but in a burst of inspiration one of us declared, "Hey, let's build a tree house!"

There were trees in abundance up in the woods behind Granddad's house, and we located four that could anchor the corners of a relatively spacious, sort of rectangular tree house. Raw materials were no problem; there was a sawmill across the road with a large pile of mill ends slated for the burner. (Back then, sawmills burned all their mill ends.) After several trips up and down the hill between the sawmill and our building site, we had transferred enough scraps to build our house. Nails and hammers were scavenged from Granddad's garage, but we needed extra large nails to pound into one of the trees for a ladder. Fortune came to our rescue in the form of several rotten railroad ties on the branch line across the road, which easily gave up their spikes—perfect for a sturdy ladder. (Fortunately, no trains were derailed due to missing spikes—none that we ever heard of, anyway.) Allen had a heavy shop hammer, the perfect tool for driving the spikes into a tree.

With all our supplies and tools in hand, it took us about two days to build the tree house to end all tree houses. It was about eight feet above the ground and had a real door, which opened onto a "bridge" connected to the tree with our railroad spike ladder. We clambered up our ladder, walked across our bridge, went inside, sat down, and congratulated ourselves on our planning, skill, and overall brilliance. We had a tree house of our very own!

A couple of days later the weather turned cool, a light rain began falling, and our tree house needed heat. Fortunately, I had been playing around with gallon shortening cans and knew how to make a stove by cutting an air hole in the side, filling the can about half-full with kerosene, throwing in some newspaper, and lighting it off. We built one in short order, placed it in the far corner of the tree house on a stack of bricks, and soon it was toasty warm inside. Too warm, in fact. Dillard stood up to go outside and fetch a stick to close the hot lid and put out the fire. What happened next was a disaster: on the way out of the door, Dillard accidentally kicked over our can of spare kerosene, which began running down toward the stove. In a mild state of panic he made a dive for the stove and ended up kicking it over into the kerosene on the floor. We watched in horror as the floor immediately went up in flames.

I still don't recall who was first out the door—I think we all went out at the same time. I do remember that Allen *jumped* the eight feet to the ground and sprained his ankle. I immediately followed, but was a bit more coordinated and had a softer landing on a bed of moss, barely missing Allen. Dillard clambered down the spike ladder, missing every other spike, with Darwin right behind him. But Darwin's pant leg caught on one of the spikes, and there he hung, upside down, until Dillard climbed back up to rescue him. Finally on the ground, mostly in one piece, we looked up at the smoldering tree house and then at one another, wondering what to do next. We finally decided to run down to Granddad's for some water containers that we could fill from the creek at the bottom of the hill. This was not well thought-out, as the only two containers we could find in our haste each had a small hole at the top and wouldn't fill very fast. I didn't wait for mine to fill all the way—when it was about a third full I beat it back up the hill and swung it toward the fire. About a cupful of water came out and splashed uselessly on the ground. We stared up at the tree house walls, now almost completely engulfed in flames. Darwin spoke for all of us: "We'll start a forest fire!" he wailed. "*What'll we do?*"

Good question, Darwin—we were all wondering the same thing.

Meanwhile, back at Granddad's house, Dad and Uncle Kenny noticed the smoke. They hurried up the hill to find the fire threatening to burn through the tree house and start on the trees. Quick-thinking Kenny ran back down to the house and brought up a couple of axes, which he and Dad used to chop down two of our support trees. When the trees fell, they ripped the blazing tree house apart, and the pieces fell to the ground (including Allen's hammer, minus a burned-out handle), where they were quickly extinguished. When the last spark was finally put out, Dad proceeded to lecture us on the dangers of building a fire in the woods, and only the fact that the woods were wet from the rain prevented the fire from getting out of control. But I think Dad was secretly amused, because it was the sort of thing he would have done when he was a kid.

A couple of days later, we began work on a new, bigger, higher tree house. Without a stove.

But the story doesn't end there. Earlier in the year the four of us had joined the Oregon Green Guard, an organization that recruited kids to help prevent forest fires, with awards for actually doing so. Allen and Darwin wrote a short letter detailing their exploits in helping put out the tree house fire. Left unmentioned was how the fire started in the first place. Dillard and I, being somewhat older and wiser, remained silent, hoping nobody would start asking questions that we'd rather not answer. About a month later, Darwin and Allen received certificates in the mail—suitable for framing—congratulating them on their courage and resourcefulness. Dillard and I just shook our heads and laughed. And Allen never quite forgave us for burning the handle out of his hammer.

I've learned a lot of lessons in my childhood that have helped me in adult life, but one I remember most was learned long ago in the woods behind my granddad's house: "*Never build a fire in a tree house.*"

Looking for Natalie

Aris DeNigris

I know that you once were here…and I've looked everywhere, but there…
     yet I cannot find you!
But how is it that I still hear your footsteps softly running up and down
     the stairs…hiding under the table…trying to pretend you hadn't
     heard me call?
Your laughter that filled the rooms, and our hearts...and
     the tree-lined avenues as you walked…and skipped…with daddy…
     while holding his hand on the way home from school.
That first day of school when you said, very seriously, "I'm going to listen."
     And you did!
The ghost stories you begged me to invent, while you pretended fright…
     under a tent of bed sheets…until it became too scary for both of
     us to pretend.
     Then, just as suddenly, you were gone…and one day your little friend
     from school came to the door with her mother and rang the bell,
     asking in a forlorn voice, "Is Natalie here, I'm looking for her?"
Sadly, I shook my head and said, "No, honey, Natalie isn't here…
     I'm looking for her too!"

Growing Up

Judith O'Neill

Even as an old man, Forrest could tell you the exact day and hour he grew up. One minute that hot July day in 1941 he was a kid just a month shy of his 20th birthday, looking at the world like any 19-year-old—everything in front of him and nothing bad could happen that couldn't be fixed. He was strong, happy, feeling the world solid under his feet. The next minute, things changed.

It was the day they lost the baby.

She wasn't still a baby, actually, his little daughter, Susie. She had turned two a few months earlier, but they all still called her "the baby."

Forrest had come home from his night shift delivering bread and found his dad and mom sitting at the kitchen table, like always this time of the morning: smoking, drinking coffee, and talking war. His dad was carrying shrapnel from the Great War, so they weren't happy about another one—the Krauts, again, too. His wife, Jill, and his oldest sister, Adele, had already gone off to their jobs. His youngest sister, Jennie, and the baby were sleeping.

His mother had a plate of pancakes and hash browns ready for him, and she got up to bring them to the table while he went in to see Susie. The nice thing about this old duplex was that it was roomy. He walked through the living room and down the wide hall past his parents' bedroom on his right and his sister's bedroom and the bathroom on his left to turn into the small room they had made into Susie's when he and Jill moved in.

Susie lay sprawled in her crib on her back. Her frilly pink summer pajamas left her chubby arms and legs bare. She slept with total abandon, her face turned up, eyes tight, mouth a little open. At last, she had hair. A bald newborn, a few wispy curls had finally appeared on the very top of her head, then scatters of light curls all over, and now the dark ringlets the women curled around their fingers.

She was a good sleeper. Once she was out, nothing seemed to bother her. He stood admiring her long eyelashes and the perfect roundness of her cheeks. He could smell the sweet, clean, baby-smell of her skin.

He glanced around the room that he thought must once have been a sunroom since it had so many windows, all open this morning to bring in the breeze. He knew the house had been built around 1900 by some wealthy industrialist for his own family to live on one side, and his daughter and her family on the other. It was the first house built on this hilly block. Later years had seen it turned into three one-floor apartments on each side as other houses rose on the rest of the block. Forrest marveled at its sturdy construction, because they had people living both above and all down the side, and they rarely heard anyone. He closed the door softly behind him and returned to the kitchen, where his breakfast and a steaming cup of his mother's good coffee waited.

After he ate, he sat for a while with his folks. He was tired from man-handling the heavy racks of bread out of the truck and into the stores, but he would get a good six or seven hours sleep if he went in soon. So he said his "goodnights" and walked back down the quiet hall to the bedroom he shared with Jill. He made sure the blinds were pulled and the windows open. He took off his clothes down to his shorts and pulled back the cover and sheet on his side. Jill always made the bed before she left in the morning, even though it would be unmade an hour or so later. He sat on the edge of the bed and adjusted the fan on the bedside table so it blew over him. He lay down, pulling only the sheet up to his waist.

The one worry that crossed his mind as he drifted into sleep was that this upcoming birthday might be a problem for him. Jill was three years older than he, but she didn't know it. She thought they had been born in the same year because that's what he told her the first night he met her at the dance at the Froghop. The most stunning of a group of drop-dead gorgeous girls who came over from the Kansas side of the river, he had known just by looking that she wasn't going to go out with a sixteen-year-old. He had repeated the lie eleven months later to the Justice of the Peace in Stanberry, and then again on Susie's birth certificate. Adoring Jill and not wanting to cause trouble, his family had backed him up. Jill was going to be pretty an-noyed at all of them when she found out. He would have to think how to handle this. The breeze coming through the windows was still cool as he fell into sleep.

He was awakened by screaming. His heart lurched and hammered against his chest, and he threw off the sheet and leaped up just as his youngest sister crashed through the door, slamming it back against the wall. "Forrie, Forrie," she sobbed. "It's the baby! She's gone!"

From outside he could hear his mother and his father shouting, "Susie, Susie," over and over, his mother's voice shrill, his father's gruff.

"Gone?" he said. "How can she be gone?"

"Stop asking stupid questions," Jennie cried. "Gone like we can't find her anywhere. She was playing in the yard and now she's just gone!" And his tough little fifteen-year-old brat of a sister broke into a rush of tears and screamed, "Come help us—don't just stand there. Get out here!"

He was already pulling on his pants and reaching for his undershirt, and he ran with her through the hall and kitchen and down the steps into the back yard. His mother was sobbing and running around the brick sheds at the far edge of the lawn, peering in the windows and rattling the locked doors. His father was out in the alley behind the sheds.

"Did you look at the well?" Forrest shouted and his father yelled that he had, but came back into the yard and ran to where Forrest was already on his knees beside a round concrete circle set into the ground. They tried to budge it, but even with both of them clutching the iron ring in the middle, they couldn't move it. They tried to shift it, but it was sunk a little below the grass and wouldn't shift. It probably hadn't been opened since running water went into the house sometime in the 1920s, Forrest thought. He crawled around it, searching with his hands for any dip or sinking of dirt, but it set solid. He had inspected it several times before, as it always made him nervous to see Susie sitting on it, playing with her dolls. Then he quickly crawled along the wall separating their yard from the neighbor's, looking for tunnels or holes.

"When did you last see her?" he called to all of them. "Where was she when you last saw her?"

His mother turned from the sheds to answer him. "She was playing with her buggy." She pointed to the tiny doll buggy full of teddy bears abandoned by the side of the house. "I was hanging out the wash, and I went in to wring out another load." For the first time, Forrest saw a half row of clothes hung on one of the lines stretching across the yard. "One minute she was pushing that buggy all over the yard, I could see her from the washroom," she indicated the ground floor room under their porch that held the wash machine, "and I could hear her."

"She was singing," his sister said. "I could hear her from the kitchen."

"I ran the next load of clothes through the wringer, carried the basket out, and she was gone." His mother began to weep and turned to renew her search of the sheds. "Oh, Susie, Susie," she cried, "where are you?"

Forrest took the few steps up to the laundry door, glancing down at the foot or so of latticework nailed along the length of the bottom of the house, and slammed open the screen, but only the squat white washing machine, double-sinks, and a long table occupied the small room.

"Did you look out in front?" he asked, jumping back down into the yard.

His father shook his head. "I ran along the fence on this side, and then out into the alley." The yard was open only at the back, but the house had a set of steps on either side that led up to the sidewalk in front. His father ran for the far side and Forrest started up the nearest. He looked up to see his ancient next-door neighbor, Aunt Pat, come to the railing of her second-floor side-porch and peer down at him. His heart bounded. She sat out there all day. "Aunt Pat," he called up to her, "have you seen Susie? Did you see her out in the yard? Did you see where she went?"

She was 100 if she was a day, he thought, and mean. She was some distant relative on his mother's side, and his mother was the only one she was nice to. She didn't like the rest of them at all.

"Susie?" she said. "She was out in the yard with Edna."

"Yes," he said, fighting to keep his voice even, taking the steps two at a time, "but did you see where she went? Did she come this way up the steps or go out into the alley? Was anyone else in the yard? A stranger?"

She was immediately alarmed. "A stranger? Is she lost? No, no I saw her with her buggy and Edna hanging up clothes. I was napping in my rocker when you all started yelling."

He was at the top of the stairs and out onto the sidewalk. His father came around the other side of the house, shaking his head, and they both scanned the separated front porches in growing despair. His father pointed down the hill and started down that way at a trot, while Forrest turned up the sidewalk. *Could she have gotten this far?* It seemed impossible, but he kept running, his eyes raking the yards, the street, the houses across the street. Behind him, he could hear Aunt Pat screaming at her daughter, "Oh my God, oh my God, Bertie, come out here! Those damn Logstons have lost that beautiful baby. Bertie! Bertie!"

On the porch of the third house sat three elderly ladies, drinking from tall glasses and fanning themselves with paper fans. Miss Stevens had come to visit her sisters. Miss Stevens had been Forrest's third grade teacher and he loved her. He thought her still beautiful with her ton of cloudy white hair piled high on her head. She stood up and called to him when she saw him running up the sidewalk.

"Forrest, what's wrong?"

"Have you seen my little girl out here, Miss Stevens? She's just two. She's gotten out of our yard, and we can't find her."

Both younger sisters came to the railing, shaking their heads. "Little Susie? Oh, no!"

"Do you want me to call the police, Forrest?" Miss Stevens asked him. "There's a phone in the hall."

Why hadn't he thought of that? He nodded. "Please," he said as he ran on.

And Jill, he thought, with a terrible sinking inside him, *someone should call Jill.* Oh God, he couldn't face Jill and tell her Susie was gone. She couldn't be gone. Surely, surely he would find her. Where could she have gone in a few minutes? What could have happened to her? Where could she be?

At the top of the hill he glanced back down the block, and he could see his father at the bottom, talking to some men gathered around him. They suddenly scattered in all directions, and his father turned the corner and was lost to view.

Forrest looked up the shady streets branching away from the corner. Which way should he go? Would she cross the street? He turned and trotted along the sidewalk. It was level here at the top, but no one was on a porch, no little pint-sized girl was running in front of him. Down at the end of the block, kids were skating. He realized suddenly that he didn't know what Susie was wearing. His mother would have dressed her when she woke up. He had no idea in what.

Where could she be? Had someone grabbed her out of the yard? Had she just gone with someone? Lured by candy? A puppy? A kitten? She was very friendly and very curious. In his mind he could see her looking up from her buggy, her brown eyes interested, her curls bouncing as she went to see what some stranger was offering. *What was happening to her right now? Was she scared? Was she calling for her mother? For him?*

A wave of nausea and dizziness hit him. He couldn't get his breath, and he had to lean against a big maple. *Was she dead? She couldn't be dead so quickly.* But even at nineteen he knew how fast you could be dead. Leaning against the tree, his head down, he saw that he was barefoot. He had run all this way and hadn't felt a thing on the bottoms of his feet. He started to run again, looking, looking.

When he came to the head of the dusty alley that ran behind their house, he turned down it. He needed to know what she was wearing, what time she had disappeared, what time it was now, how long she had been gone. Maybe they had found her, maybe she was at home right now. He ran in the dirt, looking into back yards, pleading with everyone he saw for any news of her. No one had seen her.

At Aunt Pat's back yard, her daughter, Bertie, met him at the gate. Bertie was a large woman, and today she had rolled her thick hose down around her ankles in two doughnut rolls. She was one of the nicest women Forrest had ever met, and his family believed firmly that she had to have been adopted. There was no way she could be related to Aunt Pat. Bertie was shaking her head and crying. "I've looked everywhere, Forrie," she told him. "I've searched all around the house, but she wouldn't come over here. I know she wouldn't come over here. She only comes over here with Edna." Her round face was swollen and streaked with sweat and tears. He wanted to comfort her, but no words came.

At the end of the alley, he saw that Jennie had turned up it with their old beat policeman and both of them were loping from side to side, the officer poking at bushes and shrubbery with his stick and looking into shed windows, Jennie taking the lids off trash cans and peering inside. Nausea struck him again.

He ran into his own back yard and saw that Mr. Rollins, the man who lived in the basement on the other side of his house and worked nights, was also out in only his slacks and undershirt. He had apparently found keys to the sheds and was trying to shove in the doors. Forrest's mother had obviously been searching the basement washroom again and came out the screen door followed by one of Miss Stevens's sisters, who was trying to calm her.

He started toward his mother to ask what clothes Susie had on when he heard Susie laugh. Everyone in the yard froze. She laughed again. There was no mistaking the high, little-girl giggle, and they all turned toward the house. His mother ran along the back of the house, bending low to pull at the latticework and calling, "Susie, Susie, are you under there? You come out of there right now."

The latticework held firm until she got to the corner, and then, as she pulled at it, about three feet of the white criss-crossed wood popped up, and out sprang his laughing daughter, clutching one of her teddy bears. "Baby hide," she squealed. "Baby hide from Nana."

His mother grabbed her up and buried her face in Susie's neck, while Susie wiggled and laughed.

Forrest's legs gave out, and he sat down heavily in the grass. Color flooded back into the world. Susie had on a yellow sunsuit and a matching ribbon was tied into her curls. She was delighted with herself. He could see her tiny white teeth and her flashing dark eyes. He saw, too, that someone had called Jill and his sister, Adele. His wife, with Adele right behind her, was running down the side steps. They both held their wide-brimmed hats in their hands. Their bright summer dresses stood out against the gray stone of the steps, and he could see clearly the scattering of freckles across his wife's cheeks and the bows on her high heels. Both women lifted frightened faces to him as they came around the house. He pointed, and they turned as one and ran to the baby.

He could feel the scratchy, dry July grass on his feet and under his hands. The sun was hot on the top of his head, the back of his neck, and his bare shoulders. Sweat ran into his eyes and blurred the brilliant colors of the group around Susie as they passed her from one to another. Holding her tightly, crying and laughing at the same time, his wife turned her head to look at him.

He was going to have to be truthful with Jill. She would be furious, but she deserved to know how old her husband was. This marriage business was going to be serious stuff, after all.

Up above him, he heard Aunt Pat screeching, "Bertie! Bertie! Get up here! Those crazy Logstons have found that darling baby."

Baby at the Table

Carol Christian

a baby eats with
sticky hands
and a chocolate
pudding face

with applesauce
behind
his ears
hair plastered
with the residue
of mashed peas
laced
with Cheerios

his elbows harbor
streaks of pureed
beets
his Onesie stained like
hippie shirts
tie dyed and sold
as art

momma takes
pictures
of her darling

daddy picks him up
with love and
pride smeared
across his face

and holding
baby out like a
soiled puppy
puts him
gently in the tub

Sugar Jets

Lynda Riese

"Please, Daddy, please," my little brother whines, his green eyes large as the marbles he plays with on our front stoop. "Please, can we get some Sugar Jets?" We sit at the yellow formica kitchen table, our dinner of spaghetti with garlic bread finished, tomato sauce sticky on the blue Melmac plates.

My brother's seen the cereal commercial on TV where a little girl and boy hold hands and fly through the air, white smoke trailing behind them, and he's sure that if he eats Sugar Jets he'll be able to fly like his hero, Superman.

"Oh, all right," my father says, as he rolls his shirt sleeves up to his elbows, then scratches his ear that was bitten by a mosquito. He's in a good mood because it's Friday and no work tomorrow, and because he's just finished his dinner, a dinner he likes for a change. He doesn't say anything about the meat in the spaghetti sauce even though it's Friday and Catholics are supposed to eat fish. I guess I'll have to confess eating meat to Father Bell tomorrow.

"Oh, boy." My brother jumps up from his chair, bouncing up and down like he's jumping on a pogo stick, then runs around and around the kitchen, flapping his arms, his red Superman T-shirt coming untucked.

"Well, let's go," my father says and takes my little brother's hand. "Do you want to come, Deda?" he asks me as lights dance in his dark eyes. He looks at me and winks. I wonder what he's up to, and guess he's going to let my little brother think he can fly.

"No. I'd better do my homework." That's a lie, but I don't want to have to sit next to him in the car.

"I need my cape. I have to find it," my brother says, running through the living room that's filled with furniture my grandparents didn't want anymore as he looks for the ratty white towel he uses for his Superman cape.

"You can find it later. Let's go." My father pushes him toward the front door, and when they leave I watch them through the living room window as they walk down the steps across grass still damp from my father's watering to where our blue panel truck is parked crooked in the driveway, as if my father was in a hurry to get into the house after work. I hope I don't have to pretend I can fly. I don't want to be part of my father's game.

"You clear the table," Mama tells me as I walk into the messy kitchen. I stack the dirty dishes from the chick-yellow table, putting the silverware on top like Mama showed me, and carry them carefully to the sink. Mama sits on my brother's stool, her pink flowered dress lifted up to her thighs as she rubs her neck with a fist.

"Do you have another headache, Mama?" I ask, as she rubs and rubs.

"I think one's starting. It's hot as hell in this kitchen." She sighs, fanning herself with her open hand, and I see sweat shining on her forehead. She looks tired, dark smudges under her eyes as if she'd been rubbing them with mascara on, so I say, to be nice, "I'll wash the dishes tonight. You can dry."

"Okay. That will save my hands." Mama has a nasty rash called eczema on both her hands. She treats it by smearing Noxema on the tiny bumps, the same whitish goo that she uses to wash her face. Sometimes she scratches so much, her skin cracks and bleeds. She even gets this rash on her feet, and when I'm feeling mean, I call her "fungus feet" like my father does.

I rinse off the plates and use a stained blue washrag that smells like baby puke to wipe off the sticky tomato sauce that makes me think of blood, my grandmother's blood when she was murdered, but I guess you don't bleed when you're strangled. Then I think of the blood of Christ, and what will I confess to Father Bell? I usually lie, even though that's a sin too, because I can't think of anything.

"Johnny really thinks he'll be able to fly if he eats Sugar Jets," I say as I turn on the tap, pour glistening flakes of Ivory soap into the sink, and make bubbles by swishing my hand back and forth.

"He's going to be one disappointed little boy," says Mama, standing next to me, a towel in her hand, waiting to dry the first plate. Though my brother drives me crazy, I feel bad he thinks he'll be able to fly if he eats a dumb old cereal. Maybe I should tell him it won't work.

"It's mean to let him think he can fly." I rub a plate hard that's sticky with blood-red goo, then rinse it off and hand it to her. "Just like you let me think there was a Santa Claus." I stick out my tongue at Mama while her back is turned, feeling it stretch and pull. She wipes off the plate, then sets it down on a clean space on the cluttered stove.

"I wish you'd stop talking about Santa Claus. I'm sick of hearing about it." Mama passes a hand across her forehead, pushing up her bangs.

"But, Mama, it was awful. I was the only kid in class to raise my hand." I even believed the Easter Bunny hopped through our back yard hiding eggs until last week when Mr. Fiorito, my fourth grade teacher, asked, "How many of you still believe in Santa Claus?" My hand shot up without thinking, without looking around to see what other kids would do. Mine was the only hand up, and I wanted to cut it off and throw it out the window. "You lied." I add more soap to the dishwater for more bubbles. "And now I get teased. Frank Martinez calls me a baby, and John Kaplan calls me Mrs. Claus."

Mama laughs. "They'll forget about it. Just promise me you won't tell your brother."

"I promise." But a light switches on in my head and I think of the light bulbs that float above comic strip characters' heads when they get an idea. Maybe I could blackmail Mama by saying I'll tell. Maybe she'd let me do anything I want just to keep me quiet.

But what do I want? Money. Money to buy doughnuts from Helms Bakery truck, money for ice cream bars from the Good Humor man, my favorite a milky strawberry with shredded coconut on top.

I try to stop thinking about food because Mama says my stomach's getting round as my friend Beverly's mother, who's having a baby. So I think of Santa Claus again and how bad I felt when I understood my parents were just pretending.

"Why do parents lie and say there's a Santa Claus when there isn't?" I ask Mama as I reach down to scratch a mosquito bite on my thigh. "Why would you let Johnny think he can fly?" I wash the last glass in the soapy water and pull the plug out of the sink. Glug, glug, the water gulps, then whooshes away.

"Just for fun," Mama answers, as she stacks the blue Melmac plates and puts them in the cupboard, standing on her toes so she can reach. "Don't be so serious."

"But you and Daddy are having fun by lying."

"It's not really lying. It's making kids happy by giving them something fun to believe in." Mama sighs and shoves the clean spaghetti pan into the cupboard.

"But then they find out the truth and feel dumb." I think of Christmas Eve, how my parents must have laughed behind their hands while I put out cookies and milk in case Santa got hungry, laughed as I waited tucked snug in my bed to hear Santa's bells when he landed his reindeer on our roof. Now they'll laugh at my brother, who'll try to fly after he eats Sugar Jets—my brother who's nutty about flying, who watches the noisy crows that flit from tree to tree in our back yard, watches for airplanes, how he jumps up and down flapping his skinny arms when he sees one high above our house, and shouts, "I'll fly, I'll fly, way up to the sky."

I wish I could fly, too, though I'd never tell anyone. They'd laugh just like the kids in class laughed when I said I believed in Santa Claus. I can feel my face get hot remembering their hoots.

The front door slams and my little brother bursts into the kitchen, his face flushed, his eyes as bright as the sparklers we light on the Fourth of July. My father follows, smiling a smile I'd like to rip off, carrying a brown grocery bag with the Sugar Jets inside.

"Liar," I say under my breath as my father winks at me again.

"Hurry, hurry," my brother shrieks as Mama takes down a white bowl with a blue rim from the cupboard, and my father opens the paper bag and sets the box of Sugar Jets on the kitchen table, the box that shows a little girl and boy holding hands and flying, just like in the commercial.

"Do you want some?" Mama asks me as she pours out cereal that looks like rabbit turds into the bowl. "Get some milk from the fridge." I do as she asks, careful to avoid my father's eyes as he leans against the kitchen sink.

I shake my head no, but then I say, "yes," hoping to fly myself, even though I know I'll never get off the ground. I want to believe in magic, want to believe if you wish something hard enough it can happen, like when I wanted Frank Martinez to like me. I'd lie in my bed at night and whisper to the walls, "Let him like me," over and over until I fell asleep. I'd like to grow wings so I could fly to Frank's house and land on his shoulder like our parakeet, Hoppy. I'd shake my green feathers and sing a song in his ear.

Mama sets the two bowls filled with Sugar Jets and milk in front of my brother and me, my brother so excited he eats too fast. He gulps, then chokes, milk dribbling down the yellow S that snakes down his Superman shirt.

"Slow down," my father says, laughing as my brother sneezes sloppily, a piece of cereal sticking to his chin.

I eat slowly, carefully, rolling the sweet bits of cereal around on my tongue, saying, *I can fly*, over and over in my head, hoping, wishing for wings silky as an angel's, then feeling dumb for having such a silly wish. My father catches my eye, and I smile down into my bowl, hoping he can't hear my thoughts.

When we finish, my brother jumps down from his high yellow stool and runs around the living room, calling out, "Where's my cape?"

"I'll find it," Mama says, rushing off to the bedroom Johnny and I share, coming back with a torn, dirty towel draped across her arm. "Hold still while I pin it." My brother wriggles his arms while Mama uses a safety pin to fasten the towel around his neck. "There," she says, patting him on his bottom. "You're all set."

"This is so dumb," I whisper to Mama as we all troop out the front door and into the warm summer night, where crickets chirp and nest in the jacaranda trees like birds.

"Just pretend. It will please your father." Mama rubs the back of her hand with a wrist.

My father turns on the porch light so we can see what we're doing; moths and fat June bugs buzz around it like bees. He lights a cigarette and smoke floats up, zigzagging, then disappears.

"Let's go, let's go," my little brother says in a breathy whisper as if he knows there's magic in this summer night. Should I tell him now that he won't be able to fly? That this is all pretend? But instead of telling, I take his hand. We stand on the bottom step of the front porch, our parents smiling in the doorway, Mama leaning her head on my father's arm.

"One, two, three," I count as we flap our free arms. The wind sings in the trees: Believe, believe.

A breeze lifts us up, our feet dangling like strings on balloons. Up, up we float; our father waves his arms to call us back; Mama's mouth is moving, but we can't hear what she says.

We drift high above the houses on our block, past Edna's house where lights wink in the windows, past Lila's house that's dark, past Neva's where Sparky barks in the garage, past the Panetta's where shouts fly through an open door. Above the OK Market where Mama buys her meat, the green stucco library where I check out books, above St. Hilary's where God hides.

Up, up we soar, past the moon who wears our mother's face, past Venus, past Mars, until we touch the stars.

BUTTER AND SUCH

Carol Christian

Yellow is the shame
That followed me
As a child
From my soggy
Morning bed

Yellow is the lemonade
Bonding my sometimes
Fractured family
Together in the sweltering
Evening heat of summer

Yellow is the sawdust
From my Daddy's woodshop
Where wood takes on new shapes
Under his talented hands

Yellow is the glow of a
Light bulb that carries
Me through
A book that
Cannot be put down

Yellow is the
Soft flannel quilt
Grandmother pieced
Together from old
Pajamas for me

Yellow is noon time
When we take lunch
And coffee to my Father
Who harvests
The golden wheat

Yellow is sweet pudding
The moon and stars
And the tiny Daisies
That bloom only a few
Weeks in the high plateau spring

Yellow never grows old
Yellow dreams of butterflies
And sweet cream butter
In a bright square smooth blue bowl

Yellow is the daffodils in the spring
And the last leaves of fall
Yellow is depression defeated
And happiness grown deep

CHILDREN (NOT) RAISED

Connie McIntyre

My grandparents *had ten, raised eight,*
the phrase once as common
as a milk cow out back or bath water
heating on a wood stove—
this cousin *had seven, raised six,*
those neighbors *had eight, raised five.*

Youngsters balanced on barn rafters one day
then burned up with fever the next.
Toddlers wandered too near
stamping hooves or vats of boiling lard.
Newborns appeared in hushed bedrooms,
their breaths tiny gasps, or nothing.

Half a century later, a mother tells
the story, dabs her wrinkled eyes
with a lace-edged hanky.
A father goes to his grave
never again speaking
the child's name.

LOVING LESS THAN PERFECT

Sheila Rae Reynolds

I saw the world through the eyes of a five-year-old in 1959. Midmorning sun spilled through the dinette window and onto the linoleum floor, where I lay under the imaginary tent of the table. I looked up from my coloring book to see my mother scurrying around the kitchen. I loved the nearness of my mother. Through the legs of the table, I could see steam rising from two five-gallon soup kettles on the stove. Mom watched the clock as she added one more dash of salt to the soup.

"Sheila, please put your things away now. We need to be on our way," she said, without looking up as she wiped the kitchen counter in rapid circles.

"Why?"

Mom hung the dishcloth over the faucet and helped me slip my arms into the sleeves of my Pendleton wool shirt.

"Because I promised to make food for the men building our new church, and it's almost lunchtime," she answered, as we rushed out the door into the crisp chill of autumn.

When Mom lowered the tailgate of our white Ford station wagon, I climbed up and crawled in next to the back seat. I never tired of the carnival ride effect of sitting in the cavernous rear end of the station wagon. Mom lugged the hot kettles out to the car, holding their metal handles with her potholders. Up the tailgate came, and we were on our way.

Within just blocks of our home, Mom slammed on the brakes to avoid a collision with a car failing to yield the right-of-way in the intersection—a moment forever measured by before…and after. The force of this sudden halt caused the kettles to slide toward me. I sat paralyzed. It all happened within seconds. The weighty cauldrons pinned me to the back seat, sloshing hot soup on me. I screamed from the burning pain. Mom jammed the car into park and scrambled to reach me. She opened the back passenger door, reached over the back seat and lifted me onto my feet mid-street. By instinct, she yanked the wet long-sleeved wool shirt from my body, but when she did, the skin from my right arm peeled off with it. My next memory is of Mom carrying me through the back door of our doctor's office.

The nurse swept me from my mother's arms into an examination room. I heard Mom struggling to tell the story in fractured sentences between sobs.

"A car almost…I hit the brakes…burning her…please help!"

The doctor touched Mom's shoulder as he rushed by her, hurrying toward the table where the nurse was pulling off my clothes. They worked quickly; the injury choreographed their tasks. There was very little talking, for the nurse anticipated the doctor's need for instruments, ointment, and gauze.

I was scared by everything: the pain, the intense look on Dr. Lieske's face, the tight grasp of Nurse Alice's hands on my squirming body, my mother's tears, the shiny instruments and the smell of antiseptic. The only comfort was that both Dr. Lieske and Nurse Alice were kind and familiar. The doctor was both family healer and respected friend. His gentle voice, soft touch, and silver hair were grandfatherly. From birth to death, he was there, making house calls with his black bag when necessary.

Dr. Leiske tried to soothe me, asking, "See those tiles on the ceiling? Why don't you count them for me?"

I tried. "One…two…three…ooouuuch!" I struggled against the doctor's every touch. Again I tried. "One…two…" I heard my mother sob.

I'd never heard my mother cry. Nurse Alice guided Mom toward a chair in the corner. I could no longer see my mother. Could she see me with the doctor between us? I felt cold. Did she feel cold too? I heard the soothing voice of the nurse talking to her.

"Yes…yes…okay," my mother said, her voice thick from crying. She gulped for air in between words, but kept telling the nurse how things had happened, as if, given the impossible opportunity to replay the morning's events, she'd know what to do…slow and careful. She said something about the kettles. Her voice rose only when she said, "…and Sheila always sits back there…I didn't think!" and then her voice faded.

I suffered third degree burns on my right arm and second degree burns from my right thigh to the knee. At the hospital, the plastic surgeon spoke with my parents after he examined me. My parents stood on one side of my bed, and the surgeon on the other. Words I did not understand volleyed back and forth over me. This man was serious. My parents acted differently with him than they did with Dr. Leiske. Did they look afraid? I didn't like him.

The surgeon asked for consent to take a skin graft from my right hip to replace the damaged tissue on my arm. I understood later that my mother tried to persuade the surgeon to take the graft from her body, but he insisted that my own skin offered the best chance for a good take. The graft would leave an additional scar "about the size of a very large pancake," he explained. My parents had no choice but to consent to surgery.

I was in the hospital for weeks. Even though ointment was applied to my blistered flesh after surgery, the gauze would dry between dressing changes and adhere to my raw wounds. The nurses soaked my bandages to loosen the dressing, but they still had to tug at the gauze during the daily change. My mother stood by to hold my left hand during every painful procedure.

The hospital allowed my mother to stay with me through the nights, and I felt comforted having her in a cot next to me when the lights were lowered at bedtime. Over my lower body was a protective cage-of-sorts to keep the sheets and blankets from weighing heavily on my bandaged leg. The bedding was draped over this device like a tent. Several times a day, the nurses exposed my wounds to a gentle heat lamp.

I could not turn in bed by myself. This seemed particularly difficult and frightening at night, when I would wake to a large ward of children, some crying in the shadows. When I tried to change my position, Mother's head would pop up over the bed rail. I stopped struggling when I saw her through the haze of sleepiness. My mother was just a silhouette in the soft glow of patient night-lights. She'd lower the bed rails, then lift and reposition me with the support of pillows. Always, she stroked my hair and rubbed my back until I drifted again into a fitful sleep.

When my parents were able to take me home, Mom assumed the daily routine of dressing changes. Compelled by necessity to inflict more discomfort on me each day may have reinforced her regret that she had not anticipated the danger of the hot soup and insist that I sit in the front seat of the car with her. My dad had been a combat medic in WWII and a POW, but perhaps seeing his daughter in pain was more than he was able to watch. He was such a tender and affectionate dad, but when the miserable daily dressing changes started, he retreated to another room. Mom did not have this luxury.

Once my wounds healed, she continued to rub lanolin oil on my arm daily to keep the scars supple and reduce the scarring. I enjoyed the pleasure of those quiet moments with my mother and the hypnotic sensation of her touch.

Within a month of my return home, I was playing outside with my neighborhood friends, unconscious of my disfigurement. My brother, cousins, and playmates treated me the same as always. The only inkling I had that something was amiss was the pitying affection from an uncle, who would call me over to him and, with misty eyes, softly stroke my arm. His own daughter, my favorite cousin, was just two months younger than I. His sympathy and gentle touch spoke of his love for me, but his actions made me aware, if only for a moment, that something about me was different now. My left arm had the smooth perfection of childish skin. My right arm had the unsightly irregularity of skin stretched too tight in one place and the puffiness of keloid scarring in another. The purplish hue of the scars made them all the more noticeable.

I became self-conscious of my scars one pivotal day in sixth grade. The last one to enter the classroom after recess, I heard a classmate's loud and public chiding, "Here comes cottage cheese arm!" Stunned by the heartlessness of his comment, few in the room laughed. I was mortified. I never again felt comfortable with an exposed arm. These hurtful words left a lasting impression, not to be overcome by thousands of affirming ones.

By high school, I was a leader in my class and enjoyed popularity. However, my well-developed figure and pretty face did not make up for the overriding secret I hid under my clothes. As often as possible, I would wear long-sleeved clothing in front of my peers—not an easy feat in 103-degree California heat.

The unspoken dilemma of my youth was that the person I wanted to turn to for reassurance was also the individual who would be most grieved by the reminder of her consequential lapse in judgment. Now, I'm convinced that my mother would have let me cry and share with her the stories of cruel name-calling at school, but I said nothing then. Without this sharing, my self-loathing went unrelieved. I was caught between wanting to protect my mother's feelings and the need to unburden myself to her.

Mom loved to buy new clothes for me, and I loved to receive them. Often I would come home from high school to find one or two new outfits spread out on my bed. With obvious pleasure, Mom would say, "Which outfit do you like best?" A teenage girl's dream! Regardless of her generosity, I felt irritated when she tempted me with short-sleeved clothes. Sometimes I would simply select the ensemble with longer sleeves; but on occasion I would emphasize again, "Mom, I don't like to wear short sleeves because of my arm!" It was frustrating, I'm sure, for both of us. She always replied with some version of, "Honey, you're so pretty. No one is going to notice your arm!"

I knew my parents sincerely saw me that way, but their compliments did not make up for the opinions of my peers. I just couldn't accept myself as is, and my mother could not undo what had been done; so these experiences were most memorable because of what was left unspoken between us.

My parent's outward indifference toward my scars revealed their desire to ignore the negative and accentuate the positive. I did not understand the strength of their message then. So I retreated into myself on this subject and, in silence, sought the courage to live with the embarrassment.

In my effort to make peace with my disfigurement, I attached spiritual significance to the event. My religious education instilled in me the belief that all things happen by God's permission. I was taught that even bad things have a purpose in our lives. I sat in Bible class as the teacher quoted from the book of Psalms, "Those whom God loves he disciplines." I wondered what I had done as a five-year-old to warrant such retribution. I felt confused. How comforting it would have been to discuss my questions with my parents, and to hear them tell me, "You are not at fault for crawling in the back of the car…you were not being punished for a sin…bad things simply happen!" But I did not share my questions with them. Instead, I searched for meaning and came up short. It took years to understand that this accident was not a divine grooming.

Once in college, I compared myself to the flawless young women I saw on campus. I believed that my disfigurement was a stumbling block between me and true love. This was reinforced when, during my sophomore year, I fell "in love" with a fella who broke up with me one week after seeing my scarred arm for the first time. Coincidence? I didn't think so at the time.

In the spring of my senior year, I met Jim. We've been married thirty-five years now, but I could not know that then. We were crazy about each other immediately, but would it last when he really knew all about me? We were still very early in the relationship when he suggested we go swimming at his athletic club. Once there, I rushed into the lady's locker room to change into my swimsuit. I wanted to be in the pool so the water would cover me when Jim came out of the men's locker room. Soon, I relaxed and was having fun in the pool, until Jim said, "Let's go sit in the sauna."

As we walked from the pool to the sauna, I summoned the courage to address the subject of the scars on my arm and hip. Without a doubt, Jim had noticed them by now. I was grateful that we were alone in the sauna. Jim listened without interrupting as I rambled through the story and described my feelings. I talked without a break because I feared that to pause meant I would then have to hear his response. When I ran out of words, the moment of silence was as suffocating as the steamy hot air in the sauna. Jim motioned for me to extend my arm in his direction. He cradled my arm between both of his large hands. He stroked it from shoulder to wrist, as if to familiarize himself with every bump and deviation of skin.

"Sheila, I've noticed your scars and the way you try to hide them from me."

I avoided Jim's eyes.

"Do you really think these scars matter to me?"

He paused for an answer. I couldn't reply. I was so close to crying. Words would not come.

"Maybe this is too early to say, but I will, anyway," Jim continued. "I am beginning to love you, and that has nothing whatsoever to do with your skin!"

I felt such a wave of relief. I had the overwhelming urge to cry out loud and laugh at the same time. With Jim's few words, I felt set free—free from years of secrecy, embarrassment, and self-condemnation. This man knew that my soul was not disfigured just because my body had scars.

Several months later, my mother and I traveled together. We had just turned out the lights in the motel room and were lying on our backs in the bed we shared. We talked and talked in the darkness. I wanted her to know about this wonderful guy I was dating. I turned on my side toward her, propped my head up on a cocked elbow, and told her the story of the sauna. Then, over my excited ramblings, I heard her muffled cry.

"Mom, are you okay?"

My mother was not one to cry easily, even though we were speaking heart-to-heart, daughter to mother. Her silence was long. I heard her swallow repeatedly, struggling with the tears welling in her throat, perhaps trying to speak without crying. She was still lying on her back, face to the ceiling, when she said, "You'll never understand how long I've been praying that you would finally come to peace with your body. I've hoped you could forgive me for my mistake. I've longed for you to meet someone who will love all of you, just as Daddy and I do. It sounds like you have."

Tears rolled down my cheeks. The room was dark, except for a pale streetlight filtering through the flimsy motel curtains. Even though we were just inches from each other, the cover of night offered us a confessional: a safe time and place to share our deepest feelings. Here, for the first time, Mom exposed a depth of sadness and concern I had never known before. At last, my mother and I were able to cry together over it—all of it, the years of hiding, the regret, the guilt, and the embarrassment. Our tears of relief seemed to comingle with the satisfying silence that followed.

I don't know what my mother's last thoughts were that night; but I drifted off to sleep comforted again by her nearness, as I had been through the hospital nights so many years before.

Pedestrian

Bobbie Jean Bishop

I answer the phone, listen to my adult grandson sketch details of
your crosswalk mishap, words like comatose stumbling on his

tongue. I imagine you with medics, helicopter whirring like some
metal angel, heaven-bound across Los Angeles skies. Hours of

freeway miles between us, I'm stuck in slow motion packing a bag,
garnering directions that lead to detours through a ghostly bar-

closing morning. In a maze of dark interchanges, we backtrack on
city streets resolved to reach an empire no map book can describe—

Mission and Marengo—blocks lined with parking meters and
streetlight stars. My watch tells meaningless time, everything out

of my hands now, but this cup of coffee from an all-night vendor.
Sirens stab the air, wailing toward the USC/LAC Medical Center, a

sprawling complex where we climb one of numerous stairways.
Glass doors open on a lobby like a small village; body scanners

screen us and a clerk doles out wristbands. Bearing these bracelets
of passage we board an elevator to the trauma unit where I'll pace

for weeks in hallways too white to endure. It's been hours since
life catapulted you, my one and only daughter, to a frontline

gurney. Amidst a jungle of dangling IV's, breathing tube eclipsing
your mouth, my eyes sweep your face swollen like overripe fruit,

fresh tattoos on your scalp, blood dried in your hair. You lie in
state like a queen in the lap of Injury while three teams of

specialists race with the hands of an impartial clock. Other families doze in waiting rooms, a tide of plastic cartons and crumpled

napkins lapping at their blankets. As recruits we encounter these veteran strangers, linked by similar sagas, on the tightrope of vigil.

AT THE DUSKY HOUR

Rita Ries

the October fog strolls about
chilliness closes windows
the dogs antsy around
demanding their dinners early
lentil soup warms on the stove.
The day's busyness simmers down
satisfactory day or frustrating,
what accomplished—anything?
Maybe I just sigh relief.
Whatsoever
my fragrant soup awaits,
the lure of rest in the offing,
my pets crunch their meal
then, sated, sprawl in the way.
I settle at the round table
in my cozy burnt orange room
safe and warm, comfortable.
No bombs fall in my neighborhood.
The day expires into history
at the dusky hour.

Terrifying Moments

Mary Baker

The Director of the Senior Center in West End Valley announced that a film company was going to make a commercial at nearby South Main Street. The film company making the commercial invited the seniors at our center to volunteer as participants in the film. I was the only one from our center to volunteer. I thought it would be a fun time.

At 7:30 a.m. on a Saturday, about thirty-seven people gathered in the West End Valley parking lot to film the commercial. Just as the film company was about to settle people in their proper positions, a worker began blocking off South Main Street. At this point, a car came speeding through, driving erratically. I heard moans and groans from those gathered near South Main Street. Every face displayed fear. Everyone started running in panic toward the diagonally parked cars. My heart was just pounding. The lady next to me said her heart was pounding, too. Police cars came, their shrill sirens screaming. I was scared out of my wits.

The police were in hot pursuit of the black car.

My mind raced, filled with gloomy thoughts. Was that maniac driving the black car going to tear through the parking lot and kill some of us? Would there be gunfire, and would I be one of the wounded? Later, I was told the offender of the law did look as though he was indeed going to drive through the parking lot.

We ventured out from behind the parked cars, only to be told we had to return to our hiding places. We finally came back out when we were told it was safe. The director wiped his brow with a sigh of relief. One cameraman had caught the whole police chase on film.

We spent the next two hours making a commercial for iced tea. A young, good-looking girl was the main actress in the film. She was a gifted gymnast, too. The thirty-seven other people made up the background. The whole crowd was now attentive to the director's instructions.

This day could have turned into a tragedy, but the Lord protected all of us from harm.

An Empty House

for Svlvia and the "Kids"

Eleanor Little

There's something that's sad in a house left alone,
inside doors open, windows closed.
Outside, grass grows tall and dry
where children once played after school.
I can hear them laugh, echoes in time.

No more Buick, black and yellow in the drive,
no morning fragrance of coffee and toast.
Sunlight moves silent, counts minutes and hours,
passes crumbs left alone on the floor—
where day by day they dry like bones.

Yesterdays are most often found
among baskets filled with days gone by;
todays come each morning, on time.
But where are my friends of long ago?
Gone on a highway, gone to the snow.

A Neat and Tidy Crime

Phylis Warady

Nancy paused just inside the door of Harvey Mosher's flat. She picked a path through discarded bits of red cellophane ringing the Boston rocker. Her eyes snagged on the rocker's seat cushion, which bore permanent indentations made by the elderly vet's brittle bones.

Tears crowded her eyes. Mosher had been gassed in a long ago war and suffered severe bouts of asthma as a result. He'd sworn the lozenges that came wrapped in red cellophane had helped him breathe. Last Monday though, they'd failed him. An ambulance spirited him off to Veteran's Hospital, where he'd died during the night.

Wednesday morning, Nancy was dressing Josh, her wiggly toddler, when a petite woman tapped on her screen door. "Greta Hiller?" Nancy asked.

The woman nodded curtly. She wore a tailored suit. Its violet hue matched her eyes.

Nancy was glad she'd changed from her ratty terrycloth robe into a sundress. "Come in," she invited, flinging open the door. "I half expected a call last night."

"I did get in last night," the woman admitted, "but I was too exhausted to phone. You received my wire?"

"Yes. Coffee? I was about to have a cup."

"No, thanks. I'm anxious to get into my uncle's flat."

Balancing Josh on her hip, Nancy slid the key off its nail and handed it to her.

Greta Hiller did not reappear until midday. Nancy was bathing Josh.

"Will you be free soon? I've been going through my uncle's personal effects and have questions."

"The screen door's unlatched. Come on in. As soon as I put Josh down for a nap, I'll fix lunch."

"Oh, I couldn't impose."

"There's no place to eat nearby."

"Very well, then."

Greta's eyes inventoried the cramped kitchen in a manner that made Nancy feel as if she lived in a hovel. Stuffing beefsteak tomatoes with white tuna, she found herself wishing they didn't have to eat off the kitchen table.

Her guest sat rigidly erect on a straight-backed chair. "Tell me, Nancy, where did my uncle keep his money?"

"His money?" The question stunned her. "I really don't…he did have a coin purse. He kept it in his sweater pocket."

"A coin purse? I don't mean his loose change. I mean his *money.*" She said "money" as if each letter were capitalized.

"He lived on a pension. There wouldn't be much left over after he paid rent and bought groceries."

The violet eyes darkened. "I'm not stupid, Nancy. You had a key. I don't want trouble. If you tell me where he hid his money, I'll even give you a reward."

"How dare you?" Nancy's temper smoldered. "His doctor insisted I have a key. Someone had to check to make sure your uncle wasn't having an asthma attack. Someone had to call an ambulance when he got sick. Someone had to send you a telegram."

Totally unruffled, Greta Hiller said, "I don't mean to upset you. But if you didn't go through uncle's papers, how did you know how to contact me?"

Mosher's niece didn't believe her. Nancy felt sick to her stomach.

"Mrs. Hiller, I cleaned out his fridge and washed his bedding. His sheets are in the dryer, if you want them. I did not snoop. I got your address off a Christmas postcard lying on the table beside his rocker."

The nerve of the woman!

"Nancy, I'm not accusing you of anything. Uncle distrusted banks, so if he had any money, it had to be in his apartment. Perhaps you're right, though. I went through all his junk with a fine-tooth comb." She set her fork on her empty plate. "I had counted on finding his stash. Ah, well, here's the key. I'm booked on the night flight."

Nancy stared at the key resting on the plastic tablecloth. "What about funeral arrangements?"

"Money doesn't grow on trees. It'd be different if he'd left me something. As it is, I'm out my travel expenses."

"But you're all the family he had."

Greta Hiller shrugged. "He was a veteran. Let the government bury him."

"And his personal things?"

"That trash? Take what you want…burn the rest."

After Greta Hiller left, Nancy decided to fold Mr. Mosher's bedding before Josh woke from his nap. She pulled the vet's pillow from the dryer…and sneezed. Darn it! One of its seams must have popped. Too bad she hadn't noticed before she'd tossed it in. Now she'd have a mess of feathers to clean. And his sheets were too thin to be of use, even as rags. Nancy tossed the bedding in the incinerator and lit a match.

When Josh woke, they went for their daily walk. Coming home through the alley, she was still keyed up. It taxed her patience whenever her curious toddler paused to examine something. As they reached the incinerator, Josh broke free from her grasp and scooped up a scrap of paper from the ground.

"Don't you dare put that in your mouth!"

Catching hold of him, Nancy straightened his fingers, one by one. Ignoring his wail of protest, she opened the iron incinerator door, intending to toss in the scrap. But a curious crackle stayed her hand. Faint recognition set cogs spinning. She smoothed the disreputable-looking scrap. A crisp twenty-dollar bill!

Dazed, she put Josh in his fenced-in yard. Thoughts rising and falling like a roller coaster track, she began to laugh. Her laughter held a touch of hysteria. Mr. Mosher *had* stashed some money. Inside his pillow, of all places! And she'd inadvertently burnt it up.

"Take what you want, burn the rest," Greta Hiller had said.

Nancy stared at the twenty-dollar bill. Then, as slowly, as magically as dawn breaking on a new day, her face brightened. Just enough to buy flowers for the old vet's grave.

Uncle Homer

C. A. Peters

Uncle Homer owned a gas station on U.S. Route 30 at the West Virginia end of a long bridge over the Ohio River. The junction was a real choke point, so he prospered even in the Great Depression. When gasoline rationing came in 1942, he closed the station and went to work in a nearby steel mill. Even though he was pushing the upper age limit, he was drafted because he had no children. He could have gotten a deferment for "essential war work," as many men did, but Uncle Homer declined, even though he allowed, "with war-time wages and overtime I was making more money than I ever had in my life." My father always said he declined the deferment so he could escape from a nagging Aunt Alberta, but they remained married until she died late in life, so I suspect that was just one of my dad's stories.

My uncle ended up in Europe with the "Rail Splitters" of the 84th Illinois National Guard. Before they went overseas, the older guys were offered an early out. Once again, he declined and went to Europe with his outfit.

He told me, "When they could, they put us geezers back at battalion and even in the rear at regimental headquarters. We just could not hump the hills and sleep out with the kids in the line companies." He always added with a laugh, "Sometimes they tried to make cooks out of us! That may be why army food has such a bad reputation."

Now leap ahead to July 4, 1976 and the gathering of our extended family at a farm on Yellow Creek in Eastern Ohio. All of our many gatherings on the "crick" had several things in common: lots of swimming, grilled food, volleyball, plenty of booze, kids, fireworks, all accompanied by the banging away of 22-caliber rifles and various handguns firing at beer cans floating in the creek. This particular party was unique only because it was the 200th birthday of our country's independence and even more raucous than usual.

Knowing about Uncle Homer's service, I again cajoled him, as I did at every picnic, "Show us what you can do with a rifle, Colonel," which was my affectionate nickname for him. He always declined my challenge. On that Fourth of July, however, he took my .22 single-shot rifle and dropped into a perfect prone position on the stream bank. He raised his right elbow high and up and over, like a contortionist, to tightly nestle the stock to his shoulder. Anyone taught to shoot on a military range would instantly recognize that maneuver. Then, with three quick shots, he proceeded to sink three cans, all at a respectable distance. He stood up, ensured the rifle was empty, returned it to me, and walked to the makeshift bar for another drink.

That evening, sitting next to him at the celebratory bonfire, I said, "That was some shooting, Colonel."

After a moment he quietly said, "I was always good with a rifle. When I was a kid, I banged away at the squirrels with an old one shot .22, and when I was drafted they polished my technique. I always shot high expert." Following a longer pause, he continued, "In the spring of 1945 I was with the motor pool back at battalion. We were in a little German village and started getting sniper fire. No one was hit, but it was incessant and annoying. You don't want to be the last guy in your outfit killed, and we knew the war was about over. Anyway, I saw movement in a window, took aim, snapped off one shot, and the firing stopped. When we went to look, I had killed a skinny, blond kid, maybe twelve years old, dressed in parts of a Hitler Youth uniform. He had an old Mauser hunting rifle, taller than he was, lying beside him. No wonder no one was hit! I never fired a gun again until today."

After a while I said, "How about a bourbon?"

He quickly agreed.

I added, as a compliment, "Shooting like that, you should have been a Marine."

He replied, "I tried to volunteer, but they said I was too old."

Sorghum Harvest

Evelyn Buretta

Looking at the ripened field, almost tasting the flavor,
the farmer slashed off leaves and tasseled seed tops.
Bending low, he hacked the stalks close to the ground,
then stacked them into two horse-drawn wagons.

Mill horses panted as they pulled the stone around
and around, crushing the cane stalks. The thick mass
oozed into hot vat after vat, boiled and refined into
a bronze syrup, the family's substitute for sugar.

Expecting eight gallons of molasses for the winter,
the farmer's head slumped when he received only
seven. The mill proprietor's hat nearly covered his eyes
as he said, "Well, that's what your stalks got."

A buyer came in later, shook hands
with the mill owner, got a wink and a nod,
paid seventy-five cents for a gallon of molasses
skimmed from the farmer's sorghum harvest.

THE MISSING GIRL

Andrew J. Hogan

The Chief had gone off duty. I was listening to the Nixon impeachment hearing on the radio when I caught the call from Riley Trout. I was surprised he'd made bail so soon.

"Where's my daughter?" He was screaming at me.

"What daughter?" I said. "Who're you talking about?"

"My daughter, Cassie, was here during the raid last night. What did you do with her?"

We'd raided Riley's house the previous night looking for illegal drugs. I hadn't remembered finding a kid in the house. We knew Riley's wife was in the Pima county jail on a check-kiting charge. Besides, she hadn't lived with him for maybe a couple of years. Nobody was looking for a kid during the raid.

"We didn't find a kid in the house, Riley. We had to shoot your dog. He was threatening one of the deputies."

"The dog was protecting my daughter," he said.

"You're home now?" I said. "I'll come out."

Before I left the office, I called Tiny Eggleston at the Pinal County Sheriff's Office. Tiny's deputies on the narcotics task force had provided "support" for the raid on Riley's house; they broke down the door and secured the premises while the entire Tigre Police Department—that's to say the Chief and I—waited out by our patrol car. We were there because Warden Murphy insisted the Tigre Police Department lead any drug raids within the township boundaries.

The Warden was head of the biggest employer in eastern Pinal County: the Southcentral Arizona Correctional Facility, situated on the polluted remnants of the Hargreaves copper and molybdenum mine in Tigre. All of the east county members of the board of commissioners either worked at the prison, or were married or related to someone who did. Now that the mines had either played out or closed down due to low prices, the Dude Ranch, as the minimum security prison was nicknamed, provided the best jobs around. The out-of-work miners worked in the fresh air of the Dripping Springs Mountains, babysitting drug users, non-violent pushers and dealers, and a few white-collar criminals from Phoenix and Tucson.

When Chief Johnson and I had entered through the busted front door the previous night, Riley was in handcuffs on the floor. Everybody jumped when we heard two shots from the back yard. Then the message crackled over Tiny's walkie-talkie: "Had to shoot the god-damned dog."

Riley started screaming and thrashing around on the floor. Tiny hit him on the side of the head with the butt of his shotgun. After that, everything went smoothly. Riley was arrested and later booked. His heroin was confiscated for the trial, in the unlikely event he didn't plead out. I'd looked out the kitchen window and seen the dog, some kind of pit bull, lying dead in the dirt about fifteen yards from the back door, but I didn't bother to go outside or check more closely.

Riley, semiconscious, was loaded into our patrol car for transport to the Tigre police department, where reporters from the Copper Basin News and the Florence Reminder were waiting to flash photos of the arrest and listen to the Chief and Tiny give their canned statements about local county cooperation in the fight against illegal drugs.

"Tiny, we just got a call from Riley Trout. He says his daughter's missing. He claims she was in the house last night during the raid."

"I didn't know he had a daughter. Why didn't you tell me?" Tiny said. "My squad should have known this beforehand."

"We didn't know either," I said. "His wife hasn't lived up here for quite a while. We understood she was in jail down in Tucson. Maybe he got custody somehow."

"Well, my guys didn't report seeing any kid on the premises," Tiny said. "I'll double-check and get back to you."

"I'm going out to Riley's now. I'll be back in about an hour."

Riley's house is only about a mile and a half from the station. I sent a cloud of dust billowing over the house when I pulled into Riley's driveway ten minutes later. Riley came barreling out even before the dust settled.

"Did you find her?" he said, still screaming.

"Calm down, Riley," I said. "Who are we talking about? I didn't know you had a daughter."

"Cassie…Cassie Cisneros."

I wrote it down. "Who's the mother?"

"Yvette Cisneros."

"She's the one in jail in Tucson for check-kiting?"

"No, that's Joy, my wife. I knocked up Yvette before I hooked up with Joy."

"So Cassie's illegit?"

Riley gave me a disgusted look. "Yeah."

"Your name on the birth certificate?"

"How should I know? Yvette told me she was mine." Riley lit a cigarette and sat down on a dirty white plastic chair next to the front door. He looked like he was recovering from a hangover; maybe it was the gun butt to the head. "Yvette got in a prostitution beef in Nogales, and she didn't want Cassie living with her sister—she's a junkie—so Yvette asked me to take Cassie for a couple of months until she gets released."

"Living with you is better than living with a junkie? You're a dealer, for chrissake."

Riley leaned back in the chair and blew smoke in my direction, like a smart-ass kid who knows something you don't know. "Well, Yvette's sister is turning tricks, and Yvette was worried Cassie might get hurt by her sister's gangbanger Johns. Cassie's about fourteen now."

"You put her in school, anything like that?"

"No, she was here just a week. I didn't get around to it yet."

"You got a picture of her?"

He was back to looking disgusted again. "What you need a picture for?"

"Because she's missing, asshole."

"You didn't take her during the raid?" Now he just looked stupid.

"I told you, no. I checked with Tiny, his men didn't find anybody here but you," I said. "Where's Yvette? In the Santa Cruz county jail?"

"Yeah, She's going to kill me when she finds out what happened." Riley smiled. "But she's going to sue your asses off for losing her daughter."

"Where you think she might've gone?"

"Don't know. Maybe she ran out into the desert during the raid," he said, giving me a puzzled look that might have been genuine, but with ex-cons like Riley, you never know whether they're playing you for some advantage. "She don't know her way around here yet. Could be lost. There's a lot of old mine shafts a kid could hide in if she was scared."

"She got any stuff in the house? I could get the sheriff's rescue posse over here with the tracking dogs."

"Yeah, sure." Riley went in through the busted front door and down a short corridor to a bedroom. The bed was unmade, and the nightstand was covered with empty beer bottles and a large ashtray filled with old butts.

"Shit, her stuff's gone," Riley said.

"What's her stuff doing in your bedroom?"

"Oh, right." Riley turned and walked across the hall to an even smaller room with a stained mattress on the floor and some cardboard boxes against the wall. He looked around. "Nothing here, either."

"We're going to need a picture for the missing persons report," I said.

Riley gave me a blank stare.

"Do you have a picture?"

"No, you'd better call Yvette."

"Okay, can you at least give me a description?"

"Sure, I know what she looks like."

I radioed the Chief at home before leaving Riley's house and told him we had a problem. He said he'd meet me at the station.

Chief Johnson came from Tucson to head up the newly created Tigre Police Department in late 1970, about a year before Pima County Sheriff Waldon Burr resigned following his indictment for accepting bribes from prostitutes, selling deputy appointments, and suborning perjury. Back then, Chief Johnson was the assistant chief of detectives in Burr's administration. Johnson's former boss, Chief of Detectives and Undersheriff Roy Murphy, had taken the job as warden of the newly opened Dude Ranch earlier the same year. Undersheriff Murphy left shortly after the county prosecutor convened a grand jury in late 1969 to investigate corruption in the Sheriff's Department. As Chief Johnson once explained to me, Warden Murphy had recruited his former subordinate to lead the Tigre Police Department to "maintain a secure political perimeter around the Dude Ranch."

Back when I was a kid here in grammar school, Tigre was a regular town. The Hargreaves mine was active. People like my father and uncles had good-paying jobs. Tigre had a post office, a Baptist church, a movie theater, a couple of schools, a laundromat, a general store, even a doctor—all pretty much controlled by the Hargreaves mining company.

I was just getting ready to go to high school in '57 when the mine shut down. Tigre became a ghost town almost overnight. My family moved into Mammoth up on Highway 77, so I could attend high school. After that I got drafted and went into the MPs. I did a tour in Vietnam and another in Germany. In 1970 I was passed over for a promotion and decided it was time for me to get out and come back home with my new wife.

If it weren't for the Chief and the Warden, I'd most likely be living up in Phoenix or maybe down in Tucson, pumping gas or working in one of the new Circle K stores that kept popping up everywhere. The Dude Ranch brought Tigre back to life. The Chief needed a deputy, a good paying job for these parts, with benefits. The Chief looked like he might be only five years or so away from retirement. I saw a secure life for me and my wife and son.

Driving back to the station, I tried to rethink events of the previous night, especially the trip from Riley's house. We'd gone about a quarter mile and were turning onto Mine Road, when Riley moaned in the back seat. The Chief was driving, and I looked back at Riley. The brake lights had come on as the Chief slowed at the intersection, and I remembered seeing somebody on the opposite side of the road. I hadn't paid much attention; I knew we had reporters waiting for us at the station.

The chief was at his desk when I arrived.

"What's up with the girl?" he said.

I told him of Riley's claim that Cassie Cisneros was his daughter by an old girlfriend now in the Nogales jail, and that she'd been staying with him for about a week. "Tiny's double-checking with his squad, but so far nobody remembers seeing the girl."

"You get a description?"

"Yeah, but it was so general as to be useless," I said, opening my notebook. "Short for a fourteen-year-old, maybe 4 feet 6 inches, brownish hair, not sure about the eyes (probably brown), average skin (not brown, not fair), didn't look particularly Mexican like her mother, but not Anglo, either. No birthmarks, scars or distinguishing features he could remember, still a girl, not much of a chest yet."

"Christ, there are thousands of girls within a hundred miles of Tigre fitting that description."

"I know," I said. "I'll call Nogales. See if we can get a picture and a better description from the mother."

"Great. I'd better call the Warden, fill him in. This problem could be embarrassing."

"Oh, one other thing," I said. "The girl's things were missing. Riley went looking for them in his bedroom."

"Do you think…?" he said, raising his eyebrows.

"I've never known Riley to be interested in young ones, but you know he likes to sample his own product. So maybe when he's high he's not too particular?"

The chief picked up the phone to call the Warden. I got on the other line and contacted the Santa Cruz County Jail.

Most of the older homes and businesses I remembered as a kid living in Tigre have deteriorated to the point of being uninhabitable. The only new construction has been the Dude Ranch and the police station. The old gas station, where I had hoped to work as a high school student, was rehabilitated into one of those new Circle Ks. Like most of the one hundred and fifty residents of Tigre, I lived in a trailer bought by the Dude Ranch to house the prison staff. I was in the process of fixing up my parents' old house. Because it faced north, it had a nice view of the Dripping Springs Mountain, with a hill on the east side blocking the view of the old mine roads and the prison.

The Dude Ranch operated a bus between Tigre and Mammoth three times a day to bring in staff for each of the prison's three shifts; it was free to anybody who needed a ride. We didn't have enough kids to start our own school, so my son took the bus to Mammoth each morning during the school year.

A day passed before we got the special delivery envelope from the Santa Cruz County Jail. There was a description of Cassie Cisneros provided by her mother, and a grainy 8x5 color photo of Cassie taken two years ago, sandwiched between two women, presumably her mother and her aunt, both of whom were holding bottles of beer and looking more than a little wasted. The photo wasn't going to be much help. Yvette Cisneros' description was only marginally better than Riley's; she mentioned Cassie had a half-moon scar below her right knee from a bicycling accident. There were no fingerprints on file for Cassie; her mother didn't remember her blood type, except that it wasn't rare.

I made the best enlargement of the photo I could with our little Xerox machine and ran off some posters with the picture and the physical description to distribute in Tigre and Mammoth. The evening clerk at the Circle K in Tigre said she hadn't seen the girl, but the driver of the evening shift bus between Tigre and Mammoth said he thought there might have been a young teenage girl on his bus the night of the raid. He wasn't positive, though, because he had been flirting with a woman who works in the kitchen at the Dude Ranch when the girl climbed on board the bus. The girl sat way in the back and left by the rear door near the Mammoth Texaco, where a lot of the prison workers park their cars during the day.

The evening shift clerk at the Texaco thought he remembered seeing a girl hitchhiking toward Winkelman just after the prison bus arrived. He thought he remembered a Pinal County Sheriff's cruiser pulling over to talk to the girl. I called Tiny to find out who was on highway duty that night, but there were no Sheriff's patrol cars in that vicinity at that time. However, the state police outpost in Winkelman showed Trooper Mark Cosette patrolling near Mammoth on the evening of the raid. I asked for a call back when he came on duty.

Before it closed in the fifties, the Hargreaves underground copper and molybdenum mine had been in more or less constant operation since the late 1890s; it produced a massive pile of tailings that had filled a couple of pretty good-sized canyons.

Tigre was the perfect place to put a prison. The old mine land was claimed by the county for back taxes and sold to the state for a dollar. A bulldozer came in and smoothed out the mountain of tailings. Plenty of water was already available from the old mining operations. Nobody much cared about the environmental problems on old mining sites. As soon as the prisoners started showing up, they were put on work gangs to seed the slopes of the tailings mountain with creosote and buffel grass to prevent erosion. On the bare plain atop the tailings mountain sat the Dude Ranch, surrounded by steep and unstable cliffs, except for the one well-traveled and easily guarded road into Mammoth. But then, Dude Ranch didn't hold prisoners who were dangerous or likely to try an escape.

After the mine closed, Tigre became an unincorporated area without a town council, and this left Chief Johnson as Tigre's only township official. Our Police Department relies completely on funding from the Dude Ranch. We're the Dude Ranch's external security force.

"Deputy Pettis, this is Trooper Cosette returning your call."

"We have a girl that's gone missing, last Monday evening," I said. "She may have gotten on the evening shift staff bus for the return trip from Tigre to Mammoth. A witness said he thought a sheriff's car stopped to talk with the girl outside the Texaco, probably around 20:15. Nobody in the sheriff's office was on duty in Mammoth at that time. I checked with the Winkelman outpost, and they said you might have been through Mammoth about that time."

"Sure, I remember her. Teenager, not legal yet; brown hair, brown eyes," he said.

"Sounds about right. I've got a photo you could look at, though it's not very good," I said.

"I've got some business in Florence the early part of the shift tonight. Can you leave the photo at the Texaco? I'll leave a message for you at the department when I get over there." All the deputies knew the Tigre police station was only open during regular business hours.

"I'll do that," I said. "Could I ask why you stopped to talk to her?"

"I was heading north on 77 when I saw her standing by the side of the road. Looked like she was hitchhiking," he said. "She had on a kind of short skirt and a short-sleeved shirt over one of those tube tops. You guys don't have teenage girls in Tigre or Mammoth out at that time of night, not looking like that. So I thought I'd check it out. You know, maybe a girl visiting her father at the Dude Ranch who missed her ride home."

"Right," I said. "Did she say anything to you?"

"Nothing useful. She spotted the cop-lights on my cruiser before I reached her. She turned away and was getting ready to turn down Childs Street when I caught up with her. Gave me some story about visiting relatives, the Bullochs, who just lived down the street. After I pulled away, I realized Bulloch is the name of the real estate agency up a couple of houses from the Texaco, across the street from where I stopped her. I circled back down Clark Street to Childs, but when I got there, she was gone. A call came over the radio about a drunk driver leaving San Manuel for Mammoth, so I left."

"I guess you don't know if she got back on the road or not?" I said.

"Sorry. I caught the drunk driver and took him to the outpost in Winkelman, but I didn't see her again."

"Okay, when you get a chance to look at the picture, give me a call," I said.

I called Bulloch Realty about the girl, but Percy Bulloch said they hadn't had any visitors lately, and they didn't have any relatives with girls the age of our missing girl.

The Sheriff sent a search dog out to Riley's house. We didn't have any articles of clothing or other personal items from the girl, so the deputy had the dog smell the old mattress in the second bedroom. The dog just ran around in circles; if there was a trail, the dog couldn't find it. My missing persons investigation was a dead snake in the road.

When I got to the station the next morning, Chief Johnson was already there. "Cliff, there was a message for you from the Highway Patrol—Trooper Cosette. He looked at the picture you left for him over at the Texaco," the Chief said. "He said probably it was the same girl, except the girl he talked to looked older, tarted up with lipstick and eyeliner, had a pretty nice rack, although, who knows, it might've been mostly tissue paper. Nice rack helps if you're hitchhiking."

"The picture sucks, taken with a flash on a cheap camera. It's old. Girls change a lot when they go through puberty," I said.

The Chief looked at my missing girl flyer. "Could be most any girl with some spic blood in her. They're a dime a dozen around here."

"I could send a missing child report to all the law enforcement agencies in Arizona," I said.

"It'd be a waste of time. Either they'd pick up every half-breed chica in the state or, more likely, nobody would pay any attention to it. If the girl's on the run, she'll find her way back to Nogales. Send the Nogales police the flyer and wait to see if she turns up."

~

A week went by and the girl hadn't turned up. I was in the office with the Chief, shuffling papers, when a call came in; it was the county attorney, and he wanted to talk with the Chief.

"Arvin, how are you?" the Chief said. He sipped some coffee while he listened. "No, we haven't found her yet." He started tapping the end of his pencil on his desk. "Frankly, we're not even sure she exists. We got a description from Riley that could fit thousands of greaser girls in the state. Except for Riley, nobody around here has even seen her." Now he was drumming the pencil. "I understand it could get messy, but does Riley even have standing to bring a complaint? He's not the custodial parent. Christ, we don't even know if he's the father. His name's not on the birth certificate." The Chief started looking more concerned than angry. "Okay. I'll need to talk to the Warden about this. I understand, we don't want a big political mess like the one in Tucson. Right. I'll talk to him and get back to you."

The Chief dialed another number. "Hi, Betty. Is he there? I've got something important about that missing girl." He held the receiver away from his ear for a moment, and then put it back. "Okay, I can be there for lunch at 11:30." He paused. "Sure. See you then."

The Chief hung up and turned to me. "Riley's got some kind of civil rights lawyer representing him in the drug case. The lawyer found a beaner group down in Tucson interested in the missing girl. They're saying maybe we killed her during the raid, and now we're covering it up. I'm going to have lunch with the Warden, figure out what to do."

"I'll double-check with some of the local departments just in case somebody might have seen something," I said.

A couple of days later the Chief got a public documents request from the Alianza para los Derechos Humanos de Mexicano-Americanos for our records on the Cassie Cisneros missing persons investigation. The Chief denied the request on the grounds the investigation was ongoing, but the county attorney told us the Alianza would sue and probably win, since the investigation appeared to be at a dead end.

I tried to keep the investigation alive by calling the local police departments on the girl's likely route back to Nogales, assuming the teenage hitch-hiker Trooper Cosette saw was Riley's missing daughter. If she kept going north to Winkelman, from there she'd probably hitch a ride to Florence on AZ177 and on over to Casa Grande; from Casa Grande she could hitch down Interstate 10 to Tucson, and then take the Nogales Highway back home.

A road-patrol deputy in Florence said he saw a local biker riding with a new girl who looked too young for him on the Wednesday after the raid, but the deputy was writing a ticket for an overloaded pickup and didn't have a chance to pull them over. A trooper at the Casa Grande Highway Patrol outpost saw a young teenage girl meeting our missing girl's general description hiking south on that Friday at the junction of I-8 and I-10, but he was heading north; by the time he got turned around, the girl was gone. Tucson police hadn't seen any girls on the highway matching our missing girl's description, although the desk sergeant admitted that his officers probably wouldn't have taken any notice of a female teenage hitchhiker, even if she was a little young; they saw a thousand girls like that every year.

I asked the Nogales police to check on Cassie Cisneros at her mother's former residence and at her aunt's house. They got back to me the next day; nobody had seen the missing girl. They promised to keep an eye out for her.

Another week went by with no new leads on the girl's whereabouts. The Chief got served with notice of the lawsuit filed by the Alianza. Tiny Winkelman got served as well; the Alianza was also looking for the narcotics task force records about the raid.

The Chief was in and out most of the next week. I kept working the case as best I could, but with no results. On Friday, the Chief and the Warden went together to Florence to meet with the Pinal County Sheriff and the County Prosecutor; somebody from Santa Cruz County was going to be there, too. The Chief hadn't returned by the time I went off-duty, but he called me at home about eight and asked if I could meet him at nine the next morning.

I had to get my wife to take our son to little league Saturday morning, so I could meet with the Chief. He was already in the office when I got there, the Cassie Cisneros file open on his desk.

"Cliff, we're going to close the Cisneros missing person case."

"Hey, you found her?" I said.

"No, but it's being reclassified as a runaway child case; the Santa Cruz County Sheriff is taking it over."

"Even though the missing persons report was made here?" I said.

"Yeah, well, Riley is retracting his missing persons report."

"Why?"

"Because his felony drug-possession-with-intent-to-distribute charge is getting kicked down to misdemeanor possession," the Chief said.

"And the mother is willing to go along with this?"

"Yvette Cisneros is being released from the Santa Cruz County jail five weeks early so she can search for her runaway daughter," the Chief said.

"So I guess we're off the hook?"

"Case closed," the Chief said. "The Warden's happy Tigre's image remains unblemished."

On Monday I asked the Chief for the next day off, so I could take care of some personal business in Tucson. I dropped off my wife and son at my mother's house on East Linden and took a ride down to Nogales. Yvette Cisneros' home address was an apartment building on East Calle Soto. I drove down Grand Avenue, passing the Nogales police station, and turned off onto Soto, crossing onto the "wrong" side of the railroad tracks.

The apartment building looked like an old, very rundown Motel Six. Yvette's apartment was on the ground floor with an entrance directly onto the parking lot. I parked across the street under the shade of a tree and waited. Kids would be coming home from school soon.

Fifteen minutes later a girl, maybe ten years old, unlocked the door to the Cisneros apartment, dropped off her schoolbooks, and started back out to the street. I got out of the car and flashed my badge at her.

"Say, miss, I'm looking for Cassie Cisneros. Are you related to her?"

"Yeah, she's my half-sister," the girl said.

"Is your sister around?"

"My *half*-sister ran away from home about a month ago," she said, acting like she really had important business elsewhere.

"Do you know where she might have gone?"

"Who knows?" Her sigh said, *and who cares.* "I was living with my cousins when she ran away. She was staying with my Aunt Sofi. She might have gone off to see her dad up north of Tucson somewhere. My dad lives here in town; he's a guard at the jail."

"Has she done this before? Run away?"

"Oh, sure," she said, giving me a pained, you're-boring-the-crap-out-of-me smile. "Look, I gotta go. Okay?"

"Yeah, thanks." I got in the car and headed back to Tucson.

When I returned to the station Wednesday morning, the Chief was already there.

"How'd you make out in Nogales?" he said.

I should have known I couldn't get away with anything without the Chief, or more likely the Warden, finding out about it.

"Nothing," I said. "I talked to the half-sister, but she could care less."

"When a girl like this goes missing, she stays missing. It's probably for the best."

"If she's not dead," I said.

"Maybe even then," the Chief said, making a note in the file on his desk. He looked up. "The Warden won't be so understanding the next time you second-guess him." The Chief folded the file shut and put it in the bottom drawer of the filing cabinet—closed cases.

I'd learned my lesson. Seven years later, when the Chief retired, the Warden made me chief.

THERE'S GOT TO BE A BETTER PLACE...

William Killian

When the wind whipped me out of Indiana
I vowed I would never return.
Acts of God were no less fierce in the desert—
Homes washed away in the Tucson flood of '83—
But I could no longer stand the devastation.
Winters didn't help, nor did the overcast skies
Ever bring comfort, and the humidity,
Flies, mosquitoes, and bible-belt mentality
Led me to a home away from home.

I now relive my Hoosier days at the 10 o'clock news—
Tornadoes rip through small towns
And devour poor souls
Who barely eke out a living
In areas where General Motors went silent.

In the dead of winter
I shake my head in disbelief
That I once slid from road to ditch,
Then flung dangerously back to traffic
Where I barely made it home.
Then in early a.m.
I would have to dig down deep to find my car,
Swearing *there's got to be a better place.*

My time now has over 300 days a year
Of perfect blue skies.
The mosquitoes I see die from loneliness,
The flies never crowd my life
Like they did in Koontz Lake, Indiana.
My sweat now is from honest heat,
Not from a moisture that never stops.

I have found, however, that the bible-belt
Stretches itself across the land,

And the lunatic politics of midwestern power
Do not come close to the idiocy of Arizona civics.

In my older age,
I don't know if the chaotic hot air out of Phoenix
Will send me packing to yet another home,
But I doubt it.

To the Man on My Right

Maggi Roark

It's a dinner party
not a debate.
You're not fishing.
I'm no leaping trout.

So I picture you
at ease, in a sapphire sea.
You're the ready meal—
I'm the ravening shark.

But wait.

I fear the consequence
of even one bite. I could die
from the poison
of your pompous politics.

I'll place you, instead,
in a vat of boiling oil.
Then ask you, please,
to pass the salt.

Messages in the Sand

Dorothy Parcel

For the Birds

Sparrows have a mean streak. We put bird seed in a basket and refill the bird bath every morning. The basket leaks, so a lot of the seed goes on the ground. If it didn't, only a few of the bull sparrows would eat. As it is, with the seed on the ground, they can't boss forty birds, no matter how hard they try.

The other day, I saw a sparrow sitting at the end of a branch, rearranging its lice, or whatever, when another sparrow flew up behind it and tried to knock it to the ground. Maybe there was a reason. Maybe they had political differences. Maybe the branch bird had made remarks about the other bird's girlfriend. Who knows?

A few years ago, we rarely had sparrows. Those years we had finches. Finches are beautiful, though as quarrelsome as sparrows. Some of them had purple caps, some wore red capes and hoods. We felt honored, for they rarely came this far north. I think they only migrated north because of bad weather in Mexico.

So we are back to sparrows. One final thing about the bird bath. Bird bath is a laugh. They drink out of it, bathe in it, and poop in it. To each his own, I guess.

...Oopsie

In the market the other day, I bumped into a young woman with my cart. I opened my mouth to apologize, when she turned around with a #2 can of peaches in her hand and a mean look on her face. I stepped back, ready to run, when her whole demeanor changed.

"Sorry," I said, lamely. "I wasn't looking."

"That's okay, grandma," she answered, and put the peaches in her cart. Grandma indeed!

Then, yesterday, the market had a good price on watermelons, so I chose one and went to put it in my cart when it slipped right out of my hands. Not one, but two attendants were within feet of me when the melon hit the floor. All three of us were in juicy red bits to our knees.

"Oh, I'm sorry," I said.

"Don't worry about it, grandma," one said.

"Happens all the time," the other said, putting another melon in my cart.

Grandma, again! I steamed for a while but, on reflection, having white hair and a few wrinkles had saved me some lumps. Lord knows I've been called worse than grandma. But if this goes on, I may be banned from the market for life.

...Mental – or not

A young man climbed 100 feet up a TV tower. When he came down, they arrested him. Then they took him to be mentally evaluated.

That's what the cops do now. I think I could stand being arrested if I did something that stupid, but I don't think I'd like to be mentally evaluated. I admit I have selective ideas about psychiatry, but I know they ask a lot of personal questions.

I know this because someone I know who had occasion to spar with one told me he kept asking whey she hated her mother. She finally told him her mother died when she was born, and she was raised by an aunt who she really did hate. She said he got up and stomped out.

I know a few cops and even have some cousins in that line of work, but I'd hate to get caught doing something I shouldn't by one of them. I think they'd take their time getting me to the mental person. I think this from hearing them talk about how this supervisor or that wanted things all wrapped up before they got to court.

As far as the mental evaluation goes, I don't think that would go well. At my age, my memory is a little iffy, and I have become accustomed to lying if I get caught doing something I shouldn't. Well, I don't exactly lie, but I like a happy ending. That beats saying I don't remember. I hope.

...Who, Me?

I wish there weren't so many beautiful young women on television. Especially the ones in bathing suits or what passes for underwear. It irks me that they are tall and shapely, and I was always short and usually looked as if I had been caught in a famine.

Another thing, those gorgeous people drive cars with exotic names Jaguar, Cobra, Mustang, and other animals. My Ford is more than ten years old and leaks oil no matter how I swear at it. The only animal it resembles is a snail.

And their houses—uh, mansions! My whole house would fit in their living rooms. And they're always so tidy. No newspapers waiting to be recycled, no dishes in the sink, no dogs lounging around on the beds.

I was not only born in the wrong century, I was the child of people whose genes run to longevity and not physical beauty nor the ability to make a lot of money or to hold on to it if any came their way.

I guess we have to play the cards we are dealt!

…Going to the Dogs

When my kids were small, I needed a big dog, and I saw an ad in the paper for an Airedale. I read an article about the breed, and it said they grow to less than a yard and that seemed about right. I hurried to the kennel and bought a pup. She threw up on me on the way home.

I soon learned that Terriers are, as a breed, mad. They also have their own ideas of what they'll do and what they won't. On the plus side, they are more sociable than lizards.

I have had many Airedales through the years, each one more eccentric than the last. The latest one has a skull made of some material that allows her to hit the dog door at warp speed. She has also decided that butterflies are dangerous. Her favorite trick is to come up behind me, thrust her head between my legs, and shake it. This makes me shriek, and results in a lot of dropped dishes.

I once read of an Airedale who was clocked on police radar running at thirty miles an hour. I'm sure mine could do better than that.

…Another View

We all know some of the minuses of growing old: the loss of energy, the lack of suitable clothing for our age group, the way we are invisible to everyone under fifty.

It's the little things that get us down. This week, I had to get down on my hands and knees—I had broken a string of beads. When I tried to get up, I couldn't. The more I tried, the warmer the air got. I finally crawled to the couch and levered myself up. It wasn't pretty.

We all spend more time shopping for groceries than we did a few years ago. Much of that is caused by label reading. There are all kinds of new and exotic foods. Not that we buy any of these foods. No. We don't want to spend hours on the bed, waiting for the stomach medicine to kick in.

I thought I knew all the tricks of growing old until I read an article this week, probably written by a thirty-year-old snot. His thesis was that as people grow older, we shrink and lose weight. We know that! He went on to say that our noses, feet, and ears never stop growing.

Now, that's just plain mean!

A Baby Lion

Tom Engel

I loved shooting baby animals. Now, before you react too judgmentally, you have to realize I was a Television News Photographer.

I love animals, and whenever a story came up in the newsroom about animals, I always volunteered to shoot it. Especially stories involving puppies and kittens. Oh, and a baby lion. It was a challenge shooting baby animals, I admit. They always seemed to do something unexpected, but with patience, a little planning, and some careful editing, I always ended up with a story that stole everyone's heart.

The bigger animals scared me. Not too long after my transition from editor to photographer, I was assigned to shoot some footage of zoo animals. One of the stops I made at the Pittsburgh Zoo and Aquarium was at the elephants' cage. An elephant was standing near the bars of the cage. I took a couple of wide shots and decided to get a close-up of the elephant's eye. I needed a steady shot, so I held the camera against a bar nearest the elephant. I took a moment to focus. Just as I started to roll video, my camera started to rise. I held on as tight as I could, and I started to rise with my camera. The elephant had stretched his trunk over the top of the bars and grabbed my camera. There was no one around. I didn't know what to do. I started pleading with the elephant to let my camera go. When I had risen about three feet into the air, the elephant suddenly dropped me. That was one of the scariest and most embarrassing things that ever happened to me as a photographer. I never told anyone at the station about it.

When animals get older, their unexpected moves can be dangerous. It's the baby animals that I felt most comfortable with…until the lion cub.

I'm retired now and people often ask me, "Did you like your job?" The answer is, it was a great job, and I tell them why.

It's true I traveled to some of the most interesting cities and towns in the country, ate at some of the best restaurants, and, in addition to chasing after fires and accidents, experienced the fury of a hurricane and witnessed shootouts and tornadoes. It was always a thrill to meet and talk to movie stars, but if you guessed any or all of that as the reason I loved my job, you would be wrong.

It was the unexpected story that I loved most, and an unexpected story involving an animal was best of all. So when I am asked, "Did you like your job?" I tell people how I felt about my favorite assignment.

One day I arrived at work and joined the other photogs, as the reporters liked to call us, and loaded my gear into my news car.

Like a soldier girded for combat, the news car stood ready in the station parking lot while I headed back inside, camera in hand. My camera was like an extra appendage on my body. I took to heart a company memo that directed all photographers never, never ever, to leave the expensive camera exposed, in the car or anywhere.

I locked the camera up in my equipment cage, then checked in at the assignment desk. I got lucky that day. The Assignment Director told me I would be working with reporter Jack Etzel. Jack was one of the most talented reporters in the country. He could have been a network reporter, should have been, but Jack didn't want the big time. He liked where he was, and he was king at what he did. I really liked working with him.

Jack was the station's feature reporter, and his stories were so much more challenging than hard news stories. He covered light news stories. Amusing stories. It sounds easy, but it's very difficult to write and shoot light news (sometimes called "happy news") and make it interesting. Jack was a very creative guy, and I loved working a story with Jack because he always gave the photographer a chance to be creative with the video.

Can a photographer be creative with hard news? Sure, as long as it doesn't distort the story. But most of the time hard news comes at you fast. The whole process happens too quickly for anyone to be very creative. You have to chase down the story, shoot the scene, do the interviews, edit to the reporter's script, and set up for the live shots in the newscasts at five o'clock, five-thirty, six o'clock, and six-thirty. The stress of making all the air times can be overwhelming. In comparison, Jack had one story, and most of the time they gave him a good part of the day to do it.

"There's this guy in Homewood that raises lions," the Assignment Editor told me. "He gets them when they're babies and turns them over to a zoo at about one year old—I think that's what the city ordinance requires. Maybe it's younger than one year. Anyhow, Jack has all the information."

I moseyed on over to Jack's desk, thinking, *How can I shoot this?* Jack was just putting the phone in its cradle when I sat down in a chair beside his desk.

"Did they tell you what we're doing?" he asked.

"Yeah. A guy in a city neighborhood raises lions. How did you find out about him?"

"He called us. I did some checking and found out he does what he says he does. I think this could be a pretty good story. As a matter of fact, I just got off the phone with him. He wants us to come over in about an hour. Got any ideas?"

"I might. Depends on what you want to do with this."

"I can tell you what I don't want to do with it, and that's just do an interview and roll the video of this baby over the interview. We have an opportunity here for a good story, maybe even a few laughs and some gee-whiz video. Why don't you get a cup of coffee? Maybe you'll be able to come up with something. I have to get with the producer and find out where they want us in the show, how long they want the story, and I have to give them the correct spelling of names. I'll meet you out front in twenty minutes."

I took his advice and, with a cup of coffee in hand, sat in the cafeteria daydreaming—my term for thinking creative thoughts. I pictured taking the cub for a walk on a leash and making it look like a giant. I could do it if I opened the lens wide and held the camera just an inch above the sidewalk, right beside the lion, shooting up at it. I could probably get most of the little guy in the picture and also see a lot of the neighborhood. And wouldn't it be great if someone was out walking their dog, and it crossed the street to get out of the lion's way? Maybe throw in a little music and a lion's roar.

I retrieved my camera from its cage and drove up to the front door of the station to pick up Jack. On the way over to Homewood I told him about my ideas. He didn't like the music and the lion roar. He thought that would be too hokey. But he liked walking the cub with a leash.

Jack had a few ideas of his own. "I don't want to do the interview in his house. Let's hook him up with the wireless mike and do a walking interview. I think our guy will accommodate us on that. Then you can shoot all the B-roll you want."

A story like this would require a lot of editing. It's a complicated process. In order to tell the story the way Jack wanted, we would have to shoot the walking interview first. Then I would shoot the B-roll. I would have them do the walk all over again while I got all those interesting shots I thought of when we pulled up to the house, including the shots that would show the baby lion looking like King of the Jungle. Depending on time, I would shoot from every angle I thought I would need in editing. If I did everything Jack and I talked about, the viewer would feel as though they were along for the walk. That's what we planned, and it sounded good to me.

We arrived a few minutes early. Jack helped to carry some gear. He pulled the lights and wireless microphone from the trunk while I grabbed the camera and tripod. I took a quick look up and down the street to check out all the possible camera angles while Jack made sure we had the right address. Once we were sure of the address, we picked up the equipment from the sidewalk and headed for the house.

It was a small brick home set back from a sidewalk lined with trees. The walkway was red brick, the same color as the house. As soon as we turned into the walkway, the front door swung open and a big man with an even bigger smile greeted us. It was clear our interviewee—I think his name was Bill—was excited about being on TV. Bill was at least six feet tall, maybe a little more, and had the physique of a muscle builder. He turned out to be a big powerful man with a gentle handshake and manner. A very likable guy.

We were invited into the house and sat in the living room to talk a bit. I sat down on the end of the couch beside the cellar door, and Jack sat directly across from me, beside the fireplace. Jack told Bill a little about himself and what we would need to tell his story.

Bill told us he wasn't married, that he took care of the cub by himself, and he said it wasn't too much different from taking care of a cat or dog, except for the diet. The cubs he raised had either been abandoned or rejected by their mothers. Jack took notes. We found out that Bill became interested in the baby lions about five years ago after seeing a network story on TV. Jack quizzed him about that for several minutes. He needed all the information he could get so he could ask the most important questions when he did the interview on camera.

While they talked, I checked out my equipment to make sure everything was working. After about twenty minutes, Bill interrupted Jack. "Would you guys like to get acquainted with her now?"

We said, "Sure," and he opened the cellar door.

What looked like a full-grown lion stuck its head out of the door, spotted me, and charged. It didn't have a mane. My first thought was *the female lion is the hunter.* Now, mind you, I was a news photographer who was quick with the camera. And I did act quickly. In an instant, I ignored the camera and turned to run, but there was no place to go. I put one foot up on Bill's couch and was clawing at the wall trying to bring my other foot up. Before I could get both feet on the couch, the lion wrapped its front legs around my leg and yanked me back down on the floor as easy as dropping bacon into a frying pan. The power of big cats is unbelievable.

I could think of nothing else to do but try to break its hold on me. My hands went for its legs. I thought if I could just loosen its hold, I could pull my foot free.

The big cats leg's felt like metal rods. I could not even make a dent in its skin, let alone pull myself free. Then the lion cocked its head to one side and opened its mouth, proudly showing those huge lion teeth, and went for my ankle.

In total despair I brought my head up, screaming, "JACK!" louder than Tarzan calling his jungle animals to rescue him…and I saw Jack laughing. When I turned to Bill, it hadn't yet registered with me that my foot was still attached to my leg. Bill was doubled over with laughter. He was trying to tell me something.

"Baby just playin' witcha."

I looked back down at the lion. The lion was looking up at me, and I swear she was smiling. She released her grip on me and went over to greet Jack. I had assumed that all this talk about baby was about *a baby lion.* It never dawned on me that her *name* was "Baby." I reached down to smooth out my pants and realized Baby had been so gentle that I never felt her teeth on my leg. My pant leg was not torn, and even the hair on my head was not messed up.

"You didn't hear me, did you?" Jack said.

"Just now?" I asked.

"No, when she grabbed you. I said, 'Get a shot of this.'"

"Very funny," I said, and we all had a good laugh at that thought.

Baby came back over to me, and this time I got a chance to greet her warmly. I wondered if my children would believe me when I told them that I hugged a lion. She, of course, was not full-grown, but close to full-grown.

Her head would get bigger, and she had not yet developed the muscle of a mature lion. I don't think it would have made a bit of difference if I'd had that information when Baby charged me.

Bill took Baby for a walk on a thick leash attached to a very thick collar. It occurred to me that he was able to walk her because of his great strength. If the lion wanted to chase a dog, Bill could handle it. Walking the big cat was something he normally did. So we did not fabricate that part, or any part of the story, for that matter. *I still need something for this story to be complete,* I thought, and just then an older gentleman walked out of his driveway on our side of the street with his dog on a leash. I got my gee-whiz shot when the man got close enough to see a lion heading his way. His mouth dropped open, and both he and his dog hurried across the street. It was surprising to me that Baby showed little interest in the dog. She did not pull on the leash. I remembered Bill telling Jack earlier that Baby was well fed. What I didn't hear was that part of the diet was raw meat, because of her age. And this is why Bill had called us, because she was almost one year old, and he was getting ready to turn her over to a zoo.

There is a postscript to this story. After we shot the entire story, we did what is called a stand-up-close. This is where the reporter appears on camera and wraps up the story for the audience. It is then edited onto the end of the story.

Jack asked me if I had any ideas how we should do this stand-up-close. I didn't, nor did he. It was getting late. We were running out of time.

"Listen," he said, "we're just going to have to shoot it here in the street with the lion sitting beside me."

"If we do," I said, "I'll have to shoot a wide shot in order to get you both in the picture."

"If that's what we have to do, then let's do it. It's getting late."

"Wait a minute," I said. "Let's put Baby up on the hood of the car and you can sit beside her."

Bill said it wasn't a problem. And it wasn't. Baby and Jack got right up there and sat side by side. They were the same height. I could get an extreme close-up if I wanted. It was perfect.

After I set up for the shot, I cued him. Jack started talking off the cuff and suddenly stopped. He said he didn't like that one. I cued him again, he stopped again. A third time, and Jack did the same thing. Meanwhile, Baby was getting bored. Really bored. Jack started to talk a fourth time and liked what he was saying. When he came to the part where he mentioned Baby's name, he turned his head to her, not realizing that Baby was in the middle of a giant yawn. His face went right into the mouth of the lion. If you saw this story when it ran, I'm sure you would remember a photographer once again lose it and scream, "JACK!" in the background. The station aired it exactly as it was shot, scream and all. As for Jack, he withdrew his face from Baby's mouth, turned to the camera and, with great dignity, closed out the story.

To this day I believe Jack Etzel is the only reporter in Pittsburgh to stick his head in the mouth of a lion. Well, his face, at least. Baby wasn't large enough to fit an entire human head in her mouth.

Before leaving, I gave Baby a hug, and the feeling was indescribable. I knew I would never forget this assignment. When I left Homewood and headed for the station, I felt like I had the greatest job in the world and wouldn't trade it for anything. This is what I tell people when they ask me, "Did you like your job?"

INTERRUPTION

Anne Whitlock

On the carpet
I'm surrounded
by important papers—
bills, receipts and records
when Tom, the tomcat,
ambles in from the garden,
steps on every paper,
settles himself right on top
of the mortgage bill
and lays his head on my leg.

I'm grounded, connected
soul to soul in silence
to a warm ball of vibrating fur
and two dilated yellow eyes—
to a primordial power source
from another time and space.

All at once, ears up scope,
responding to a silent alarm,
Tommy's on his feet,
cutting the current,
releasing me—
my hands move again
and I reach for a pen.

My Big Opportunity

Fred Bridges

I was patrolling the back yard looking for other Toms who were in my territory. I always gave them my best Cheshire cat smile, and then pounced on their back and rode them like a bronco around the yard. Wow, I must be getting old. I only lasted two laps around the yard on the last ride.

Everything outside was going well, but inside you might say I was in the doghouse. I could have mentioned the other type of house, except that might have offended the more genteel.

The incident where I was caught on the kitchen counter with a turkey leg and the time when I sharpened my nails on the furniture did not go over well with the lady of the house. What was I to do? A cat has to keep his nails in top form. The question now was how could I redeem myself and regain the respect of my humans? I miss the lady's soft lap, bits of toast in the morning, and lying between the master's legs on the recliner.

The best place to ponder this is under the leaves of the rhubarb. An idea came to me as I was dreaming there that would make me king of the garden. Perhaps this would be my big moment. I would rid the garden of those grey rodents. At that moment, a grey body ran between the cornstalks and into a burrow. This sent the adrenalin rushing through my body, and the sinews of my muscles began to flex. This would be my greatest moment. I would catch each one and align them by the patio door.

Carefully hiding by the burrow's entrance, I waited. Sounds of laughter floated up from below. "Who is afraid of the big bad cat?" flitted up to my ears. One by one, they ventured into the garden and were soon in my grasp. I carefully carried each one to the patio door and aligned them all in perfect order. This was my biggest opportunity, and I jumped up on a patio chair so I could watch the moment unfold. They might place a medal on my collar.

The lady of the house opened the door to let out the children, who were carrying cold drinks. The children laughed and giggled and said, "Look what Moses has brought for Mom!"

She shrieked for the master. "Fred, get those things out of here!"

My first thought was to hide under the rhubarb leaves as I watched my prizes disappear and laughter filled the patio. But the lady picked me up and stroked my back, saying, "Moses, this was your finest moment. Just don't do it again."

The Visitation of Mr. Black

Marie Thérèse Gass

One morning that summer, Madeleine was just standing there watching me brush out her raised kitty bed in the corner of the garage, when another black cat, a stranger, stuck his head through the little door and called once, softly. Not meowed, but called with one syllable. His voice sounded so much like human speech that I just stared at him.

Usually I chase other cats away, as Madeleine has indicated she doesn't want them in her domain. And some who've hung around our acre have been diseased. One morning I had to bury a grey shorthair found outside the locked cat door. By the time I discovered what was left of him after some fight he'd been in, the cat had rigor mortis, so his burial hole had to be quite wide. I planted a fern on top of the grave so no one would dig it up by accident.

I was surprised not to hear any menacing territorial growls from our kitty at the advent of this Mr. Black. I looked back at him again. He hadn't moved or meowed and seemed to be waiting for Madeleine's decision, or maybe mine. Then he stepped in through the cat door and I noticed the oddest thing—this kitty was a dead ringer for Madeleine. Hairs on my arms began to rise. No other visiting feline had even remotely looked like her. Madeleine had long silky midnight black hair which rippled when she bounded across the yard. She moved delicately, like a lady, and weighed a little less than most kitties her size. Acutely aware of everything, she was a good hunter of shrews and baby moles, yet would patiently lie on my lap listening to confidences for hours. And she loved to snuggle more than anything—always and everywhere.

I pride myself at being good at art puzzles—you know, the ones that ask you to find some minute dissimilarity between two nearly identical sketches—so I thought that finding how Black contrasted would be a cinch. Systematically, I studied the two adult cats, methodically noting Black's size, length of fur, ear stance, fuzziness of tail, all of which were indistinguishable from Madeleine's. At first, I could see no difference at all. It was only when I reexamined Black's eyes that I noticed they were slightly more hazel than Maddie's soft green, but so close that you couldn't tell which kitty you were looking at if you only saw one of them.

We live about thirty miles from the pound where we'd gotten Madeleine, so he couldn't possibly be her sibling. Or could he?

Mr. Black stood there in silence like a gentleman waiting for his prom date, definitely not about to be scared away. Then, to my surprise, Madeleine suddenly ran to the door to greet this guy, as though she'd been waiting for him all her life. They stood there nose to nose a moment. Uh…Maddie, I began, and she looked up at me as if to say, It's okay, Mom. We're going out to play. I reminded myself that she'd been spayed as she disappeared out the cat door like a sister act.

For weeks that summer, those two felines spent time together on the back deck crouched nose to nose, dozing in the sun or speaking to each other in a kind of shorthand. He would open his mouth and utter a succession of vowels, each followed by a glottal stop—no meows or yowls—and she would listen until he finished, then answer in kind. I had never heard Madeleine, or any other cat, make those sounds before. Whenever I came close, they'd stop and look at me as if to say, Hello, how are you, we're in the middle of this conversation, so goodbye for now.

One day when I could hear them verbalizing from where I was working on the other side of the hedge, I decided to find out exactly what they were doing. Who knew how long this would last and if I'd ever get to the bottom of it? Quietly, I tiptoed across the grass to the deck and sat down on the middle stair. Both black kitties were by now motionless and silent, watching me. Excuse me, I said softly, in case they also understood English, You can go on talking. I'm going to sit here and listen. I said nothing more and did not move a muscle. Black looked at Madeleine, and she made a single sound. Then they began speaking again, back and forth alternately—a long conversation, as if he'd been away for years and they were catching up. I wondered if they were trapped human souls. Finally, they rose simultaneously and touched noses. Mr. Black rubbed his shoulders gently against hers, then turned and walked away. No glancing back. I never saw him again.

Some days later, still curious, but not having been able to figure it out, I brought up the situation with Madeleine. Who was that Mr. Black? I asked. Maddie paused to glance at me, then continued cleaning her fur, not saying a word. It really wasn't my business.

Requiem for My Dog

Maurice Hirsch

I emptied your ashes into the manure spreader.
Carla's ashes, thrown
into the ocean a decade ago,
were heavy, granular,
black and white mixed.
Yours are pure white and fine as pastry flour.
The white box with the saccharine
note from the cremation company
taped to its lid held a bag
much smaller than I expected,
not much left.
So I spread them like a soft white blanket
over the week's accumulation of bedding and manure,
opened the gate to the pasture,
pulled up the levers on the spreader
so its contents would fan
in a brown-and-white arc
as I crisscrossed the field
where you had trailed behind,
waited for tasty droppings
to hit the ground, sorted through them
in your mouth, mined undigested grain
to eat with relish. You slept on the top
of the hay pile where I placed your cardboard urn today.
You pawed bales to make nests,
always greeted me with a toothy smile,
eager to give me a dog kiss. Your fourteen years
ended as I turned 70. I still look
for you hunting mice, moles,
anything burrowing,
so you could dig a hole.

Jumpin' Jack Flash

Buck Dopp

It started harmlessly enough. Stephanie drove to a pet store to buy a new collar for Mac, our nine-year-old golden retriever. She noticed a sign that read, "SALE! GOLDEN RETRIEVER MALE PUPPIES! $350 MARKED DOWN FROM $700." She saw three six-month-old puppies climbing all over each other, playing, biting, and gnawing on their littermates. In the adjacent cage she spotted a solitary puppy that, for some reason, was segregated from the rest of the litter. When he caught sight of her, he stood on his hind legs and braced himself with his front paws while squeezing his snout through the bars, trying to get a better look at Stephanie. His eyes locked onto hers like heat-seeking missiles, and he grinned so widely she could see his tonsils.

She asked if she could take the puppy to the playroom to spend a little time with him. Puppies in pet stores are known for their, "Take Me! Take Me!" look. This dog's expression said, "I'll take *you!*" The attraction was mutual and immediate. Stephanie fell in love with the little guy, and there would be no turning back.

The next day, she took me to the pet store to visit the young golden retriever. "We're not going to buy it," she promised. "I just want you to see him, he's really adorable."

"That's good, because we don't need a second dog—so it would be a waste of our time and money to get one," I said.

Stephanie nodded. "That's right. The last thing we need right now is another dog."

We took our granddaughter along with us to the pet store. I told her, "We're not getting another dog, 'cause we're too busy doing other things. Grandma just wants to show us a golden retriever she saw yesterday, and then we'll get something to eat."

As soon as the little dog was placed on the floor of the room, he started picking up every little toy, one right after the other, as if to say, "See how good I am at picking up all these toys? Aren't I special? Don't you think I'm about the cutest thing you've ever seen?"

In rapid succession, he performed every trick he knew; this was his big chance to impress us, and he wasn't going to waste it. His scheme to win us over worked. We concluded that the little showoff was smart, talented, and athletic. Then he started jumping up and down. We marveled, because it didn't seem possible that a little puppy could jump so high.

Then tragedy struck. He had launched himself like a rocket high in the air and landed with his leg in an awkward position, which snapped the bone in two. His boundless joy and energy in motion stopped. He lay crumpled on the floor, stunned. Then he started howling in excruciating pain. I picked him up and saw that his leg was crooked and hanging at an odd angle. A woman came and took him away.

We called the store later to find out what happened to him. An employee told us the doctor set the bone, put the leg in a cast, and sent him back to the store. The woman paused for a few seconds and lowered her voice to a whisper. "The manager said he's probably going to put him to sleep because he's already lost money on the dog and doesn't want to pay for more medical treatment. We still have three other males from that litter available for purchase."

"Can we visit him?" I asked.

"Sure," she said. "One other thing…the nurse told us she'd never seen a dog tolerate pain the way that puppy could."

The next day, we paid him a visit. He was alone in a cage in a dark storeroom. His right rear leg was bound in a cast made with a red gauze wrap. He wore a halo protector around his neck to keep him from chewing on the cast. We thought he might associate us with the trauma of the previous day and be afraid of us. No way. He immediately jumped up on three legs, holding his broken leg in the air. and started barking. as if to say, "I'm so happy to see you again! I knew you'd come back. Let's play some more."

We visited him again on Sunday, even though the store was closed for business. On Monday, I negotiated with the manager, offering to take full responsibility for the dog's medical treatment if we could take him home that day. "Can you give us a discount on the price?" I asked.

"I've already lost money on him. I'll waive the purchase price, but you have to agree to pay all the medical bills and, if he has to be put to sleep, you pay for that too."

"Deal," I said.

We took him home that night and named him Jumpin' Jack Flash. He wasn't supposed to walk on his broken leg, so we held him in our laps that night until we went to bed. We did that every night for the next six weeks. Whenever he got excited, he would pee on us, and he got excited a lot.

When new x-rays were taken after a couple of weeks, they revealed that the leg had not healed; instead the bone was separating. The vet said that, if the trend continued, Flash would need surgery to install a screw in the bone to hold it together. We continued to hope for the best and did everything we could to keep Flash from walking on his bad leg. In our home we carried him around in our arms like a baby and took him for walks in a baby stroller that we picked up at a secondhand store. By the third cast changing and x-rays, the bone had started to grow back together, and a month later they removed the cast permanently. His bone healed so well that, when we looked at the x-ray, we couldn't tell where the break had been. Now he runs and jumps with no trace of a limp.

We could have bought one of his brothers for $350, while Flash's medical bills ran over $2000, but we got the best value of all. He's worth every penny and more. Besides, how can you not love a dog who is willing to break his leg to get your attention?

A Visitor for the Winter or A Bad Weather Friend

Suse Marsh

It is customary in Germany to open the windows at dusk for a few minutes before pulling the drapes for the night. Forced air heat is not known there, and the reason for the ventilation is to exchange the used-up air and get some fresh oxygen into the rooms.

There was a nice size magnolia tree in front of our living/dining room windows. It was also the perfect tree for our bird feeder. The feeder always was a very busy place for all kinds of different birds and provided us with entertainment, watching and identifying the species. One evening with the windows wide open, a Rotkehlchen flew in and made the rounds of the living room before landing on an indoor plant in the corner. This was a red-breasted songbird the size of a finch, and we were stunned at his unexpected appearance. He seemed quite content on his perch, so we finally closed the windows and drapes for the night. We decided to keep our distance, and when it was time to go to bed, we turned out the lights and closed the door.

The next morning we found the bird restless, so my mother opened the window and he left. That evening the bird was waiting again by the bird feeder, and as soon as we opened the window he flew in and took his perch on the plant stand among the houseplants. We were really puzzled by this bird; his behavior was definitely very intentional. We called him Hansi, and he was our houseguest for several weeks, until the weather became warmer. Hansi was not housebroken, however, and as time went by he chose to sit on the chandelier or the drapery rod.

Spring came and we didn't see Hansi anymore. We all know that some birds migrate to warmer climates in winter and come back to the same places in the spring. Rotkehlchen do not migrate from the Black Forest area, and so it shouldn't have been a surprise for us when Hansi appeared again the following winter. He settled right back into his routine and stayed again till spring. After that Hansi disappeared for good, and we often wondered what happened to him.

Yes, we are all God's creatures, great and small.

THE COPYCAT BIRD

Kathleen Lesniak

Birds fill the world with many fascinating sights and sounds. Each bird species has its own special color, size, and song.

Mockingbirds have gray feathers. They are endowed with a large number of vocal muscles which enable them to sing a most remarkable repertoire.

Monica, one of the first daughters of the Mockingbird family, was not satisfied with her modest features. She considered gray to be a dull color. She thought she was not as pretty as the more colorful birds.

"How wonderful it would be to have feathers of bright blue, or red, or yellow!" she wished as she daydreamed during her daily lesson.

"Monica, please pay attention," her Mother scolded. "It is important that you and your brother learn about the unique talent that our family possesses."

"What is it? Please tell me," Monica begged.

"We can duplicate the calls and songs of other birds. Once we hear the musical notes of our neighbors, we are able to repeat them perfectly. We can also combine their sounds into lovely melodies for all to enjoy," her Mother informed her.

"Aha! Now that I know I can copy the voices of other birds, I shall compose a medley of *all* their lyrics to amaze them. They will envy such a masterful musician!" Monica boasted.

"Oh no, dear daughter, do not be mischievous. You must be very careful," her Mother cautioned, "for songs and calls are meant to convey messages and signal concerns, especially if danger is close by." Mother Mockingbird then began teaching the meaning of each call that she sang, stressing to her students, "You need to learn these sounds and memorize their meanings. Practice by reciting after me."

While her brother enthusiastically mimicked his mother's calls, Monica halfheartedly participated in the exercise. Her mind drifted off to her plans for the following day.

~

When morning's dawn crept into the meadow, Monica quietly ventured out alone. She had already tested her wings and was able to glide over miles of lush landscape. Today, she intended to travel farther than she had ever flown before.

She knew that the sun woke up in the east, so she soared high in the sky and flew toward the sun as it rose from the earth in its rich tones of gold. While she was flying, she heard another bird shrieking, "Thief, thief." She scanned the area and spied a Blue Jay in a thicket. She quickly landed near him. She observed the Jaybird as he devoured the small blue orbs of fruit that bulged from the bush. She approached him as he dined.

"Go away, gray bird!" the Jay shouted at her as he fluttered about.

Monica ignored his warning and instead tried to imitate his screeching sound. The Jay gave her a puzzled look and hopped away. Monica thought she must have copied his shrill call *so well* that he was allowing her to eat his berries. She was delighted to learn that the tempting treat tasted quite sweet.

"Perhaps I have uncovered a clue," Monica pondered as she partook of the fruit. "These blueberries might be the secret of how the Jay obtained such a brilliant blue suit."

The Jaybird returned and frantically flapped his wings at Monica. "You are trespassing on my territory," he protested. "My mate and I have nestlings nearby. They are waiting for me to bring them their breakfast."

But Monica stubbornly continued to invade the boundary he guarded, for she was determined to turn blue. After two duels, the Jay finally persuaded Monica to depart from the shrubbery.

She sought refuge in a huge tree that contained ruby-colored fruit that hung like a garland from its branches. There she came upon a Cardinal, who was greedily gobbling up the cherries. He paused occasionally and whistled his carol.

"Now I have certainly discovered how the redbird acquired his radiant red-crested costume!" Monica exclaimed. She attempted to befriend the Cardinal by mimicking his trilling tune. She hoped he would consent to sharing the juicy cherries.

"You cannot trick me with your mocking," the Cardinal snickered. "I can tell by the color of your coat that you are not one of my kinfolk. Find something else to eat, for I have summoned my fledglings to come and feed on this fruit." Then the Cardinal attacked Monica with such force that she plummeted to the ground.

Her tail ruffled and her pride wounded, Monica stumbled through the grove. She noticed activity ahead and soon encountered a Robin in a large orchard that was festively decorated with fuzzy orange ornaments. She was immediately attracted to the Robin's flaming red chest. She studied how the Robin busily gathered as much fruit as his beak could hold, and then carried it away to a nest close by.

Monica caught a glimpse of another Robin, who was roosting on that nest. Moments later, the Robin's partner arrived and repeated the procedure. Monica was convinced that the peaches were the reason for the fire-colored velvet vests the Robins wore. She wasted no time in learning the language the Robin parents chattered. She cheerily chirped at each of them as they filled their bills with food for their brood.

Whenever both of the Robins were gone, Monica pecked at the plump peaches and gulped down their delicious pulp. "At last, I shall be able to change my color to a more handsome hue!" Monica sighed contentedly.

Suddenly, the Robins came back together. They squawked at Monica, "Why do you try to deceive us, young minstrel? Leave us alone, for we fear our offspring are not safe with you here." They dove at Monica and drove her from their source of sustenance.

Furious and frustrated, Monica decided to return to her family. She remembered that she should head home in the direction of the setting sun. While she flew, she witnessed the glowing globe silently slipping toward the western horizon. Suddenly, rolling clouds filled the sky and cast a veil of darkness over the land. During the downpour of rain, Monica rested and sipped a few drops to quench her thirst. Then she desperately began to search for familiar sights and sounds.

As she approached each flock of birds, it was difficult to determine which family was hers. Without the sun's bright light shining on them, all of the birds along the way looked GRAY!

She landed near a nest that looked similar to hers and listened for familiar voices. Instead, she heard some hatchlings crying. Monica wanted to help the nestlings. She remembered how her parents sang soothing lullabies to her when she was frightened. Since she could not tell which species of birds they belonged to, she did not know which song to sing to them. So she decided to compose a medley of all the tunes she had learned during the day. Her music calmed the young birds, and she stayed with them until their parents returned to the nest. They thanked her for comforting their offspring while they gathered food.

As Monica resumed her search for home, the clouds cleared, and a radiant rainbow appeared. At that moment, she recognized the singing of her sibling. Her brother, Michael, was perched high on top of a tall sycamore tree, serenading his sweetheart. He leaped and floated above the tree's foliage as his love song filled the crisp twilight air.

Monica rudely interrupted him and told him of her misadventures. She bad-mouthed the other birds and complained of her sad plight as a drab-colored creature.

"It is a pity that you were not here today," Michael said. "Father gave us our last lesson before we must leave home to build our own nests. He explained how our feathers help us."

"They help us to fly," Monica retorted.

"No, that is not their purpose. Our waterproof feathers protect our skin from cold and hot weather. And birds are the only animals that have feathers!" Michael boasted.

"What does it matter?" Monica moaned. "Nobody ever looks at our gray feathers when they can gaze upon all the flocks who are robed in the colors of the rainbow."

"The colors of feathers do not affect the function they serve," Michael replied. "Tell me, did the colors of feathers help you find your way home?" he asked.

"No, they didn't…but being gray is *so* boring!" she whined.

"Have you forgotten about our powerful voices?" Michael reminded her. "Our neighbors are always looking to see who sings such beautiful rhapsody."

"If that is true, why did the Blue Jay, the Cardinal, and the Robins chase me away today?" Monica inquired.

"Because it was impolite to disturb the other birds while they were busy supplying food for their families," Michael admonished her.

"But how will I *ever* be able to feast on the fruit that makes the other birds' feathers so colorful?" Monica insisted.

"The fruit is not what produced their color. Each family has its own coloring." Michael spoke emphatically. "Do not think of gray as a lack of luster, for it is the color of many of our world's wonders."

"Like what?" Monica asked.

"Like the gray clouds that nourish nature with the refreshing rain we need to flourish," Michael told her, "and evening's gray shade that calms the world for a restful night's sleep."

"Yes, the rain refreshed me, and the shade calmed me when I was tired," Monica admitted. "So I now realize that we have *both* beauty and skill!" she exclaimed.

"You must *never* forget that our musical ability was given to us so we could perform symphonies that bring pleasure to all who listen," Michael instructed her.

"I will treasure our gift of vocal mimicry and always share it carefully," Monica promised.

Then the sibling duo sang in harmony as they took flight in search of homes of their own.

SUNDAY DINNER

Una Nichols Hynum

All the leaves in place, we gather around the dining table,
eight of us – Mother, worrying whether the eldest
daughter's latest beau is Jewish. She has baked ham glistening
with honey and crosses of cloves. Once my sister invited
a Catholic lad on a Friday when we were having roast beef.
Father makes a grand entrance in time to carve. He brings
up butchering hogs, the halves hanging in the barn.
Mother counters with the joy of raising a piglet on a bottle.
The conversation moves from molasses to nutmeg, from
Massachusetts cranberry bogs to Louisiana pecan orchards.
Small history and geography lessons, subtle rehash of the Civil War.
We roll our eyes – thankful when crystal-music starts from rims
wet with spit on a finger. Who can make the loudest squeal.

thunderstorm
on the table candle flames
rowing in the dark

The Tablecloth

John Barbee

The table has been the centerpiece of our lives every since we first blended our two families together and started life over. We loved each other deeply, but we also loved our children dearly and were determined to meld our new relationship into one big happy family. Lots of thought and effort went into each decision, no matter how big or small. My bed or hers, which refrigerator or maybe both, which car insurer and milkman? Each one of a thousand decisions was evaluated for its importance in our new life.

The most important item of furniture, we decided, was the dining room table, where we would gather each night for supper to discuss the day's problems and try to re-solve them. However, we both had tables that seated only six. What was needed was a large table that seated ten or twelve, because you can't have important deliberations if you're all crammed together at a small table.

The table, when we found it, was solid maple, magnificent, old, heavy, and bore the scars of a long and useful life. After stripping, sanding, re-staining, and the application of three coats of lacquer, it became the center of our family life. Tablecloths for this large, important part of our lives were pricey, but well worth the money. Over the years, we purchased or made many new coverings to protect this altar of our life, and always it wore a protective pad underneath the covering to preserve its beauty.

In later years, after our children were grown and gone, the two of us began eating in the kitchen, but the table was always kept suitably attired. Its leaves were never removed and stored in their flannel sleeves; the table always remained extended, waiting for the next family gathering. Sometimes, its surface was bare to show off the beauty of its wood with place mats and plants or flowers in the center; other times, it wore cloth coverings of warm tans, bright reds, or soothing forest green. Then came the day when I bought what was to become the table's best tablecloth.

There is in our rural community a very small church, attended mostly by Mexican fieldworkers who have come to start a new life in this country. The church is tattered, worn, and in need of repairs, but the joyful singing and praying that comes from this congregation on Sunday mornings is enough to gladden the heart of anyone who happens to pass by. The congregation, in their quest to keep their church financially afloat, hold raffles, bingo nights, and rummage sales.

One Friday afternoon as I passed by, they were having a sale. Stopping to see if there was anything I could buy to help their cause along, I was disappointed to find only old clothing, worn-out tools, and repaired small appliances. Then, suddenly, I noticed hanging from the top edge of the porch one of the most beautiful tablecloths I had ever seen. It was large enough for our table: heavy linen, cream-colored with an embroidered scene in the center of an old mission decorated for Christmas and the words, "Feliz Navidad," below. It was well worth the price asked, but it was still a lot of money. Telling myself it would be two presents in one—a Christmas gift for my wife, but also for our table—I dug into the secret compartment of my wallet to get just enough money to buy this work of art. After taking it home, I wrapped it in a pillow case, then hid it in my closet to wait for Christmas. But for us Christmas never came that year; it was the year my beloved wife went to be with our Lord.

For years the table sat there looking forlorn, lonesome, and abandoned, wearing a red wrapping that went untouched. Then, one day, noticing that the tablecloth was dusty, I added it to my laundry. Instead of changing to a new covering, I intended to put the old red one back on, but didn't get to it. Like the red tablecloth, my life went on, unchanging, in the same old rut until last year.

As I age, the energy of life has been slowly leaking from my old bones, and I decided to get help. A man was hired to wash my windows, a yardman to hack and prune, then, lastly, someone to dust and vacuum. My house cleaner is the young daughter of a family down the road, and she is trying to become the first in her family to get a college degree. She cleans between classes and does a great job, but she feels sorry for me because I live alone, without my family around me. A kindhearted person, she always looks for ways to do a little something extra to brighten my life. Last month, after she finished cleaning, she then asked if there was anything else she could do.

I told her where the tablecloths were and said to pick one out to cover the table, but not to reuse the old red one I had been using. Then I went to get her money.

When I returned, she stood staring into the drawer with tears in her eyes. I asked what was wrong, and she explained they were tears of joy; because the tablecloth had found a good home. She said her grandmother had spent years making it for her mother, and her mother had brought it with her when she came to this country. She had parted with her prized keepsake to help her church raise money for repairs and had always wondered where it had gone. The girl said her mother, who knew and liked me, would be pleased it had found a good Christian home.

Sometimes the right gifts are hard to pick out, but this information gave me an easy choice. I had been in a quandary about what to get my young house cleaner for Christmas. Money was an obvious gift, but although she got paid, she acted more like her work was a kindness, and she might be offended. So the last workday before Christmas I gave the tablecloth to her, to be shared with her mother and family.

The beautiful bit of art work is now back with its family, where it belongs, and I think they may have shared the story. My Mexican neighbors have always been kind, friendly, and helpful, but now sometimes ones I don't even know will slow or stop their car, wave, and call out a good morning or...

"Feliz Navidad."

Second Runner-up: Best Poetry Contest

People a la Carte

Maurice Hirsch

Both in their sixties, well coifed
and made up, in Nashville
for the SEC women's basketball
tournament, they're dressed
in orange Lady Vol t-shirts
with "We back Pat"
on the front, a tribute
to a giant who's slipping
into darkness. Their waiter approached, asked
whether they were doing the breakfast
buffet or ordering a la carte. He has
a European accent we couldn't quite place.
The one with her back to us asked
where he is from. "Kosovo."
And how did he get to Nashville?
He told his story, nothing special.
Then she said: "What religion
are you?" I flinched. Without
a pause, perhaps not wanting to offend
a customer, hurt his tip, he responded:
"Muslim." She said,
"Jesus loves you. I'll have the buffet."

KITCHENS

Judy Ray

Dusty pink, which must have some more exotic name in the color charts of interior decorators, laminates the surfaces—counter, cabinets, and table—of the remodeled kitchen in our 1940s house in Tucson. The working space is very small, a butt-bumping turnaround if more than one person attempts a task at stove, sink, cupboard, limited countertop, or refrigerator at the same time. And I think of how much time in our lives—especially those of us who prepare meals and wash dishes—is spent in these corners, or centerpieces, of our homes.

A significant space from my childhood was the kitchen of the early seventeenth century farmhouse my parents lived in for more than fifty years in Sussex in the south of England.

A black-topped Rayburn range almost always had wood and/or coal burning in the grate—the fire that cooked our food, boiled the kettle, warmed irons, and heated the water tank and large room. First thing in the morning the stove was lit, usually by placing crumpled newspaper over a few red embers still hot in ashes from the night before. The accumulated ash was riddled and jiggled out into a pan below the grate and thrown into a corner of the garden. If clinkers of coal or coke were left behind, they might be added to a pathway through the mud. Lighting the stove in the kitchen, and towards evening lighting a fire in the dining room—which served also as living room, though we did not know that term—was generally my father's chore. He could quickly coax a bright blaze with careful sequence of paper, kindling, "seconds," and finally logs or longer-lasting coal. Perhaps identification of such elemental chores with my father is why I hold Robert Hayden's "Those Winter Sundays" as my special secret poem. There, too, a father gets up early and makes "banked fires blaze."

In winter, the kitchen with the constant Rayburn was the warmest place in the cold house, yet it was often cold, too, having a painted concrete floor and an easterly door, under which the wind blew.

Yet it was my mother whose life hovered close to the kitchen range. The stove's efficiency would vary with differences in wood or coal and especially in response to force and direction of wind, which might draw the fire to blaze like a furnace, despite fixing the damper, or might send puffs of smoke back down the chimney to a slow-poke glow. Dinner, the midday hot meal, always managed to be on the table on time, but often my mother would have spent much of the morning juggling pans around the hot and cooler parts of the stove, watching a slow oven, and putting off her baking until the oven temperature rose.

On days when the laundry had not flapped dry on the clothesline outside, it would have to be finished off hanging across the kitchen or piled on a barred shelf over the stove. And there's a gesture of lifting clean laundry and touching it lightly against the cheek to test for dampness that gets passed on. My grandmother did it. My mother did it. Not saying, "This is how you test the laundry," but saying, "I think this sheet is still a bit damp."

The light oak table in that kitchen had been scrubbed hard so many times that the wood grain was deeply grooved. A cloth covered it for meals. Drawers at each end held the everyday cutlery and cloths, and usually screeched slightly as they were pulled out. Mrs. Beeton's famous old recipe book was kept in the drawer, too, a book we laughed at for its assumptions of large households. "Take two dozen eggs," we used to joke, "and a bushel of flour…" Beside a corner of the table and close to the middle of the room a very hard black oak post, a round support column, was a reminder of the long history of the house and a link with ancient oak trees on the farm and surrounding common lands.

Half of the kitchen, nearest the back door, was dark—dark with a big cupboard where the outdoor work clothes were kept, the farmyard-smelling coats, the wool or straw hats. It was a string cupboard, too—always an extra big spool of binder-twine as well as bits of saved string—and a rag cupboard, and a shoe-cleaner cupboard with polish for Sunday shoes—again, an echo of Hayden's poem, where it is the father who does this weekly, simple task of service for others.

Big Wellington boots stood under the draining board by the sink, boots that were often muddy despite efforts to get them wiped off on the grass or the mat on the way in, and a wooden bootboard with its gaping Y was available to hold the boot's heel as the foot was slipped out. Lifting the big

wooden latch of the back door, men—my father and my brother and whoever was working with them on the farm—would enter and stand briefly
in work clothes, bringing a message, sipping a quick cup of mid-morning
coffee, taking a breather before heading out for a job in the yard or across
the fields.

At these times the kitchen seemed divided into masculine and feminine,
dark and light, farm work and house work, but it was a place of connection, too, and of security—the family hearth. In the pure darkness of night,
distant from town or other houses, a warm light beamed out the kitchen
window, seen across meadows. Electricity connections did not reach that
community until after I had left home for college, so in my early recollections the light was shed from an Aladdin paraffin lamp with its fragile mantle
inside a tall glass chimney, or dimly from a candle carried to an upstairs room
with flickering orange light on walls crisscrossed with black oak beams.

Since that farmhouse time I have used many kitchens, claiming some as
mine for months or years, but I do not intend to make this a litany of such
spaces. I will mention, however, the first I felt responsible for that was mine
and not mine.

When I went as a newlywed to live in Uganda, for three years that extended to six, we rented a house at the outskirts of the city, beyond paved
roads, and were told by my teacher husband's headmaster that a "houseboy"
named Joseph was already living in a room in the back garden and wanted to
work for us, to clean and to cook. I did not want to have a servant. I had not
run a house before, I wanted to experiment with cooking once I learned my
way around the small shops and market, and I felt uneasy with hiring someone to do things we should be able to take care of for ourselves. But there was
an economic expectation that we would help others by giving them jobs.

So Joseph, shy and whimsical, became part of our household and took
over the kitchen. The small house had so many doors between its rooms
or leading to the outside that it must have been designed by an investor in
hinges. And the kitchen was about three yards away from the house, linked
by a short passage. It spoke separation, not connection. The room was small
and dark, with an electric stove, a sink, and a couple of deep shelves made
of cement, one at counter height and a lower one serving for storage as well
as a bench.

Joseph knew how to cook basic English food, and often I just left him to it, after we discussed our likes and dislikes. And he also took on the task of cooking up a big pot of what we were told was *posho* (though some people call the porridge-like mix of maize or cassava meal *ugali*) with chunks of meat thrown in to feed our dog, Rikki, a mutt who was half Rhodesian Ridgeback. But at that time I had also fallen in love with Elizabeth David's *Mediterranean Food* and, finding approximate ingredients, would experiment with her recipes while Joseph looked on, eager to increase his own culinary repertoire.

There is an odd phenomenon in our consciousness that seals a particular place and event together, even though the place might be a familiar location and the event a small blip. For example, my mind's eye often sees exactly where a coyote trotted out of a Tucson alley early one crisp Christmas morning, and where someone tripped at a sidewalk bump and took a fall.

So, too, in that Ugandan kitchen, the concrete bench, where often friends of Joseph came to sit and chat while he worked, became imprinted with sight of a snake, long and coiled. Joseph shrieked with a slam of the door, and we retreated into the house, terrified. There are, indeed, many poisonous snakes in Africa, but it was a shock to find one in the kitchen next to the vegetables. Joseph declared that his friend Musa, who worked odd jobs in *shambas* or gardens, liked to kill snakes and was very good at the task, so he was summoned and fulfilled the promise.

Shadow memories in dreams have not taken me back to that faraway place, but they have led me many times to the first farmhouse kitchen. Before the dream I might have seen excited, floury hands in the mixing bowl, other hands pouring cups of tea, the postman reaching inside the door to leave shiny brown envelopes perched on the edge of the sink, a rambler rose nodding outside the small-paned window. In a dream, the door opens with lifted latch and there will be posed a scene like those *tableaux vivants* with familiar characters (usually including my parents) around the kitchen table. There is a moment when I think I could retreat—I am never quite sure. They hold still and silent, as though they are just about to react to some important piece of news. Maybe domestic, maybe national. Maybe happy, maybe disturbing. They have played all the parts, and this is the stage.

Cooking From Scratch

Willene C. Auslam

T
he first steps toward cooking from scratch were those down from the back porch to the chicken yard. I hesitated, but knew Grandmother would not be pleased if I didn't take them.

It was the summer just before I was twelve years old when I went to visit my Davis grandparents in Miami, Texas. Grandmother was known as an excellent cook and was going to teach me some basics around the kitchen. I assumed, incorrectly, the first steps to the culinary lessons would be maybe Jello, boiling eggs, or making toast. Boy, was I wrong!

Her noon menu (called dinner in 1939) the first day would feature fried chicken. That meant we had to catch the fryer, slay it, clean it, and cut it up before frying it. Okay. I did catch the one Grandmother indicated. I'm sure she knew I could not/would not kill it, so she grabbed it, wrung its neck, and tied it to the clothesline while it flopped around and drained. Talk about cooking from scratch. Yuk!

Cleaning it and cutting it up was also yukky, but I bravely did it under her supervision. Even so, Granddaddy did not recognize his favorite piece, and I declined my normal intake of a heretofore favorite meat.

Lesson number two was also "from scratch." Granddaddy's favorite dessert was angel food cake, and Grandmother's was known to be light and airy. The first step in this lesson was to crack and separate thirteen eggs without breaking the yellow. Then, by hand, I had to whip those dozen plus one egg whites into stiff peaks, which took forever. The sweet treat did taste really good, but I decided not to serve it very often in my own home.

Biscuits from scratch, an every morning treat in the Davis household, were served with some of Grandmother's home-canned jelly or preserves. The biscuits weren't too difficult, but in later years I resorted to those from a can.

I don't remember the other dishes I had to prepare except that every day we went down those back porch steps to gather fresh vegetables from the garden. Preparation entailed washing, stringing, snapping, or some other labor-intensive process to have dinner ready by noon, when Granddaddy came home from his hardware store. Unfortunately, his favorite veggie was okra, which was very itchy to handle.

My two-week sentence finally came to an end, and I was so happy to be paroled and on the train back to Amarillo, where Mom would take over the cooking chores. I fear I did not meet Grandmother's expectations. She advised me to "always make your table look pretty and maybe people won't notice as much that you can't cook."

That was before grandparents knew their main role in life was to build up a grandchild's self-esteem.

A few years ago, a friend gave me a decorative tea towel that proclaims, "I no longer butter my bread. I consider that cooking." So if guests have a meal with me, they can eat canned biscuits which, if they want buttered, they must do themselves.

I still hate to cook—but I can set a pretty table.

Button Box

Esther Brudo

when aunt florence came
all the way from new york
she brought a suitcase full of presents
and fancy chocolates
in a purple and gold metal box with a hinged lid
like a treasure chest

when we finished all the chocolates
the box was mine
i put in tiny acorns, my best bottle tops,
pieces of colored glass, my secret decoder ring
and my lucky rabbit's foot

i was rich

decades later
now faded and tarnished
smelling still of tin
this aged treasure chest
now holds buttons

sorting through it one day
those silver buttons once on my grey winter coat
the boyfriend i had then
bright and shiny at the time
is dull and conceited as i recall him

and those gaudy pink buttons
from the jumper mom made for me
that i hated then and refused to wear
have become beautiful

Millennium

Anne Whitlock

Close the volume and open the cabinet
where random moments of a troubled past
spill out of the glass doors
and shatter the morning sun dust.
Where is my life—the long stretches
of beach sand with little rocks
left by the wandering sea birds
in the path of the waves.
When will I walk here again—
in what millennium, under what
new planets and spinning solar systems?
Who will touch my aging soul
as it crumbles into the powdered sand?
What will the white birds say
as they rise like fog from the silver crests
of waves that gallop out to the sea?
Will I come here again—will I walk under
a new sun, new stars,
and the pristine blue page of the sky?

First Runner-up: Best Fiction Contest

The Stars in Their Courses

Jim Foy

New York in the early 1950s, and the capital of the world was brimming with new art and culture: Balanchine and Bernstein, Pollack and de Kooning, poetry by Auden and a young Lowell. But we were waging war then in faraway Korea, and the city began to fill up with servicemen. I met him in a bookstore on Madison Avenue. He was wearing the same United States Navy uniform I was, the same rank with two gold stripes on the sleeves. If you're old enough or a movie fan you will remember him, a Hollywood pretty boy turned ruggedly handsome by the time he was forty, the actor Robert Taylor. I was Reserve, a Lieutenant, Medical Corps. Taylor was also a Lieutenant, a naval aviator. I had read somewhere that he had served as a flight instructor during the big war and assumed he too was called to active duty because of the Korean emergency.

We were both browsing a table of new fiction. He looked me over and spoke up. "Hello, Doc. What ship are you off of?" He could see by my sleeve insignia that I was Medical Corps.

"I'm duty officer in the sick-bay at the Brooklyn Navy Yard, across the river, been called up for the past year or so. Yourself?"

"I just flew in from California, temporary duty. I'm in the Reserve myself."

We chatted about New York and, jokingly, what a great liberty town it was for sailors. I was sure he could see I recognized him from the movies. I looked at the book he was holding, a novel, *The Cruel Sea*, and mentioned it would make a good movie someday. I was holding *The Caine Mutiny*. We laughed at the coincidence and carried on about life in the Navy and the usual gripes of junior officers. Then books came up again, and we found we shared a liking for Joseph Conrad's tales of the sea and spoke of our favorites at some length.

"Look here, Doc, could you wait a minute? I have to make a telephone call to an old friend of mine that I promised to meet today."

He was at the back of the store using the bookseller's phone and seemed to talk for a longer time than I thought necessary for his arrangements. After he hung up, he came to me with smile on his face.

"I have to get along. I'm meeting an actress friend of mine at her place, not too far from here, within walking distance. By the way, I asked her if I could bring a new acquaintance for our casual teatime visit. She didn't object and, in fact, was interested in meeting a Navy man, a doctor serving his country, and one who likes books about ships and the sea. You interested in coming with me?"

"Look here," I said, "I wouldn't want to intrude on your afternoon with a friend. I'm sure you have some catching up to do, and I'd feel out of place…a fifth wheel." I felt it odd that he made this invitation on such short notice, but his tone and manner led me to believe it was merely a drop-by visit and nothing intimate was suggested.

"Listen to me, Doc. I want you to accept a special favor from one sailor to another, away from home in wartime with nothing else to do on a Saturday afternoon but hang out in a bookstore. I'm offering you one chance in a lifetime, about this I'm certain."

"What do you mean," I came back at him, "the chance of a lifetime?"

"To meet Greta Garbo," he said, an even wider smile across his face.

And indeed I would meet Garbo that late afternoon in her hideaway in New York, where she was living more or less in retirement after abandoning Hollywood ten years earlier. In my mind I was attempting to recover memories of Garbo's movies that I saw in boyhood. To me, her life and her movies were all of a piece, a magical presence upon a screen in a darkened theater. There was an image of a younger Taylor as her leading man in "Camille" and her role in "Ninotchka," her only comedy, a brilliant one at that.

We left the bookstore, found Fifty-Second Street and proceeded east toward the river. I wanted to ask him about Garbo. Could he clue me in on how to engage her in conversation without looking like a jerk or star-struck idiot? The Garbo file in my head was meager: born in Sweden, made a film or two; came to Hollywood in the silent picture era and made more films well into the late Thirties and early Forties with MGM, where she was "a big star." Then, for some reason, she left movieland for good and literally hid out in New York, a recluse.

"Tell me, Lieutenant, what is Garbo really like?"

"Really like?" he said sharply. "Every man and boy would like to know the answer to that one, but you'll have to find out for yourself. The best and only way to find out is to meet her. I'm not going to coach you; you'll be on your own. Okay, here's one insider's advice: she's crazy about the ocean and crossing the Atlantic. Another thing, she prefers to be called Miss G. Nothing else will do."

I made a note of these negligible items and thought more about Garbo. Maybe she wasn't a recluse in the strict sense of the word. She was seen regularly walking about the streets of the city, sometimes alone, sometimes in the company of friends. She disliked being approached in public, especially by newspaper reporters or what we now call *paparazzi*. Taylor surely had an inside track, perhaps a lasting friendship with her. I wondered why I was to be admitted to her inner sanctum, if only for a short visit. Maybe it was the medical degree, setting up the proverbial curbstone consultation. I had experienced my profession as a social asset more than once. I thought to ask Taylor more, but I assumed he would be annoyed by my not crediting his personal recommendation and influence.

Our walk took us to a building close by the East River, with a doorman and desk inside, where we were cleared after the obligatory call up to her place, which was on the fifth floor on the side overlooking the river. We were admitted by a maid, and right away I was stunned by the elegance and spaciousness of the apartment. Paintings by French masters hung on the walls of the main gathering-living room, and there were fresh flowers. What I saw looked very lived-in and arranged for comfort. Other rooms seemed to branch out from there into the further reaches of the apartment. Miss G. was nowhere in sight. We found her in a room with the best river view, a library and sitting room. She was seated or coiled on a hassock at the far end of the room near the windows. She was wearing gray slacks and a pale violet turtleneck and looking up at a dapper man seated in a wingback chair. He rose immediately and came forward to handle the introductions, but before he said a word Miss G. spun off her hassock and flung herself at Taylor, who looked startled at first, then submitted to her generous hugging and endearments spoken in genuine delight at his appearance in her den. The man was George Schlee, whom I later learned was her constant companion during her early years in New York, a man of indeterminate age but older than Miss G., who was then in her mid-forties.

After disentangling himself from our hostess, Taylor introduced me by giving my name, full naval rank and corps designation, followed by handshakes with Schlee and Miss G., whose lovely firm hand consisted of all too human flesh and bones. This was the mature woman, no longer before the camera, no longer a flashing, fugitive image on a silver screen. Her vivid, beautiful face was framed by near shoulder-length light brown hair. Then there were her eyes, watchful and on you, observant but accepting, the focal point of her face and radiance. She was made up lightly, fresh and impeccable. There was a naturalness to her that did not match my shaky memory of her screen persona.

It occurred to me that there was a bit of acting in that enthusiastic greeting showered on Taylor, but during the visit there wasn't the slightest hint of another theatrical display, nor was there mention of her films and the triumphs of her career. I soon realized that, although I was once a schoolboy admirer of her pictures, this was not the occasion to offer any fan talk or make remarks about that part of her life, a life she had abandoned with emphatic finality.

Miss G. announced she would prepare tea and gracefully left the room. Taylor and Schlee wandered off into that spacious living room to examine the art on the walls. I remained in the library, curious to investigate the books: modern Scandinavian classics in their original language—Strindberg, Ibsen, Lagerlof, Undset—sets of Jane Austen, Dickens, Hardy, and a generous shelf of art and reference books. The books looked well used. A small antique desk sat in a corner.

I went to join the gentlemen as our hostess entered with a tray of tea things and plates of small sandwiches and pastries. We took seats in a semicircle of chairs arranged for conversation. We sipped tea, ate little, smoked, and a chatty exchange commenced. It started out with small talk: anecdotes and memories shared between the others. Then the three of them turned on me and opened a quiz session directed at my origins, education, and place in the world, their world. I would give them the abridged edition of my biography, the account of the stranger in their midst. I couldn't tell them about a courtship at risk of breakup because of my absence, or uncertainty about my plans for a future career. But I believed I knew what they wanted. I told them I was born and bred in Chicago, joined the Navy during World War II at age seventeen just out of high school. After boot camp I shipped out to Hawaii as a Yeoman striker and spent the next two years assigned as a clerk far from battles or engagements. I was lucky enough to be chosen for officer's training—the need was great. I spent three months Stateside and came out an Ensign. They called us ninety-day wonders. The war was nearly over by then, and I made plans to study medicine. I played my trump card. After internship I spent a year between Paris and London doing postgraduate studies in medicine with enough breaks for travel around the continent. This was my man-of-the-world credential. They took it in with agreeable nods and winks, except for Schlee, the old fox, who seemed unimpressed.

Miss G. went somewhere and returned with a bottle of wine and glasses. Taylor and I were the only takers. She indicated through body language that she wanted to see me apart from the others and moved off to the library. I followed with my glass in hand and spirits high. She was standing by the windows, looking down at the water below.

"This view of the river always reminds me of Stockholm with the barges, small boats, and yachts coming and going night and day. It's one of the reasons I chose to live here. I'm a real American now. Last year I was finally sworn in as a U.S. Citizen, though I've been here since I was nineteen. I made the commitment even though my heart still longs for Sweden. I travel there from time to time, see family and old friends from my youth. I love the voyage out and the return. The ocean is a passion of mine."

"Yes, Robert told me that about you, the long voyage home."

"And you, Lieutenant Doctor…you have been to sea and experienced something of its moods and effects on the soul? Tell me of your long voyage, wherever it took you."

"During the war I saw something of the Pacific, and I've crossed the Atlantic aboard Navy ships and ocean liners." I was avoiding a direct reply; then I remembered something I felt compelled to reveal. "I do have a story to tell about a cruise I made last spring, embarking from the Brooklyn Navy Yard. That's downriver, not far from here."

"Tell me your story. Perhaps we share the sense of adventure in such a voyage and the moments of vision that the sea can sometimes reveal to us."

I laid out my tale for her while underplaying the mundane nature of much of life on a naval vessel. "We were a squadron of three destroyers, tin cans we call them, the smallest of warships, and bound for Havana. I was the only medical officer for the three crews and my quarters and sick bay were on the lead ship. The alleged purpose was the practice of maneuvers for officers and sailors who were reserves needing a refresher course in seamanship and gunnery, but I suspected the real purpose was to get to Havana for some prime liberty ashore in a wide-open town known for its good times. I had little to do on the first leg of the cruise. I had the run of the ship, fore and aft, below and above deck.

"Good weather held, and we were in the Gulf Stream in a season without tropical storms, smooth going at thirty knots or more when we were not executing a drill or an exercise with our sister ships. I spent more and more time topside, watching the ocean in its shifting colors of bluegray-green, the sky with the distant line of an encircling horizon, the tricks light played on the choppy sea, cloud formations of all kinds, and the sun going about its daily business. Being in the center of that dome and circle induced a state of meditation, a rare concentration of the mind on infinite space, with time standing still. Best of all were the nights. The moon riding high in its own waveless ocean. The night sky had no limits with its outbreak of stars, the immensity of it. The unknown and unknowable void held me enthralled. It sounds strange, even contradictory, but I felt on intimate terms with the cosmos."

As I spoke, she made eye contact, then reached toward me without touching and said, "Anyone who goes on the ocean will have those deep feelings. Anyone can contemplate the deepest mysteries. I could make a religion for myself from those experiences, and start to heal my moods and the wounds I have received since I was a child. My beloved father died when I was fifteen, and my older sister after I first came to America."

Miss G. was calm, her grief had dissipated long ago, yet the melancholy was there just below the surface, an essential trait, a way of looking on the world. Then she found the story she wished to leave with me. "In 1932 I sailed to Sweden on a luxury ship. I was ill and exhausted from my work in Hollywood and needed to see a doctor, one I knew and trusted in Stockholm. I feared the tuberculosis that took my beloved ones from me. He reassured me that my lungs were sound and prescribed rest and diet. After a long visit with my mother, I knew I must return to America. I had the choice of a luxury liner or taking a much longer return voyage by freighter. I chose the freighter, and you must know why."

"Because it would take longer...more rest, more of the sea and solitude."

"Yes, Lieutenant Doctor, it was the voyage of a lifetime, more than thirty days from Stockholm to San Diego by way of the Panama Canal, and I was the only passenger aboard. I immersed myself in that voyage: the unpredictable ocean, the days and nights all jumbled, the passage into another world. I had booked under the name Harriet Brown, and once on board I gave up all attempts to look nice. On deck I faded into the peeling paint around me. Weather during the voyage imposed all the changes one could imagine: heat and cold, rough and calm, tempest and bright sky. One time, there was a storm and I went on deck, which was huge and filled with cargo, but I was able to walk around it. The captain came to me and said, 'By God, you're a good sailor.' I was the only one out on deck. The ship pitched and rolled and shuddered. I adored it, I was in command.

"You spoke of your nights at sea. They can be glorious with the stars in full flight. The sea is a heavy sleeper, and if you listen carefully you can hear it breathing in and out. From charts I learned the names of the constellations for the first time. There was a blue moon and the crew celebrated with drinks. By then I was one of them."

The windows were drained of light, the river a dark ribbon below us, Brooklyn lit up in the distance. I looked at her and saw that her intensity had diminished. I heard a sigh and saw a bright smile.

We were joined by the men from the other room. Parting was ceremonious with ritual pleasantries, but I was awkward in expressing my thanks on taking leave. She then took my hand in one of hers and familiarly patted me on the shoulder, saying she enjoyed our chat together. Later that night, I dreamed of the heaving ocean, but it was unlike what I remembered. The sea was different, dark and unforgiving. Only the stars remained the same, tracing their courses.

Captain's Dinner

Ruth Moon Kempher

       Served fettuccini, piles
of it, long eel-like pasta—
the menu calls it *pesca del mare*
(with fish of the sea)— it's rich with
tiny shrimps and buttery scallops
succulent, swaddled in noodles
with black-shell mussels, peeping
bringing memories of another
feast, blackest shells ever seen.
       The man from Michigan
at my shoulder has rack of lamb, with
ah, redolent rosemary, which is
not "rose" of the sea, but "dew"
of the sea—a sprig stuck up
curling petals, mini-tree—
I'd tell him but
       I'm distracted
an orchestra plays the opening bars
of "Moon River," and stops
abruptly and I can't interrupt his
tale of working out, arthritis
his loud laugh
       When was I at Cuma?
       When Taormina, looking
       for D. H. Lawrence?
       When did I see the blue
       bees on Napoleon's walls
       that house on Elba?
what I really want to do is pinch his
rosemary, herb of remembrance:
that thirst, that greed.

SID CAESAR, CAN WE TALK?

Richard Lampl

One time I actually avoided a celebrity: Sid Caesar. He was alone on the same aircraft as I, an almost empty 737 on an early morning flight in the late sixties from Las Vegas to Los Angeles. It would be easy for me to sit next to him and talk, but I didn't.

Sid Caesar and I had something in common. We both grew up in the Riverdale Avenue section of Yonkers, New York, and he was just two years older. I never knew him there, but the opportunity to reminisce about the old neighborhood was obvious. If we talked it would be inevitable that we would know people in common in this predominately Jewish section. We could talk about the delicious aroma of fresh rye bread coming from Weber's Bakery next to the firehouse where on-duty firemen shared counter sales with the ugly Weber sisters. We could remember the clatter of the bright, red-and-gold Number 8 trolley as it clanged past us on Riverdale Avenue, or the pungent smell from Pleshko's Kosher Chicken Market. We could laugh about Mr. Rau, the Yonkers High School physics teacher who always messed up his experiments.

I had admired Sid Caesar's antics in front of the camera for years, and avidly followed his performances on the "Show of Shows" and the "Sid Caesar Show." I thought he was a great comic, and I harbored a certain pride for someone from my neighborhood who had "made it."

How could I miss an opportunity to talk with him? This was my big chance. But something about his demeanor stopped me. I was not sure I wanted to approach him. He was alone, and he looked morose and defenseless. This was a very early, early-morning flight. I had seen his show the night before at the Frontier Hotel with his old sidekick, Imogene Coca, and I felt he had lost his rapport with the audience. It seemed to me he was sleepwalking through his sketches. He and Imogene Coca were doing some of their old tried and true routines that had audiences and critics raving when they were performed on TV. One skit in memory was a modified strip tease by the pixyish Imogene, where she begins and ends in a mammoth overcoat.

As it turned out, skits like this that had worked so well on TV bombed on the big Frontier stage. Sid and Imogene's facial contortions, which were so expressive on the TV screen, were lost under the proscenium arch. And his timing was off. A great comic without good timing becomes a mediocre comic. The audience reacted with polite, scattered applause. This was not the Sid Caesar the audience or I had admired for many years.

Perhaps a discussion about a few youthful memories would cheer him up, but I stayed glued to my seat. I was puzzled at my own inaction, until I realized what it was. I did not trust myself. I was unhappy with his performance. He knew he had been bad. I was afraid that, if we met, I would tell this obviously vulnerable man something he was not in a position to hear. What could I say to him? Could I say I enjoyed his performance? It would be like lying to an older brother or a favorite uncle. Anything positive I could say would sound hollow.

I would be more protective of my idol if I left him alone. Why inflict my negative feelings on him? I did not want to add to his misery. I kept myself in check and decided to let the opportunity slip by.

We remained distant during the entire 45-minute flight, as distant as we had for the many years before or since. It wasn't until years later that I understood what was wrong. I read his autobiography.

He had been worn down. The demands of being funny and creative in weekly performances for live television productions had taken its toll. He could not keep up with the pressure. He was going through self-destructive alcohol addiction and ego problems at the time, and his actions in front of the camera had suffered with him. His downward slope continued after his weekly comedy series ended. It took years of psychotherapy before he could recover enough to appear in any TV or movie part.

I still remember his better days with a smile.

"A Mind Like a Steel Trap"

Jean Marie Purcell

I wonder when someone says that to me
does it mean a person's as smart as can be,
capable of rendering his views in taut,
tight concepts, oh, so wittily wrought?
Is it about ideas clung to doggedly?
When I hear it, here's the picture I see:
a paw of some pitiable creature caught,
which has nothing to do with exalted thought
and just leads to me feeling entrapped
by an adage I do not consider apt.

Touching/Not Touching

Joan E. Zekas

I had run my fingers along all the crevices in the massive fireplaces. Maybe…just maybe…he'd left something behind. But there was nothing—no musical scores, no crumpled notes, no broken batons. I had imagined him in the rooms: his laughter roaring through the halls, his fingers tapping out a beat on a table, his daydreaming in front of the large windows. However, sixty-some years had elapsed since he had lived in the house. Nothing was left but dust.

In 1960, fresh out of graduate school, I rented a second-floor apartment on South Aiken Avenue in Pittsburgh. The beautiful old Victorian home had a broad front porch with a swing. There was a twin house next door. Coming up the front steps, you had the feeling that you were entering grandeur. And then you saw it—the brass door knocker, etched with the words, "Home of Victor Herbert while he conducted the Pittsburgh Symphony."

Easily given to romantic fantasy, I relished the idea of living in the house of such a luminous talent. Victor Herbert and his family lived in that Aiken Avenue house for six years, from 1898 to 1904, while he not only conducted the Pittsburgh Symphony, but also composed operettas and produced musical works for the stage. Herbert's biographer, Joseph Kaye, wrote in 1931 that Herbert "lived comfortably at his residence on Aikins Avenue" in Pittsburgh. The home was described as well furnished and had a billiard room in the attic. When Richard Strauss came to Pittsburgh, his wife was greatly impressed when Mrs. Herbert showed her through the house. She was particularly taken with the "array of fancy combs and toilet articles" on Mrs. Herbert's dresser.

Sunday afternoons must have been a rollicking, boisterous time in that house. Gregarious and expansive by nature, Herbert collected and entertained a coterie of musicians. One Sunday, according to Kaye, there were four highly talented visitors, including Fritz Kreisler. Herbert was himself a cellist by training. The group played, they drank, they ate, then they played some more. *The Schubert String Quintet* was played not once, not twice, but three times that day.

Mrs. Herbert prepared the dinner. She was described by Kaye as a "noble cook." An accomplished singer herself, I imagine she hummed along with the music as she worked by the stove. After dinner, the men trooped upstairs to the attic for a rousing game of billiards.

Kaye called Herbert "an affectionate father" who "took great delight in playing with his children." Daughter Ella Victoria was about nine years old when they arrived in Pittsburgh, and son Clifford Victor was about seven. When Herbert brought a train home for his son, the great composer "rolled all over the carpet with it." Clifford had a hard time getting his hands on the train, but "he had great fun watching his father's antics." Sad to say, son Clifford never did get the hang of playing the violin, even though he had many lessons. Poor Mama Herbert! She probably had to put her hands over her ears to muffle all the screeching.

Herbert's passion for music engulfed him. He was both prolific and versatile, and his output was staggering. It was a good thing his wife could turn a blind eye to the clutter. Herbert worked simultaneously on multiple compositions all over the house. In the appendix of Joseph Kaye's biography, there are pages and pages of Victor Herbert's published compositions. Listed are a total of 181 works. Forty-one of those works were operettas, and eight of the operettas were composed in the Aiken Avenue house, including *Babes In Toyland*, *Mlle. Modiste*, and *The Red Mill*. Little images of Toyland figures must have danced in Herbert's head, figures like The Sun Queen, The Spirit of Maple, and The Brown Bear. Other published pieces ranged from full-length operas to incidental music for the Ziegfield Follies.

That house on South Aiken Avenue must have vibrated with life. I'm sure Herbert hated to pack up and leave it—that house in which his talents flowered, in which his family flourished, and in which he and his musician soul mates created a kind of nirvana. Kaye, the biographer, said that, years later, Herbert's friends, Fritz Kreisler and Henry Burch, "met and mourned: 'Where are those happy days at Pittsburgh!'"

I had to move out of the grand old house after eight years, as it was being developed into a more modern structure. I now take comfort in looking at its next-door twin, which still retains a lot of the old charm.

Rest in peace, Victor. You were truly a shooting star. And thanks for the fantasies…

THE CREEK

Ila Winslow

S hould you want a quiet place to sit and read, go to the creek. When the winds blow east to west, watch closely, and you might see a sliver of a building between two tall trees by the trickle of a creek.

Let your imagination flow, and you might see a young woman holding a book, dipping her bare feet in the cool water. Beside her might be an ugly green frog. Look closer, and you will see that the green object is not alive, but is a purse and holds her shoes and bonnet.

She is here because she is waiting for her prince charming. The book in her lap is about magical things. One chapter explains that, if you wish for something hard enough, your wish will be granted.

When the winds blow north to south, the image changes to a young fellow standing in the water, a fishing pole in his hand.

Atop a knapsack are his shoes, cap, a biscuit, and a hunk of cheese. Deeper inside is a book-shaped object. Not once has that object seen the light of day since his mother gave it to him. She's gone from his world, but he remembers the quiet times with her when they both dipped their feet in the clear creek water.

Knowing the lad feared to expose his heart, I rose from the creek and, invisible to his sight, dug deep in his bag and grasped my book of magic. I removed my hand from the knapsack and took the book with me. I, the magician, knew it was time to change the creek's location.

Re-entering the cool water, I waved my hand in a circle. The winds came together so east winds combined with north winds, and south winds swirled with west winds. Together, they scoured the scene clean.

Cold Case: Rona

Neal Wilgus

> *I always perceive more and otherwise than I see.*
> — Jean-Paul Sartre

C all me Ipse Dixit. No kidding.

I have a contact in the police department who lets me know when the cops are in need of a psychic adviser. Oh yeah, most psychics are fakers whose record of cases solved is dismal, at best, but I'm that exception that helps the others skate. They claim to solve cases, but don't. I do, but can't tell.

I hadn't heard from my contact, Thorne, for over a year and had to eke out a living in used cars, but late one dreary night my old rotary phone rang, and I somehow knew. "Thorne," I said, "what's up?"

"How do you do that without caller ID?" he asked, but didn't wait for an answer. "I got one you're gonna love, Ipse. A case so cold it's deep freeze."

I grunted and waited for him to go on.

"Ever hear of a Llovizna?"

"A drizzler?" I asked.

"Weeping willow," he said. "Pendulous Plume."

"A hired mourner, so I've heard."

"Exactly."

"Feed me," I said.

"Not on the phone," he said. "I just wanted to get your attention. Can you meet me up on the palizado in an hour?"

"You did and I can," I said and hung up.

The near-full moon made the palisades miraculous—the Rio Grande in deep shadows below us, the lights of the city filling the huge valley, the looming Sandia Mountains holding up the sky, silver clouds above. The safe house on Cliffside was dark when I got there. Inside, Thorne was smoking by candlelight.

"Crazy weather," he said.

"It's those wildfires," I pointed out needlessly. "Weeks of smoke making the sun orange, the moon red. Then runoff ash turning the river black. Spooky. Whatcha got?"

Thorne blew smoke and said, "A really cold case, Ipse. Remember the case the newspapers called La Rona, about forty years ago?"

"Rona, they shortened it to," I said. "Thirty-nine years ago."

"Yeah, well it was never solved, but now there are some new developments. As you no doubt recall, the reference was to La Llorona, the wailing woman of Hispanic folklore, who drowned her kids in the river to spite an unfaithful lover. She repents and now wanders the ditchbanks and riverside, weeping for her loss."

"And warning others to avoid her mistakes," I said. "Apparently, the editor of the *Albuquerque Republic* had trouble pronouncing the double L, sounding like Y, so he cut it short to La Rona, then to plain Rona, as the case dragged on."

Thorne smiled and crushed out the cigarette. "In the so-called Rona case, though, the two kids were drowned in the bathtub, and the case got so complicated it went cold and unsolved. Sex toys called acorns were found at the scene."

"How old were the kids?" I prompted.

"Two and five," he said. "Named Joseph and Mary Lopes."

"Not Adam and Eve?"

"They were Catholic, not Jewish," Thorne said grimly. "Now the mother, Juanita Lopes, was the prime suspect, as was her boyfriend, Hoseib Alar, an illegal from Mexico, or Cuba, or Central America—an unsolved mystery of his own."

"He disappeared soon after the murders," I recalled.

"They traced him to Matamoros, then lost him." Thorne reached for another cigarette, but held off. "Nita Lopes was charged with murder, but with no witness or evidence the charges were eventually dropped."

"She was said to be very beautiful," I said. "Did she have other lovers?"

"Let's put it this way, Ipse." He smiled. "If it had been thirty years later, she might have been one of the West Mesa serial victims. Part time hooker, drug dealer, student at the University. She was struggling to raise her kids, without much help from Alar."

"But there was another well-known name connected with Nita," I prompted. "A Captain somebody or other…"

"Colonel Tom Halberd, as you well know." Thorne grinned as he finally searched out another smoke. "Retired military, local business man, small time politician. Nita was his mistress in a sort of on-off way."

"Suspect?"

"Some thought so, but there was nothing connecting him with the killings. His interest in the lost treasure at Victorio Peak gave him the nickname Col. Kidd. He's big on paranormal stuff—went to UFO conferences, investigated ghosts, crop circles, El Chupacabra. Led an expedition to track down Big Foot in Mexico about ten years ago."

"And his wife? Did she know about Nita?"

"That she did," he said, lighting up. "Veronica Halberd, well known figure in the arts community and charity work. Known as Ronca. Original name Anastasia Jones, out of Texas. A cousin or something of Jim Jones of Jonestown, Guyana."

"Any other suspects?"

"There were a few friends and customers that were what we now call 'of interest,' but they've long since gone their separate ways."

"So what's new?" I asked. "Why the renewed interest in an ice cube?"

"Several things," Thorne said. His cigarette glowed brighter as the candle began to dwindle. "First, the cops in Juarez have arrested a guy they think is Alar—a psychosurgeon calling himself Dr. H. A. Robardin."

"Ah," I said.

Thorne held up a hand. "I've been keeping track of Nita Lopes on my own over the years. It may surprise you to learn that after the La Rona ruckus died down, she got involved with an anthropology professor at UNM—Dr. Duncan Barnabas, who'd been studying the Isleta Pueblo culture for years. About fifteen years ago, the two of them and their son, Jack, moved to Las Cruces to study the Ysleta community near El Paso—just across the Border from Juarez. Barnabas published a philosophy book called *Real Reality: Immanuel Kant's Vision*—and bang—he died soon after in a car crash."

"Didn't Nita write something, too?"

"Yes, *A Real Confession*, written with Barnabas' help. She remains a devout

Catholic, but the Barnabas influence is glaring. Interestingly, after Barnabas died, Nita began visits to Juarez to see her old friend, Dr. Robardin."

"And…?"

He blew more smoke. "That leaves Col. Halberd to account for. He was last in the news when he joined a spinoff of the Dianetics movement a couple of years ago. Two days ago, he suffered a stroke and is paralyzed on the left side. Happened on his eighty-eighth birthday."

"His wife still around?"

"Ronca Halberd is at his side, overseeing his care. She's an important figure in an Evangelical movement—the First Church of Resurrection?"

"Anything else?"

"Yeah, something rather odd. Not long after Barnabas' death, the bunch of them—the Halberds, Nita, Robardin, and young Jack and his girlfriend, Sue—made a mysterious visit to the T'charcosa Badlands, also known as the Jornada del Muerto."

"The journey of a dead man," I said. "I've skirted the edges."

Thorne nodded again. "Best known for the Trinity Site, where the first atomic bomb was exploded. It has a long history of violence and tragedy, including the death of the Kid."

"Billy?" I asked in surprise.

"Apache." He grinned. "Supposedly killed on Cyclone Saddle near Cold Spring Canyon in 1906. But the Halberd party was interested, for some reason, in a place called Robledo's Peak, where the first European to die in the Jornadas was buried in 1598. They apparently stayed over two nights, then returned to Elephant Butte. They never talked about it or wrote anything for the general public."

"Rather strange," I mused. "I'll have to do my disappearing act while I mull this over. I'll get back soon as I can."

Thorne nodded and crushed out the cigarette just as the candle went out.

To do what I do, I have to get away from high tech as much as possible, but with an atomic bomb in the middle of the badlands, the modern world doesn't give me much leeway. So I went for a walk along the riverbank. Yes, the trail is closed to the public at night, but I know how to handle that— keep quiet and stay off the trail.

I went north from the Alemeda bridge into the Corrales bosque, barely able to see, even in the bright moonlight. I didn't exactly call out to La Llorona, but she was on my mind, as were those two helpless kids drowned in the bathtub. Whoever killed them, the spirit of La Llorona was there egging them on. But why?

The La Llorona legend goes back at least a century, probably a lot longer than that. The stark figure of the Weeping Woman and her terrible crime is a natural archetype, but what did it mean? How could such a tragedy keep happening over such a long time? And did a homicide like the bathtub murders really fit the pattern or was it just media hype? In the dark shadows of the bosque, anything seemed possible.

For some reason, my thoughts began to focus on young Jack Barnabas. He had survived, where the children fathered by Alar (or was it Halberd?) had not. So perhaps it was not the mother's crime, but the boyfriend's. Not unusual for the live-in male to resort to abuse and sometimes murder of another man's child or infant. Jack might have been bored to death by his father, but not physically attacked.

I moved away from the river as the undergrowth grew thicker, and my attention turned to Nita herself. Originally from the Riverside neighborhood in the South Valley, she had done well in school and worked at various jobs to help her family survive as she was growing up. That much I remembered from the newspaper stories, but how she did at the University and why the part time prostitution, I could only speculate. Hispanic culture is overwhelmingly Catholic, but had plenty of room for folk tales and superstition. She was apparently equally at ease with Alar's psychosurgery and Barnabas' philosophical reality show.

I could make out the lights of Corrales now and moved back toward the riverbank, contemplating the image of Nita's body ending up on the West Mesa. Fortunately, that hadn't happened, I thought—when I suddenly became aware of the presence of someone else in the shadows of the riverbank. At first, it was just a presence I could feel, but when I stopped moving, I could hear a soft, almost inaudible moaning. Images flashed through my mind—the motherly Nita, Jack's beautiful young Sue, even the elderly Ronca Halberd—all gone in an instant. The stranger stopped when I did, so I moved forward again, silently, to see what might happen. The figure, which I could see clearly on the river's edge, moved with me.

My impulse was to flee, but running through the bosque in the middle of the night was not an option. Instead, I began to move slowly away from the river, keeping my eyes on what I thought was a female figure in dark robes. She seemed to be watching me.

The moaning never stopped.

All thought of the murders and the cast of characters involved had disappeared from my mind—all I wanted was to get away. I didn't know how this could be happening, but I knew I wasn't dreaming or imaging things. The woman in dark clothes at river's edge was real, and I had no idea if she meant me harm or was there to offer her help. I only knew I had to get away. And I knew one other thing—the woman I saw there in the moonlight and shadows was La Llorona.

I didn't get to sleep till almost dawn, and then slept fitfully till midafternoon, spending the evening at the University library. I began by looking through some of the old newspaper stories about the bathtub murders, where I ran across a picture of Col. Halberd, who was being questioned by police about his "acquaintence" with Nita Lopes. He was smiling, and denied everything. They were just friends. He was quoted as saying, "Would I kid you?"

Ronca Halberd said, "No comment."

A quick check of Barnabas' books gave me nothing, which is what I expected.

For the next two days, I did more digging in the library and used bookstores with little results. Dr. Robardin had begun to be noticed as a psychosurgeon about a year after Alar disappeared, but no one made the connection. Robardin was famous for curing people at mass meetings by pulling bloody chicken livers from their guts. Some of the pictures were spectacular, but Robardin allowed no critical inspection of his work.

I found a copy of Nita's *A Real Confession* and spent an afternoon reading through it. I was surprised to see it was dedicated to both Dr. Barnabas and Col. Halberd, but reading it cleared that up. Nita managed to follow Catholic orthodoxy in explaining her own life struggles, while at the same time describing her realization that Real was not really real, but that unexplained mysteries like UFOs really were real. She made one passing reference to La Llorona, but never revealed who murdered her kids.

I put down Nita's *Confession* and fell into a state of revery—a realm between sleep and dream, where everything about the case swam together in the black river of the red moon. Remote viewing, out-of-body experience, Really Real awareness—it didn't matter. I just let everything swim. The babbling inferno of unconsciousness, riverrunning…

…down Second Street past the yellow sign in front of the Basilisk Temple, court of the underground dragon…the Jornada vampire with eyes of fire declares himself Conquistador…the new ark selli stones of dodona…the aegis of the cloud-gatherer…Erasabeth's underdimensional song, "The Praise of Conches"…burial ground of the good Wizard of Oaxaca Zapotecs…at the Court of Asa, Ipse Dixit and itsy Biscuit…busily and neat, the Dongo Kid at Vittoriale Peak…rio bonito/town and family massacre/grim weeper walking…the primary Filotelic act—Truth or Daresequences…the old profit of fickle Cassius Longlance the sublime, who stabbed JC…a silly fool's play about a starline crossing the badlands, the angst of Ankh…old bloodroot out to get the great escape goat gruff…diary of Father Ambrose Fort, the Wildgooze del Apache…across endless seas/another cry of slaughter/banshee answering…aha, Sir Rush live at goregotha, 2K plus…Billy Holmes on the range, Sherlock, where D. D. and the Crookes play at native shell games, travelogue supreme…survival of the finnest wno forged the javalance shroud…madamegamex urnest strides through red hell, leaving the best behind…the burning city and the ghostfaced bloviation of Jerome St…dumb bonney Oaks and the Atlantean flavor of V'Nula…young Dr. Metnuselah's kids, a clear sacrifice…young Sleepenstein, the final kid map…the blue footed booby hatch red chile con carnage…a mountain of gold/a room full of skeletons/Victorio peak…

But it's not Victorio Peak I see next, but Robledo Peak, where I see or sense or feel the band of seekers moving across the badlands—the Halberds and company, along with two dark-looking men with rifles who I'd never seen before. The Halberds ride horses, Nita a donkey, the others on foot, carrying supplies and herding livestock—a cow and two young goats. I seem to float above them—they all unaware.

They reach the base of the peak at dusk and set up camp in an oak grove just as the new moon is sinking. Before the sun comes up, the camp is alive—the riflemen on guard, Halberd and Robardin slaughtering the cow, the women preparing a meal. A small altar is constructed at the base of the largest oak, and some kind of ceremony is conducted by Ronca Halberd. Then they withdraw to their separate tents to meditate or pray. Siesta is followed by the evening meal and another ritual at the altar.

As the moon rises, a chanting begins. Torches are set ablaze around the campsite. Candles are placed on the altar, and each membeer, including the riflemen, steps up to sing and chant and sometimes howl. The ceremony lasts several hours, and the climax comes when the two young goats are brought to the altar. After more chants and howls, the goat kid's throats are cut. The blood is caught and consumed by the worshipers.

Mercifully, my vision fades at this point, and I fall into a deep sleep, which lasts until the following morning. I see the moon out my window, setting behind the volcanos of the West Mesa.

When I'd somewhat recovered, I took up *A Real Confession* again to see if I could find some hint of what I'd observed or experienced or dreamed. To my surprise, a small pamphlet slipped out of the back page—an announcement of the opening of the Robledo Museum of Resurrections at an exclusive address in Los Ranchos de Albuquerque. I'd seen the address before—it was the Halbert's palatial home in the North Valley. The pamphlet made it known that visitation to the Museum was by Special Invitation only. It was dated almost ten years earlier.

So it was time to call Thorne again and see if we could make some sense of it all.

"What took you so long, Ipse?" he asked when we sat down again at the safe house on the palizado.

"You won't believe me anyway," I told him through the cigarette haze. But I gave him a quick summary and asked what he'd come up with.

"You won't like this," he said, "but they've exhumed the two victims to extract DNA samples. The results prove the father of both kids was Col. Halberd, not Robardin or Barnabas—or anyone else."

"Interesting," I said. "That makes it even more important for me to get that Special Invitation to the Robledo Museum. Think you can swing it?"

He smiled in the smoky shadows. "I have a few contacts. Are you up to Ronca face to face?"

"The idea scares the hell out of me, but I think I can handle it," I said. "I need to ask her about a lot of things, but especially about this." I took out a torn piece of paper, half of which had once been a poster for the Robledo Museum. A large picture of Col. Halberd took up most of it. He was smiling wickedly and held a hand-lettered sign saying, "I kid you…" A hand on his shoulder could only be from Ronca's missing half. "I found it with the Museum pamphlet."

Thorne studied it a moment and blew more smoke. "I'll give you five dollars for it."

"Not even five thousand," I said. "Which reminds me—when do I get paid? I'm flat broke."

He smiled again and pulled out a thick envelope. "Got ya covered, Ipse. Here's a cash advance to cover your expenses. Sorry it couldn't have come sooner. There'll be a bigger check when we get this thing resolved."

"I'll hold my breath," I said, taking the money.

"By the way," he said and grinned, killing his cigarette, "better get a haircut—and buy a new shirt."

It felt like it should be Halloween, but it was actually the fourth of July in the Druid month of Oak when I finally got past the gates of the Halberd estate in my rental car and was escorted to a medium-sized building called the don jon, some distance from the main house: the Museum.

Inside, Ronca Halberd beckoned me into a large, plush office and waved me to a seat.

"Ipse Dixit," I said by way of introduction. We didn't shake hands. "I'd like to learn about the Museum. Dr. Wilberforce at the University suggested I talk to you directly."

"He called me and informed me of your interest. Tell me a little about yourself."

I rattled off the cover story we'd concocted and which she'd no doubt checked thoroughly. Apparently, my backup team was pretty good. When I'd finished my spiel, she stood up and began pacing the room—a tall, elderly woman, slim and still attractive despite the ravages of time. I took no notes, but absorbed her counterspiel, somewhat awed by her regal presence. She spoke with great conviction about coming to this country as a teenager and finding her way to a fortune by way of several books and a financial and investment empire. Then she began to rant about the power and strength to be found in the mighty Oak—the true spiritual source, she said, of all that was important in life.

As she carried on in her mystical way, a few pitches for her books and financial advice thrown in, I took the opportunity to look around at her rather bizarre office. The main theme was Egyptian, with the Nile depicted in photographs and reliefs and the god Ptah of Memphis shown in various guises. But there was a Native American theme running a close second—Aztec, Myan, Zarahemla, Anasazi, and modern Pueblo all represented in pictures, plaques, baskets, and blankets. One corner seemed to be devoted to UFOs, and a whole shelf of Scientology books shared the space.

"That, briefly, is a sketch of what we're all about," Madame Halberd said at last. "Have you any questions?"

I thanked her profusely for her presentation, then dropped my bombshell. Or, at least, hand grenade. "Before I offer my support for your work," I said, "I have to ask about reports that the Church of Resurrections has at times used dangerous illegal drugs and engaged in sexual activities that might amount to prostitution or sexual slavery."

No explosion, just a prolonged silence. Finally, she fixed me with a cold stare and said, "You're referring to the so-called Druid Dungeon affair that the local television and newspaper reporters had such fun with a few years ago. It amounted to nothing. We freely acknowledged using some harmless psychedelic substances in our religious rituals, and there is a sexual component to our practices. All harmless and legal."

"And the charge of sacrifices being made?"

"Hogwash! Of course, we sacrifice for our beliefs and practices, but there is no physical abuse of any kind, animal or human." She fell silent for a moment, then concluded, "It's my poor, dear Col. Oak who has made the great sacrifice for us—but he will return to his leader role, I assure you."

"I'm sure he will," I said.

"Are you?" she barked, suddenly fired up. "I don't detect any real enthusiasm on your part. Do you really have any interest in our work? Are you just another reporter looking for another media circus? I thought your connections were legitimate, but perhaps I was wrong." She glared at me.

"No, I really am interested," I started to say, but at that moment her purple cell phone rang and she held up her hand as she answered it. I was a bit relieved, because my next IED was a question about her role in the death of the two Lopes kids. I wondered if duck-and-cover would be enough after that.

But Ronca cut me off with an explosion of her own—a threat, roar, an eldritch boast like the cry of a buck in rutting time. Then I made out her cry of, "No, he cannot die, he can't! How could the Oak have fallen?" She threw the cell from her and fell forward onto her desk, the news of her husband's death driving me and my outrageous questions back underground.

I sat stunned, not knowing what to do. She seemed in a state of shock that might have killed her, too, and I realized I'd better call for help from her secretary or staff — or 911.

Then I heard it—that low, almost inaudible moan coming from the stricken Veronica Halberd. A moan I'd heard before, I thought. Yes, just days before in the shadows of the Corrales bosque. The soft cry of the weeping woman—La Llorona!

I did call for help, of course, and for 911, and in almost no time a score of people were moving through the office and outside, restraining Ronca before she could do herself or anyone else harm, sedating her and placing her in an ambulance that quickly left the estate.

In the turmoil that followed, I found myself alone in that bizarre office, surrounded by all those ancient and alien relics and symbols.

I stumbled around to the other side of her desk and something caught my eye. Under the glass was a picture of the ancient Egyptian prince Anknnaf, another of a gold breastplate from Guatamala, a snapshot of Col. Halberd with Nita and her kids, and a couplet, hand written on the back of an envelope:

> *I take the world in one great stroke—*
> *nothing can stop the mighty Oak!*

But my attention was riveted to a piece of paper under the glass—the missing half of the poster I'd found showing the Colonel's wicked smile. This half of the picture showed a smirking Ronca, holding her part of the paper, on which she had written, "I kid you not!"

Changing Arrangements

Claudia Poquoc

There are no new problems that fill in our days,
as a lizard-sized dinosaur darts past my door.
Only ancient human struggles arranged in new ways.

Old Woman of the World stirs her brew in a cave.
She loves life, the mess it makes, no matter the laws.
There are no new problems that fill in our days.

"Spinning nature and culture, makes sacred", She says,
as She threads an evergreen cloak leaving flaws.
Only ancient human struggles arranged in new ways.

Old Woman restores myth when memory frays.
She weaves a new tapestry where edges are raw.
There are no new problems that fill in our days.

We clutch to Her fringe giving glory and praise,
when all looks forsaken and death lies in the draw.
Only ancient human struggles arranged in new ways.

The story from birth that our soul portrays
She spins, we conceive, using head, hand and heart.
There are no new problems that fill in our days
only ancient human struggles arranged in new ways.

BEFORE THERE WAS A BEFORE

David Braun

before there was a before
the beginning, there was nothing;
no more than nothing,
much less than nothing;
an infinity of nothing
all over space but indefinably small.
so much smaller than nothing.
you could say there was no point at all
(isn't that something to gawk at in awe)
for an eternity of untime
and in an infinitesimally
brief instant; almost no time at all;
then there was an infinitesimally
minuscule something, almost nothing;
but then everything and everywhere and all
eternally lasting forever and longer.
now we know that nothing's still
there sneaking in and out of of our
sight, but we don't know how
long its been all night.
now i'm not god, so i know
i didn't do it, but i'm still
curious how he did; and where he was
before the before it all happened,
and how he hid it.

CONTRIBUTOR'S NOTES

BILL ALEWYN lives in Arizona with his wife and their eight cats. This is his fourth appearance in *OASIS Journal*. Last year his short story, "Venus," was awarded Best Fiction in *OASIS Journal 2011*. His play, "An American Execution," was the first place winner in the 2012 Beverly Hills Theatre Guild/ Julie Harris Award Competition. [1]

WILLENE CHRISTOPHER AUSLAM grew up in a family of storytellers who related true accounts of family members, some of whom were no longer living. She did not want those memories to be lost, so put into writing the well loved oral stories for future generations of the family. She has participated in writing classes and groups in Fort Worth, Texas, and continues to do so in the retirement community where she now lives in Portland, Oregon. Some of her stories have been published in *Reminisce*, *Good Old Days Magazine*, and *OASIS Journal 2011*. [265]

MARY MARGARET BAKER: At the age of fourteen, her creative leanings began to emerge in writing, art, and music. She has studied painting and writing, and has a diploma from the Institute of Children's Literature. One of her poems is in an Anthology. Her writing has appeared in a local Pittsburgh Bulletin about five times. She recited two of her poems at a poetry meeting. She has written two children's books and two family tree books. An active Senior, age 78, she uses a cane and enjoys hanging out with family and friends. "Terrifying Moments," is based on a scary experience she had. [203]

JOHN BARBEE: I was a country boy who moved to the city to get an education and a job. But you can't take the country out of a man, so when I retired it was to a small, rural farming community. The area is populated by farmers, fieldworkers, teachers, and truck drivers, who keep horses, chickens, goats, and sheep. There are dairies, egg farms, and fields of potatoes in this pleasant valley that reflects a time long past. These people are good citizens that work with their hands and are kind, helpful neighbors. My story, "The Tablecloth," is fiction, but the people in it are very real. [257]

VIRGINIA BARROWS began writing non-fiction and poetry in 1974 from her great interest in spiritual and philosophical themes, winning an award in 1974 for her published poem, "Children of the Cosmos." She facilitated a group in the metaphysical philosophy, "A Course In Miracles," for thirty years, and was invited to be a weekly guest speaker on a local Cambria California radio station for several years. She has completed a volume of poetry, *The Kindled Heart*, and a glossary, *Our Forgotten Sacred Language*. She is delighted her submission, "The Butterfly Tree," was chosen for publication in *OASIS Journal 2011*. [30]

TABINDA BASHIR: "Sheru..." happened around March 2012 during our vacation in Pakistan. All names and events are real. My stories have been published in Pakistani magazines and some issues of the "Moon Journal," here. I won "The Daily Herald Citizens' Award" twice, and have a chapbook, "Turning Point." Two stories, "Bound" and "Odyssey," appeared in OASIS Journal 2010 and 2011, respectively. A shorter version of my biography, "My Journey," is published in *Jane's Stories Press Foundation*'s chapbook, "Bridges and Borders." "Odyssey" is set to be published in *Jane's Stories* anthology. [19]

DOLORES GREEN BINDER started making poems when she was nine years old. Her book of poetry, *An Obelisk in the Garden*, was published by New Quarto Editions. She has worked with young people as Artist in the Classroom and with adults as a workshop leader. Her programs were sponsored by Yale University, Albertus Magnus, and the Connecticut Commission on the Arts. Ms. Binder was selected as a Role Model for Women in Careers by the Yale University Women's Organization for her work as a poet, a teacher of poets, and a pioneer in helping women find their own poetic voice. [140]

BOBBIE JEAN BISHOP: My poems have been published in a variety of small journals since 1974 and were included in two Doubleday anthologies. I won my first poetry contest in 1986 at the University of Texas, and a recent prize for a poem in *OASIS Journal 2011*. I wrote the poem, "Pedestrian," in response to a family crisis: in 2009 my 45-year-old daughter was struck by a car in a crosswalk in front of a school. [200]

DAVID BRAUN was raised mostly in Austin and Port Arthur, Texas and has lived most of his adult life in Austin, Corpus Christi, and - his current home

- San Antonio, Texas. He received his M.A. in Psychology from The Univsity of Texas (Austin) and applied this while engaging in research, teaching, consultation, and psychotherapy. He has four siblings, three children, and three grandchildren. He has been a scribbler all his adult life. Having retired, he now has time to write and edit at leisure and focus. [157, 297]

FRED BRIDGES: My education includes a BS from Utah State and an MED from the University of Oregon. I am retired from the military, having served in both the Navy and Army. During my civilian career as an educator, I taught math, science, and PE. Writing was not in my resume until I discovered that the real point of writing was to tell a story in your own words and style. When I realized this, writing became fun. The story, "My Big Opportunity," is part fiction and is about our beloved cat, Moses. [239]

ESTHER BRUDO: This year I have two poems in *OASIS Journal*. "Button Box" deals with how the passage of time colors our recollections and alters our perception of what has happened in our lives. "Younger Sister" recaptures my perception as a child and teenager of my relationship with my brother. How precious this relationship has become in older age may be the subject of a future poem. [34, 267]

VIVIAN BULLOCK: My home is in Sun City, CA. Five years ago, when I was only ninety, my son, Jerry, decided to come live with me to keep me out of trouble, such as using a ladder to change a light bulb or forgetting to check the oil in my car, etc. It was a wise decision. I have always enjoyed writing for my own pleasure. However, last year I sent a poem to *OASIS Journal*. They accepted it, and this year they have accepted other submission of mine. Thank you, OASIS. [29, 121]

EVELYN BURETTA, after retiring from the US Army Reserve and from a national defense corporation as a technical writer, had time for creative writing. She is a member of the St. Louis Writers Guild and has publishing credits from previous *OASIS Journals* and two other publications. She uses poetry prompts from classes, internet, and other sources. She writes memoir pieces for an eventual book. Writing inspirations come from everyday surroundings, childhood experiences in rural southern Illinois in the 40s and 50s, and stories from her father. Her current "Sorghum Harvest " is an example. Evelyn resides in St. Louis, MO. [210]

JACK CAMPBELL: Through the years of a satisfying career, I would occasionally write poetry or prose for special days. When retirement loomed, my "well to go to" was overflowing, and I have not stopped writing. My joy still remains in the fulfillment I get from birthing a new effort. Selling my work would probably be a high, but I don't dwell on it, or need the money, which leaves me free to please myself and not an editor. The writing must continue, as long as the well I go to is "half full," and even if it's half empty! [105]

JOHN J. CANDELARIA began a 30-year healthcare career in 1962 as a US Army officer, retiring after twenty years. He continued his career as an association executive, a healthcare consultant, hospital administrator, and clinic director. John is an accomplished public speaker who received the Distinguished Toastmaster Award from Toastmasters International. He is schooled as an instructional designer. John begins his fourth year as an OASIS tutor, and the poem, "A Tale of the Oasis Tutor," is based on those experiences. As a poet he writes in free verse and form. John lives in Corrales, New Mexico. [28, 47]

SALLY CARPER: My dear friend and long-time neighbor toolk ill and everyone thought we were going to lose her. Suddenly she returned. Not the friend I once knew, but I was so happy I put pen to paper and out came a poem. I have had other submissions selected by *OASIS Journal*, but this is the first poem to be published. It came straight from my heart, and I dedicate it to my friend, Betty Jarnigan, and the friends and family who love her. [84]

CAROL CHRISTIAN: "Yellow and Such" is a poem about the color yellow and its many meanings to me. The memories evoked are both good and bad and reflect my complex feelings about home and family. "Baby at the Table" is a snapshot of both my children and grandchildren as they first began eating solid foods, a proud and celebrated moment for all. I dedicate them both to my supportive family, friends, and fellow writers. [184, 190]

SUSAN CLARK: I've been writing since I was twelve. Before that I made up stories to tell my sisters to help them go to sleep—a different one each night, like Scheherazade. Art is another thing I've done since childhood. Sometimes I combine art and writing. For over thirty years I worked as an LPN; seventeen of those years were in psych. Nursing was a source of inspiration for many poems. I also worked in Med-Surg, private duty, with the elderly and dying. I learned more from patients than they did from me. I am now 63, on disability, and battling cancer. My friends, books, and music are what feed me. [128]

ARIS DENIGRIS is 81 and lives with her husband of 63 years in a retirement community for active, independent retirees. Before moving, they lived in a large Victorian house. "My granddaughter, Natalie, and her parents lived downstairs in our home for three years when she was five. Natalie was a really special little girl—funny, super bright, and talented. Then her parents moved away. That was ten years ago. Now we communicate by phone or e-mail. She is still special—now 18, entering college—and I still miss her at every stage, but especially between years five and eight." [176]

BUCK DOPP retired in 2009 from a 27-year career in the telecommunications industry and relocated to Lake Havasu City, Arizona with his wife of 38 years, Stephanie. Buck is chairman of the Lake Havasu City Writers Group and has had two other stories published in *OASIS Journal*, "Smart Shopper" (2011) and "Skinny Post" (2010). *Long Story Short Ezine* has published "Dance Partners," "Eye-Opener," "Christmas Angels," "The Winner," "Pigskin Professor," "Which is Better?" and "Running Elk." *Offerings of the Oasis*, published in Kingman, Arizona has included his stories, "History Lesson" (2012) and "Massacre on Lake Victoria" (2010). [245]

MARY ROSE DURFEE: One of the greatest pleasures for me is taking a ride with someone else driving. There is so much to see, but the unusual is what catches my eyes. So it was with my story; "The Boat of Many Colors." It is an honor to have been accepted for publication for the fifth year now in *OASIS Journal.* What an encouragement to keep writing at age 96! And more memories of the past century keep popping up. [163]

TOM ENGEL began his career at WQED-TV in Pittsburgh, in the same studio, but a little before Mr. Rogers introduced the country to his neighborhood. From there, he worked for eight years in radio as a disc jockey, and then made the transition to television. He began as a film editor at WPXI-TV in Pittsburgh. When video tape replaced film, Tom became a news photographer. After he retired, he joined "The Squirrel Hill Writer's Group" and started writing a novel, "The Lot." After critiquing sessions, he would often tell stories about past assignments. "A Baby Lion" was one of those stories. [231]

JIM FOY is a physician-writer, a retired professor from Georgetown University School of Medicine. His poems have appeared in medical journals and literary magazines. "The Stars in Their Courses" is fictional biography. All details of the actress's life story were discovered in research and are factual. The author served in the US Navy Medical Corp and his voyage is based on personal experience. He once had a passing encounter with the actor in the story, but everything else is fiction. The life of a celebrity behind the persona/mask is a challenge to the creative writer. Empathy can be a starting place. [269]

JIM FRISBIE and his wife, Rinya, are United Methodist pastors living near Portland, Oregon. They have two grown sons. Jim has traveled extensively and has many outdoor interests, including backpacking, skiing, canoeing, sailing, working with horses, and building and flying his own airplane. The poem, "Coming Home," is a reflection on his homecoming after spending his junior year of college in West Africa and hitchhiking through Europe. Jim has had poems published in *Alive Now!*, local and national church publications, and the University of Wyoming anthology, *Hard Ground*. [66]

CALVIN FULTON: Having received an award for a nonfiction entry last year, I decided to write a fiction piece for this year. With the encouragement of my writing workshop group, this story went through several versions and rewrites to its present form: a story about a writer writing a story that has an O. Henry twist. Acceptance of "The Road Less Traveled" has given me the impetus to try a larger work, which is currently in progress. The *OASIS Journal* is a great place for new writers to gain experience. [77]

MURIEL GANOPOLE: My natural curiosity has been fed by rich and varied travel opportunities. I've even been to Antarctica, thanks to a scientist/writer son. I was married for years to an academic whose travel provided me and our three children with an incomparable education. At 50, in life transition, I went to Alaska to teach school, married a retired geologist, joined a writing group, and stayed 25 years. Now retired in Oregon, books, music, and *writing* frame my days. I am grateful for my innovative and encouraging memoir teacher here in Portland, and thrilled to have my "friendly skies" piece published. [63]

MARIE THÉRÈSE GASS loved living on that woodsy acre with Madeleine, children, and husband, building and planting, sitting outside in the cool evenings, inhaling the trees and grass in summer. Memories now, since her husband sustained a TBI falling off the roof twelve years ago. A semi-retired teacher, Marie has been writing in recent years, and playing in visual arts with her grandchildren. She lives on a tiny lot in a small house in a development and every day misses the acre of forest that used to be home. Three nonfiction books are available on amazon.com and other places. (caregive@easystreet. net) [241]

DIANA GRIGGS has found that writing about her mother's journey with Alzheimers has brought a sense of peace. She is grateful for Mary Harker's OASIS poetry class and the support of her Bluestocking Poets. [88]

ANITA CURRAN GUENIN was born and raised in Providence, Rhode Island. Her poems and essays have been published in *OASIS Journal 2009* (best poetry winner), *OASIS Journal 2010* and *2011*; "Frogpond," *2012, The Journal of the Haiku Society of America*; *Southern California Haiku Study Group Anthology 2010*, "Island of Egrets"; *SCHSG Anthology 2011*, "Scent of Rain"; *SCHSG Anthology 2012*, "Deep in the Arroyo"; and *San Diego Poetry Annuals 2010-2012*. [92]

JOHN J. HAN (Ph.D., University of Nebraska-Lincoln) is Professor of English & Creative Writing at Missouri Baptist University in St. Louis. An award-winning poet, he has authored three haiku volumes: *Little Guy Haiku, Chopsticks and Fork*, and *Thunder Thighs*. His poems have also appeared in the *Mainichi Daily News*, the *Asahi Haikuist Network*, *Simply Haiku*, *Mariposa*, *Geppo, Shot Glass Journal, The Fib Review, The Laurel Review, Cave Region Review, Prune Juice, Elder Mountain, Lucidity, Taj Mahal Review, Wilderness*, and numerous other periodicals and anthologies. *Simply Haiku* designated him as the world's sixth-best English-language haiku poet for the year 2011. [122]

TIINA HEATHCOCK: When not writing in her lakeside home in Haliburton County, Ontario, she has devoted her time to arranging events to mentor young writers and provide an opportunity for people from various forms of the arts to meet and to perform together. Her first collection of poetry, "*up North*," was published by Passion Among the Cacti Press (2004). Her second collection, "*afterimages*," came out in April 2005. She has also been published in *Quills*, and various anthologies, magazines, and newspapers. In the past, she was Writer in Residence for the Dorset Library. [154, 155]

TILYA GALLAY HELFIELD was born and raised in Ottawa and now lives in Toronto. Her short stories and essays have appeared in *TV Guide, The Fiddlehead, Viewpoints, OASIS Journal 2010* and *2011,* online, and on *CBC Radio One*. Her memoir, *Metaphors for Love*, is presently being considered for publication. She is a multi-media artist who has participated in 13 solo and more than 76 juried group exhibitions in Canada, the U.S., Spain, Brazil, Japan, and Korea, and has won several awards. Her work is found in 27 public collections and in private collections in Canada, the U.S., and Europe (http://www.tilyahelfield.com/). [39]

JEANNE HENDERSON lives in San Marcos, California, with her husband. She graduated with a degree in language arts and is a retired teacher and stock broker. Now she is putting her energies into writing. She enjoys writing stories about people and their humorous eccentricities, as in the story, "Morning Coffee." Her OASIS writing class has encouraged her to complete a book of memoirs and several short stories, two of which have been published in *OASIS Journal*. Jeanne took over leading the writing class two years ago and has found the experience enjoyable and inspiring. [93]

JACQUELINE HILL is a member of *Writers Anonymous*, a workshop sponsored through the UCLA Writing Project. Her poems and essays have been published in *Oasis Journal 2010* and *2011*. Her work has also been published in *phati'tude Literary Magazine, Chaparral, Reverie*, and *Does Heaven Have a Post Office?* Born in Ohio, Jacqueline is a retired Southern Californian educator. [49]

MAURICE HIRSCH has three poetry collections—*Taking Stock, Stares to Other Places, Roots and Paths*—and is working on his fourth. His work is in *OASIS Journal 2011* and *2010, Winter Harvest: Jewish Writing in St. Louis, 2006-11, New Harvest: Jewish Writing in St. Louis, 1998-2005*. He lives on a horse farm and is a lifelong photographer with his work in juried shows. "'People a la Carte' comes from being a photographer and observing what's going on around me. Dogs have been part of my life from the beginning. 'Requiem for My Dog' is one of a series of five I've written about them." [244, 260]

ANDREW HOGAN received his doctorate in development studies from the University of Wisconsin-Madison. Before retirement, he was a faculty member at the State University of New York at Stony Brook, the University of Michigan, and Michigan State University, where he taught medical ethics, health policy, and the social organization of medicine in the College of Human Medicine. Dr. Hogan published more than five dozen professional articles on health services research and health policy. He has published fourteen works of fiction in *OASIS Journal, Hobo Pancakes, Twisted Dreams, Long Story Short, The Lorelei Signal*, and *SANDSCRIPT*. [211]

UNA NICHOLS HYNUM, born in Providence RI, long-time San Diego resident and participant in Mary Harker's Poetry Workshop at OASIS. [256]

TERRIE JACKS: I have taught school, worked as a substitute, and currently I'm a volunteer tutor. Also I volunteer my time reading to children in preschools. When my two sons were young I made up stories to entertain them. Now, my grandchildren are entertained with my stories and poems. Sometimes they suggest the theme and help me writing it. As for my credits I have compiled a dozen collections of poems and stories that I presented to my grandchildren for Christmases and birthdays. Also several of my poems have been published in the Missouri Baptist Universitys literary magazine, *Cantos*. [102]

Helen Jones-Shepherd, born in New York, received her BA and MA in English Composition and Literature from Cal State University, and after retiring from teaching several years ago, she returned in 2009 as an Adjunct faculty part-time at a Community College. Between grading essays, she continues to write poetry, memoirs of world travels, essays, and some short fiction, and has been published locally and in other editions of *OASIS Journal*. "Oh, No, My Battery's Dead" was written as she recalled this humorous, yet life-changing incident from many years ago. [119]

Carole Kaliher, born in New Orleans, Louisiana and the fifth of six children, always loved to read and write. Transplanted to California in 1946, she worked for Pacific Bell Telephone and married Jim Kaliher on December 26, 1959. While rearing six sons, she attended college classes and currently enjoys her fourteen grandchildren. After losing her husband to emphysema in 1997, she followed his advice to "Get back to your writing." She's been published in local papers and magazines and facilitates a writing class in Sun City, California. She's been writing avidly for ten years and was previously featured in *OASIS Journal 2008* and *2011*. [97]

William Killian has been a parish minister, hospital chaplain, marriage and family therapist, working actor of stage and screen, published poet and lyricist, and professional basketball player. His publications include *Breakthrough: Stories & Reflections* (2012), *From the Balcony* (2011), and *All the Faces I Have Been: An Actor's Notebook* (2010). He resides in Tucson, Arizona with Linda, his wife for over fifty years. They have three children, two daughters-in-law, and six grandchildren. [129, 224]

Richard Lampl: This year is his fourth successful submission to *OASIS Journal*. He is grateful for the opportunity the anthology provides for older writers. He believes the mental exercise of writing is as important as physical exercise of the body for a productive, long life. Currently, he enjoys a carefree writing style compared to the rigid requirements in his former job, writing testimony appealing to the U.S. Congress on behalf of the aviation association for which he worked, or his other job, editing an aviation magazine in Washington D.C. [277]

PATRICIA LENT came from an Oregon Pioneer Family on her father's side. The ancestors passed on a love and a preservation of nature. They also passed on a love of literature. The OP Lent School is named for her great-great-grandfather. Her father was a non-published poet who read Kipling to her for bedtime stories. She started journalizing at the age of nine and studied writing and the great authors through grade school (where she was the editor of the school newspaper), high school, and college. She thanks Pat Arnold, her present instructor, for giving her the confidence to actually call herself, out loud, a writer. [167]

KATHLEEN LESNIAK: After retiring from a 33-year career, I joined OASIS and became a volunteer tutor. Tutoring is a rewarding experience! Each student is unique and precious, but one exceptional child inspired me to write this story. She was adopted from Russia and very eager to learn to speak, read, and write English. To become like the American students, she astutely observed and imitated them. During this same time-frame, a mockingbird family built their nest near our home. I enjoyed feeding them and listening to their remarkable repertoire. This blending of story lines was a joy to compose and share with the students. [251]

ELEANOR LITTLE was born in Detroit, Michigan during the depression. She began writing poetry in 1998, after she retired, and offers thanks to OASIS poetry teacher Mary Harker for her direction. Eleanor studied classical piano in Michigan, later played in a Dixieland jazz group in San Diego, then organized her own jazz group and a jazz trio. She played guitar and sings in various choral groups. She also loves to write, read, and garden. She enjoys time spent with family, friends, and 'Cheyenne', a new mini-Poodle. [204]

CLAIRE WARNER LIVESEY was born in Los Angeles, grew up in Carmel, California. Attended Mills College and U.C. Berkeley Library School. Children's librarian at Alameda Free Library for fifteen years. Married Herbert Livesey in 1958. Moved to Tucson Arizon in 1970 for reasons of health. Began studying poetry writing with Ann Dernier and then at the Poetry Center on Cherry St. [12]

ELLARAINE LOCKIE is a widely published and awarded poet. Her seventh chapbook, *Stroking David's Leg*, was awarded Best Individual Collection for 2010 from *Purple Patch* magazine in England, and her eighth chapbook, *Red for the Funeral*, won the 2010 San Gabriel Poetry Festival Chapbook Contest. Her recent chapbook, *Wild as in Familiar,* received *The Aurorean's* Chapbook Pick. Ellaraine teaches poetry workshops and serves as Poetry Editor for the lifestyles magazine, *Lilipoh.* "The Last War" was published and nominated for a Pushcart Prize by *Mobius, the Poetry Magazine* and before that won a First Place in the Chicagoland Poetry Contest. [10]

DENISE MARCELLI: Sixty-seven years ago I was born in St.Boniface, Manitoba to French-speaking parents. When I was 13, our family moved to Toronto, Ontario, Canada. When I was 18, I gave up my daughter, Brenda. I met and married my husband, Joe, forty-six years ago. We moved to many different places while raising our children. We now have 10 grandchildren and 3 great-grandchildren. I enjoy writing poetry, short stories, and memoirs since I joined the writer's group in Baysville, Ontario. I'm currently writing my family book and writing memoirs for my children. [53]

SUSE MARSH was born, raised, and educated in Germany in the beautiful Black Forest region. In 1961 she visited an uncle in the United States, where she fell in love with an American engineer. They were married in 1965 in Germany. The Scribes group at OASIS is a great inspiration for her, and her work has been published in *OASIS Journal 2004* and *2010.* She still visits Germany yearly and feels fortunate to know two different countries and their cultures in depth and, most importantly, to have family and friends to make it home. [249]

SERETTA MARTIN's writing has appeared in a number of publications, including: *Margie, American Journal of Poetry, Web del Sol, California Quarterly,* and *Best of Border Voices. Foreign Dust Familiar Rain* (2002), a limited edition books of her poems and illustrations, is still available on barnesandnoble.com and amazon.com. Currently, she is bustling with the editorial staff of *Poetry International Journal* and *San Diego Poetry Annual,* as well as teaching poetry through bordervoices.com and cpits.org. She hosts a 3rd Wednesday, 7 p.m. poetry series at Upstart Crow Bookstore, Seaport Village, San Diego. Her website is serettamartin.com. [127, 166]

CONNIE MCINTYRE has crafted a host of poems—some are prizewinners, and some are published. An author and publisher of books for children and families, she is founding co-director of The Grannie Annie Family Story Celebration, a nonprofit writing and publishing opportunity for young people. "Children (Not) Raised," like many of her poems, grew from years of listening to her parents and her thirty-seven aunts and uncles tell stories about the old days. This poem was written in honor of the three uncles she never knew. [192]

Margaret S. McKerrow: Born in Ireland, raised in England, lived in Canada and Arizona, and now thankfully calling San Diego my home. I always think of myself as a fledgling writer and am grateful for the encouragement I have received from Mary Harker and the many talented poets in her OASIS class. I have been published in the *San Diego Poetry Annual* and *OASIS Journal* and am excited to be accepted again for 2012. This year my life has been dominated by my son's illness and being able to express myself through the written word has indeed been a life saver. [85, 87]

Tucsonan Susan Cummins Miller, a research affiliate of the University of Arizona's Southwest Institute for Research on Women, writes the Frankie MacFarlane, Geologist, mysteries published by Texas Tech UP. The latest, *Fracture*, was named a Finalist for the 2012 WILLA Award in Contemporary Fiction. Susan won the 2012 Will Inman Award from the Tucson Poetry Festival, and her poems have appeared in regional journals and anthologies, including *What Wildness Is This: Women Write about the Southwest* and *Roundup! Western Writers of America Presents Great Stories of the West from Today's Leading Western Writers.* Her website is www.susancumminsmiller. com. [18]

J. R. Nakken has been writing since she retired at Y2K. She promised herself high-speed internet the first year she earned a thousand bucks from her writing, and is still sending e-mail on Juno dial-up! "I keep body and soul together with some editing and a new gig: writing advertising copy for a newspaper chain. Currently writing book #2 in my Jacey Cameron series (Kindle and Nook) for middle-graders. 'Twilight Cactus' is a fictionalized version (read: romance was added!) of a personal incident that left me awestruck. I'm pleased it will be included in *OASIS Journal 2012*." [123]

Eleanor Whitney Nelson, a longtime Tucson resident, holds degrees in English (BA) and Geology (MS). Her short stories, memoirs, and poems have appeared in several anthologies, including *The Story Teller, A Way with Murder, Chicken Soup for the Soul (Dog Lover's* and *Loving Our Dogs)* and *OASIS Journal 2004* and *2006-2011.* Her story, "Preconceived Notions," was originally sketched out in a letter to her family in 1983, describing one of her more eventful experiences as an exploration geologist. This year, twenty-nine years later, she developed and refined the account in her writers' critique group, St. Philip's Writers' Workshop. [55]

Kathleen O'Brien began writing two years after the death of her husband in 2000. "Some Lies About Loss" was written last year at the Women's Writing

Retreat at Pyramid Lake, New York. She wrote "Cruising" the day after returning from a trip to Cape Cod this June, wanting to capture the joy and excitement of being alive. Hobbies include: reading, writing poetry, dancing, gardening, volunteering for hospice. She writes that she is becoming addicted to the iPod game, "Bookworm." A former teacher and LPN, she retired in November and looks forward to taking a belly dancing class in September. [104, 131]

JUDITH O'NEILL, a retired teacher and technical writer, has published short stories in *Ellery Queen's* and *Alfred Hitchcock's* mystery magazines and in numerous short story anthologies. One of her stories was nominated for an "Edgar Allan Poe Award" by the Mystery Writers of America and appeared in *Best Mystery and Suspense Stories, 1989.* Her short story, "William," received the Third Runner-up Award in the F. Scott Fitzgerald Literary Awards Competition 2011, and a poem, "Morning Commute," appeared in *OASIS Journal 2011.* [177]

BARBARA OSTREM: Writing is fun. Finding the definitive word or phrase is a pleasure. The class I have attended for eight years has become a group of friends as well as inspiration. My beloved husband died four years ago after 52 years together. "Fairway Exchange" is one of many memories of our experiences. Now my life is enriched by the families of our two grown daughters and the special friends I see each week. I'm fortunate to live independently in a cozy house with good neighbors and an assortment of backyard critters. Soon to be 78, I am indeed lucky - and blessed. [101]

DOROTHY PARCEL has been writing, and teaching writing, most of her life. She wrote fiction for young people for a long time. Later, for a few years she was a technical writer at a drug company. After that, she taught writing in Adult Education classes. Now, in her eighties, she writes short essays about anything that catches her interest. She is most grateful to have shared the company of other writers for most of her life. [227]

CHUCK PETERS, 79, retired as director of the Allegheny County (Pittsburgh) nationally recognized $176,000,000 Mental Health-Retardation-Drug and Alcohol-Homelessness and Hunger programs in 1995. The former Marine lives on Pittsburgh's South Side in a prize-winning home he and his late wife, Georgi, renovated in 1990. He has three adult children and five grandchildren. "Uncle Homer" previously appeared in Chuck's self-published iUniverse Inc. 379-page book, *I Never Had to Duck: Adventures in the Peacetime Marine Corps,* a memoir of his "undistinguished service with the Corps." "Hitchhiking" is from *Me Want Milk*, a memoir (in progress) of growing up in an Ohio River town. [69, 208]

BARBARA PONOMAREFF was born in Germany and lives in the Greater Toronto Area, where she writes novellas, short stories, and poetry. Her latest novella, *In the Mind's Eye,* was published by Quattro Books in 2011. "Lac Seul" grew out of her first coming across this evocative name in a newspaper article; it presented itself to memory tenaciously until the story was written. [89]

CLAUDIA POQUOC has been writing poetry for 30 years in San Diego and teaching it both in San Diego and Nevada through California Poets in the Schools (CPITS) and Border Voices Poetry Project. Her published song and poetry book, *Becomes Her Vision,* includes a CD. Her recent publication, *As We Conceive Her...,* is a collaborative poetry/photo journal. Her poems appear in the *San Diego Poetry Annual, Magee Park, OASIS Journal,* and other publications. [296]

JEAN MARIE PURCELL: The saying, "A Mind Like a Steel Trap," has bugged me for years. I hope I explained why in my poem. I prefer verses that are easy to understand, explicit. Even if it's considered old-fashioned these days, I still love rhyme. My main job was teaching mentally challenged kids in the Los Angeles area. I started writing seriously about seven years ago and am trying my hand at plays, lately. [279]

DAVID RAY: My poem, "Sex," is playful autobiography, but also a testimonial to innocence. I don't think it exaggerates one's nostalgia, at least mine, for remembered scenes whether they happened or were fantasized. Jean De La Bruyre wrote that "Life is wholly spent in wishing." We hated to lose it, Innocence, unrecoverable and forever mourned. My latest book is *Hemingway: A Desperate Life,* and others include *Music of Time: Selected and New Poems,* which offers selections from fifteen earlier books, and *The Endless Search,* a memoir. More information or book orders at: www.davidraypoet. com [142]

JUDY RAY was born in Sussex, England, and lived in Uganda for some years before moving to the United States, the country of her poet husband, David Ray. Those first two locations are the inspiration for her essay on "Kitchens," included here. Judy's most recent poetry book is *To Fly Without Wings* (Helicon Nine Editions), about which Richard Wilbur wrote: "The poems of

To Fly Without Wings see with a fine descriptive eye, but also and always…
with compassion or joy." More information is at: www.davidraypoet.com/
JudyRay [261]

Sheila Rae Reynolds enjoys gardening, nature photography, and
cherished friendships in addition to writing memoir. She credits her weekly
Memoir Writing Group as the inspiration for "Loving Less Than Perfect,"
and dedicates it to her mother, Gladys, who passed away in 2007 with Sheila
at her bedside. She lives in Wilsonville, Oregon with her husband, Jim, who
still loves her just the way she is. [193]

A native Californian, Lynda Riese lives in San Diego with her newly-retired
husband and two springer spaniels. An antique dealer who loves the hunt,
she specializes in vintage and antique jewelry. She writes to make sense of her
life, preferring the personal because her experience is the only lens she has to
look through. "Sugar Jets" is a scene from a almost-completed novel/memoir
in stories that gathers dust in a drawer of her desk. The poem, "No Mary,"
grew out of her experience growing up Catholic. She's published in *Calyx*,
Onthebus, *Poet Lore*, *Potpourri*, and other small press magazines. [52, 185]

Maggi Roark has lived forever in San Diego with children (now grown),
teenage grandchildren, and collections of my unpublished words. Her poem,
'To the Man on My Right," was inspired, as you might guess, by a dinner
partner of insufferable opinions. It was very satisfying to dispose of him
without offending (or inspiring) any other guests. [226]

Albert Russo has published worldwide over 65 books of poetry, fiction,
and photography, in English and in French. His work has been translated
into a dozen languages, including German, Italian, Spanish, Greek, Turkish,
Bengali, and Polish, broadcast by the World Service of the BBC, and published
on the five continents in 22 countries. His photography books have garnered
several prizes, among them the Indie Excellence awards. [156]

Nancy Stein Sandweiss is inspired by the sights and sounds of daily life
and tries to capture the ironies and complexities of relationships and the
world at large. A visit to South Africa provided images of spectacular natural
beauty and a colorful, vibrant culture—as well as terrible poverty. "A Single
Strand" was prompted by an encounter at a roadside rest stop, where I was
touched by a young vendor's shy but hopeful manner and sobered by my
inability to make a difference. [54]

STEVEN SNYDER, a Tucsonan, runs a janitorial service, teaches fiction and poetry tutorials, and loves to hike the mountains of southern Arizona. His poems and stories have been published in many journals, including *OASIS Journal 2008-2011*. The poem, "Waiting," is one of his therapy poems. [153]

JANET THOMPSON is a boarding school survivor, whose life experiences include over 44 address changes and two marriages. She was a 1951 Polio epidemic victim, college dropout, office manager, and self-employed bookkeeper. In more incarnations, she was a historic property renovator, urban pioneer, slumlord, water well drilling partner, financial winner and loser. A volunteer, now retired, she writes a newsletter, reads, and relishes politics. "The Horsehair Bridle" is from her larger memoirs, *The Glass is Half Full* (subtitled "She Wove the Threads and Knots of Her Life With No Pattern"). At age 82, she self-published her story on-line through *Fast Pencil*. [35]

MANUEL TORREZ, JR.: My lovely wife, Esperanza, has always inspired me in my work. She is the one that keeps me going. We live in San Antonio, where I still work at one of the local Home Depots as a sign artist. "Bar Suez" is my fifth story to be published in *OASIS Journal*. At the present time, I'm working on a short story in Spanish. I've had one poem in Spanish published in *La Prensa* of San Antonio. I've had fourteen poems in English published in the *San Antonio Express/News*, *OASIS Journal*, and *Voices along the River*. I feel that I still have many stories and poems to write. [143]

GORDON WARADY: In college, I dearly loved writing sonnets. Raising a family left little time to write, but within the family circle I did sometimes play storyteller. Recently, my darling wife rescued this 'gem' buried in a box and shipped it off to Imago Press. Can you possibly imagine my stunned surprise upon receipt of a letter informing me that my essay had made the cut? All thanks to her meddling, "Illusions of Grandeur," initially written decades ago to mark her dual offer of publication of her first novels—to my delight—is about to achieve a wider audience. [117]

PHYLIS WARADY: I've always wanted to write. Majored in Journalism and after high school graduation wrote straight news and an occasional feature for the local weekly. Yet nursed a secret desire to write fiction. *A Neat and Tidy Crime* is one happy result. It gleaned 1st place in the 2003 Ray Bradbury Creative Writing Contest. Its commemorative plaque graces my office wall. Whenever discouraged, I gaze at it, my main focus upon the late Sci-Fi author's bold signature. And my spirits rise. What's more, nine years later, I feel honored by its inclusion in *OASIS Journal 2012*. [205]

Mo Weathers spent his childhood roaming through the forests and plains of Oregon. Following a hitch in the Navy, he attended the University of Oregon, graduating with a degree in Mathematics. After graduating, he served 22 years in the Air Force, retiring in 1987. Mo and his wife, Lois, live happily ever after in Milwaukie, Oregon's Rose Villa retirement community, where Mo has been taking memoir writing classes from Clackamas Community College for the past two years. "Up in Smoke…Down in Flames" chronicles one of his early, less successful attempts to stay out of trouble. [173]

Sarah Cifarelli Wellen: I have not only been published in newsletters, anthologies, and newspapers, but I have also won several poetry contests. I still have a copy of the $75 check I received for a true story published by the *New York Times* in 1982. Occasionally, I give poetry readings. My self-published book of poems, *Reflections*, came out in 2007. The poem in *OASIS Journal 2012*, also called "Reflections," is a description of an actual experience, and, yes, I did feel foolish! [62]

Jeff Widen, Chicago-born and Los Angeles raised, is a retired sports medicine doctor who practiced in Ashland, Oregon. A journalist for 30 years, he wrote a newspaper column on sports injuries. Active in the 12 Step recovery community, he's published "anonymously" in its national magazine and other periodicals. He now lives in Portland, Oregon with his wife, Lois, who edits most of his works. He takes a Creative Writing course at the Milwaukie Center from Pat Arnold, who mentors him and his colleagues. He loves writing action stories that reflect his many life experiences. [13]

Neal Wilgus writes poetry, fiction, satire, and reviews in Corrales, NM. His first story in *OASIS Journal*, "Galapagoed," won the fiction contest in 2006. Long interested in the Southwestern folk legend of the Weeping Woman, La Llorona, he wrote "Cold Case: Rona" for an Albuquerque anthology, *La Llorona* (Beatlick Press, 2012), but missed the deadline. Published widely in the small press in the US and UK over the past fifty years, Neal is the author of six chapbooks of poetry and satire as well as the conspiracy theory classic, *The Illuminoids* (Sun Books, 1978). [285]

Ila Winslow: I am age 75, divorced, single since 1985. During chemo treatments in 1985 (ovarian cancer) my sister encouraged I write for mind therapy. Ten years of Creative Writing classes. "The Creek" is the result of a class assignment. I've not been published but have received eight Honorable Mentions from 1999-2008 stories to Alfred Hitchcock's Mysterious Photograph contests. Background: 1959-1969 Women's Army Corp; 1971-1995 clerical for Portland, Oregon Police Department. Interests: Mysteries - both adult and children. I enjoy quiet summer days watching birds, bees, bugs, while reading and thinking in my patio. [283]

JOAN ZEKAS: God bless our wonderful librarians! They were as enthusiastic as I was, in finding the material to verify that Victor Herbert actually lived in this house. The drawing I did became an obsession to re-create the house as it existed in the late 1800s. Our Pittsburgh Scribes group is a phenomenon. We are in our 24th year with writers new and old and others who've gone and left their spirits with us. Kudos to Leila Joiner for her dedication in creating yet another *OASIS Journal*. [281]

ORDER INFORMATION

Copies of *OASIS Journal 2008* through *2012* are available at:

www.amazon.com
www.barnesandnoble.com

Copies of *OASIS Journal* from previous years (2002-2007) may be ordered at a discount from the publisher at the address below as availability allows. Please enclose $10.00 for each book ordered, plus $3.00 shipping & handling for the total order to be sent to one address.

Please make checks payable to Imago Press. Arizona residents add $0.91 sales tax for each book ordered.

Proceeds from the sale of this book go toward the production of next year's *OASIS Journal*. Your purchase will help us further the creative efforts of older adults. Thank you for your support.

Imago Press
3710 East Edison
Tucson AZ 85716

CPSIA information can be obtained at www.ICGtesting.com
Printed in the USA
BVOW070142190912

300803BV00001B/3/P